SPEEDWAY PUBLIC LIBRARY

3 5550 43053 7186

P9-DJV-356

641.812 PILL
Pillsbury appetizers

SPEEDWAY PUBLIC LIBRARY
SPEEDWAY, INDIANA
ink mark noted back of first page   11/02 8/8

WITHDRAWN
Speedway Public Library

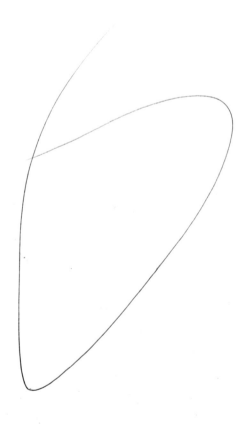

CHEDDAR	Rich, creamy flavor that sharpens with age. Golden, orange or creamy white with smooth, firm texture; melts well.
CHÈVRE	A soft, pungent, spreadable cheese made from goat's milk. Usually sold in a small log shape, sometimes coated with herbs or cracked black pepper.
COLBY	Similar to Cheddar but more golden with milder flavor.
COTTAGE CHEESE	Soft textured, mild flavored with slightly acidic small cheese curds
CREAM CHEESE	White-colored, rich and slightly sweet with smooth, creamy texture. In addition to the plain variety, cream cheese spreads are also available mixed with herbs, pineapple or smoked salmon.
EDAM	Pale yellow interior; inedible wax exterior. Buttery/nutty flavor with smooth, firm texture. Often made from part-skim milk.
FETA	Sheep's milk cheese, tart and salty with crumbly texture. Often sold covered with water.
FONTINA	Semisoft to hard, slightly yellow with delicate, nutty flavor.
GOUDA	Light, buttery and nutty with smooth, creamy texture and pale yellow interior. Red wax indicates mild flavor; yellow or clear wax, aged or flavored; black wax, smoked.
GRUYÈRE	Mellow, buttery, nutty. Slices, cubes and shreds well without crumbling.
HAVARTI	Creamy, slightly acidic, pale yellow. Smooth, supple texture that slices, cubes and shreds well without crumbling. Sometimes flavored with dill.
MASCARPONE	A very soft, white cheese with a texture between cream cheese and sour cream. Used in dips, spreads and dessert fillings.
MONTEREY JACK	Semisoft and creamy with a buttery, slightly tart taste. Creamy white color. Sometimes flavored with hot pepper, basil, etc.
MOZZARELLA	Semisoft and creamy with a buttery, slightly tart taste. Creamy white color. Sometimes flavored with hot pepper, pesto, dill, etc. Fresh mozzarella is more tender and has a sweet, delicate flavor.
MUENSTER	Semisoft and smooth with orange or white surface and creamy white interior. Mild flavor. Slices, cubes, shreds and melts nicely.
NEUFCHÂTEL	Soft, rich, nutty, slightly sweet with smooth, creamy texture; resembles cream cheese but has more moisture and less fat.
PARMESAN	Hard grating cheese with pale yellow color and buttery, sweet, nutty flavor that intensifies with age.
PROCESSED AMERICAN	Similar in flavor to the natural cheese from which it is made. Smooth, elastic texture; slices, melts and shreds well.
PROVOLONE	Ivory to pale beige with full flavor that sharpens with age. Has firm texture and melts well.
RICOTTA	Creamy, slightly grainy with mild flavor and a bit of sweetness.
ROMANO	Creamy white, hard, granular cheese with sharp, piquant flavor. Grates and melts well.
SWISS	Ivory-colored with dime-sized eyes. Firm with mellow, buttery, nutty flavor.

Party Beverages

Every party needs beverages, whether you offer a few choices or provide a full-service bar. If you plan to serve alcoholic beverages, be sure to offer alternatives such as fruit juice, soft drinks, ice water, sparkling cider, iced tea, hot mulled cider or nonalcoholic punches. If you're offering coffee and tea, include decaffeinated versions, too, especially in the evening.

ESTIMATING QUANTITIES OF BEVERAGES

As a general rule, plan on one to two drinks per guest per hour. A 750-milliliter bottle of wine holds four 6-ounce servings; a liquor bottle of the same size will yield 17 1½-ounce drinks. A gallon bowl of punch averages about 24 servings.

LEFT TO RIGHT: MARTINI COCKTAILS, PAGE 260; MANHATTAN COCKTAILS, PAGE 262

COCKTAILS AT HOME
Stocking the Bar

Tools
- Bar spoon or stirring rod
- Bottle opener
- Coasters
- Cocktail shaker/strainer
- Corkscrew
- Electric blender for frozen drinks
- Ice bucket with tongs
- Jigger measure
- Juicer
- Paring knife
- Straws
- Swizzle sticks
- Toothpicks

Spirits

Basics
- Beer
- Gin
- Rum
- Scotch
- Vermouth
- Vodka
- Wine
  (red and white)

Extras
- Bourbon
- Brandy
- Cognac
- Liqueurs and
  fruit-flavored brandies
- Sparkling wine
- Tequila
- Whiskey

Mixers
- Angostura and orange bitters
- Bottled, frozen or packaged drink mixes
  for margaritas, daiquiris, etc.
- Club soda
- Cola
- Fruit juices
- Ginger ale
- Lemon-lime soda
- Mineral water/seltzer
- Tonic water

Garnishes
- Coarse salt
- Cocktail onions
- Fresh fruit (including lemons, limes,
  oranges and berries)
- Granulated and powdered sugar
- Maraschino cherries
- Stuffed cocktail olives

GLASSWARE

Glass	Use
3- or 4-ounce stem (martini) glass	Manhattan Cocktails, page 262 Martini Cocktails, page 260 Blue Hawaii Freeze, page 266
6- to 10-ounce on-the-rocks glass	Scotch on the rocks Old-fashioned Bloody Mary
10- to 14-ounce tumbler glass	Gin and Tonic Cocktail, page 260 Soft drinks
8- to 10-ounce all-purpose wine glass	Wine Wine coolers Soft drinks
Champagne flute	Sparkling wine Champagne cocktails Champagne punch Sunrise Mimosas, page 262

Guide to Wine Selection

Here is a simple guide to different wines from around the world. As you go down the list, the wines become drier and stronger in taste. Mild-tasting wines are typically fruitier, smooth and mellow. Strong tastes are typically drier (not sweet) with more acidity, bitterness and, at the end of the red wines, tannic or astringent (the mouth-drying sensation).

WINE TYPE	DISTINCTIVE REGIONS OF PRODUCTION
Sparkling Wines and Champagnes	
Sweet	
Asti Spumanti or Spumante	Italy, sometimes U.S.
Moscato d'Asti	Italy
Demi-Sec Sparkling Wines and Champagnes	U.S., France
Extra-Dry Sparkling Wines and Champagnes	U.S., France
Inexpensive Sparkling Wines	International
Dry	
Blanc de Noirs Sparkling Wines and Champagnes	U.S., France
Brut Sparkling Wines and Champagnes	International
White and Rosé Table Wines	
Sweet	
White Zinfandel and Other Blush Wines (sweet to almost dry)	U.S.
Rosé (sweet)	International
Riesling (sweet to almost dry)	U.S., Germany
Gewürztraminer (sweet to almost dry)	U.S., Germany
Chenin Blanc (sweet to almost dry)	U.S., France (Vouvray)
Dry, Light to Medium Intensity	
Rosé (dry)	U.S., France (Tavel Rosé, Rosé d'Anjou)
Riesling (dry)	U.S., France (Alsace), Germany (labeled "trocken")
Gewürztraminer (dry)	U.S., France (Alsace), Germany
Pinot Blanc	U.S., France (Alsace and Burgundy), Germany
Pinot Grigio	Italy
Dry, Medium to Full Intensity	
Pinot Gris or Pinot Grigio	U.S., France (Alsace), Italy
Viognier	U.S., France (Condrieu)

Dry, Medium to Full Intensity *(continued)*

Semillon (medium intensity, often oak-aged)	U.S., Australia, France (white Bordeaux)
Sauvignon/Fumé Blanc and Meritage (a wide range of styles, from light to medium intensity, often oak-aged)	U.S., France (Sancerre, Pouilly Fumé, white Bordeaux), South America, South Africa
Chardonnay (dry, light to full intensity, typically less fruit and oak flavors than U.S. or Australian versions)	France (White Burgundy: Chablis, Puligny or Chassagne Montrachet, Pouilly-Fuissé, Macôn), South America, Italy, South Africa
Chardonnay (slightly sweet, very fruity, usually oak-aged)	U.S., Australia
Chardonnay (dry, medium to full intensity with lots of fruit and oak flavors)	U.S., Australia

RED TABLE WINES

Dry, Light to Medium Intensity

Gamay, Gamay Beaujolais (mild and fruity to medium intensity with mild tannins)	U.S., France (Beaujolais)
Dolcetto (mild and fruity to medium intensity with mild tannins)	U.S., Italy
Pinot Noir (light to full intensity, fruity with mild to moderate tannins)	U.S., France (red Burgundy), Australia, Germany
Tempranillo (light to full intensity, fruity with mild to moderate tannins)	Spain
Sangiovese (light to full intensity, fruity with mild to moderate tannins)	U.S., Italy (Chianti—light to medium intensity; Brunello di Montalcino—full intensity and tannic)

Dry, Medium to Full Intensity

Zinfandel (a full range of styles, from light to full intensity, fruity with mild to moderate tannins to strong tannins)	U.S.
Syrah, Shiraz and Petite Syrah	U.S., France (Rhône), Australia
Nebbiolo (medium to full intensity, moderate to strong tannins)	U.S., Italy (Barolo, Barbaresco)
Merlot (light to full intensity, mild to moderate tannins)	U.S., France (Bordeaux: St. Emilion, Pomerol, Médoc), Australia, Italy, South America
Meritage (medium to full intensity, moderate to strong tannins)	U.S.
Cabernet Sauvignon (medium to full intensity, moderate to strong tannins)	U.S., France (Bordeaux: Médoc), Australia, Italy, South America

DESSERT WINES

Very Sweet and Intense

Riesling and Gewürztraminer	U.S., Germany (Beerenauslese, Trockenbeerenauslese, Eiswein), France (Alsace), Austria, Canada
Semillon, Sauvignon Blanc	U.S., France (Sauternes, Barsac, Monbazialac), Australia

FORTIFIED WINES

Sherry (sweet to dry as indicated)	U.S.
Sherry (sweet: oloroso; medium: amontillado; to very dry: fino)	Spain
Madeira (sweet: Malmsey; medium: Bual; to dry: Sercial)	Madeira
Marsala (both sweet and dry versions)	Italy
Port (full range from dry to sweet, mild to strong tannins)	Portugal
Port (sweet, full intensity, medium to strong tannins)	U.S., Australia

Copyright © 1999 by Wine Logic, Inc. All rights reserved.

Serving Punch

WARMING A PUNCH BOWL

To warm or temper a punch bowl before adding a hot beverage, fill the bowl with hot tap water. Let it stand for about 10 minutes; then drain. Transfer the hot punch to the warm bowl. Tempering serves two purposes: It minimizes the chance of stress cracks from hot liquid hitting cold glass and helps to hold the heat in the punch a little longer.

You can also temper teapots and coffee mugs in the same way.

NICE ICE

To make a decorative ice ring for the punch bowl, arrange fruit in the bottom of a ring-shaped cake pan or gelatin mold. Choose a combination of pineapple chunks, peach slices, mandarin sections, maraschino cherries and fresh or frozen berries. Add enough water or fruit juice to partially cover the fruit. Freeze. Add water or fruit juice to fill the mold; freeze until firm. You may use contrasting colors of juices for added interest. To unmold, dip briefly in hot water; remove ice. Invert to float it in the punch bowl.

Tips for Perfect Coffee

For many people, a meal or party is not complete without a cup of coffee.

Start with clean equipment. Coffee gets its flavor from essential oils contained in coffee beans. These same oils, however, can cause a stale flavor if they're allowed to build up on your coffee equipment. Wash all equipment, especially metal pots, in hot, soapy water after each use.

Use fresh coffee. Store whole beans and ground coffee in an airtight container in the refrigerator or the freezer. Unopened cans of vacuum-packed coffee and jars of instant coffee will keep one year at room temperature if stored in a cool, dry place. Once opened, coffee will maintain its freshness 2 to 3 weeks in a cool place, 8 weeks in the refrigerator and 6 months in the freezer.

Use high-quality paper or gold filters for the best flavor. Poor-quality filters can add an "off" flavor.

Serve coffee immediately after brewing. To keep remaining coffee warm, use an insulated jug or carafe rather than keeping the pot on a warmer.

COFFEE BAR

Keep regular and decaffeinated coffee hot in thermal carafes, then set out a selection of:

- Granulated sugar or cubes, plus sugar substitute
- Cream, milk or whipped cream
- Anisette, amaretto or coffee liqueur
- Cocoa powder blended with sugar or cinnamon sugar for sprinkling
- Cinnamon sticks for stirring
- Whole nutmegs and a small grater
- Shaved bittersweet chocolate

Serving Tea

TYPES OF TEA

Tea varieties fall into three main categories: black, green and oolong.

Black teas, the most popular in the United States, have a rich aroma and amber color when brewed. Varieties include Ceylon, Darjeeling, English Breakfast, Earl Grey (flavored with oil from the rind of bergamot, a citrus fruit) and Lapsang souchong. Varie-

ties of black tea flavored with spices are also available.

Green teas, gaining popularity because of their reputed health benefits, have a slightly bitter flavor and pale green color when brewed.

Oolong tea is a cross between black and green tea. Popular varieties include jasmine and Formosa oolong.

HERBAL "TEAS"

True herbal teas are not made with tea leaves but rather with a blend of herbs, spices and aromatic ingredients. Many require longer steeping to fully develop the flavor. Herbal teas are usually caffeine-free, but some may be mixed with regular tea leaves.

Not every herbal tea is a good choice for those wishing to avoid caffeine. Pregnant or nursing women and people on medication, in particular, should consult their physicians about the ingredients in herbal teas.

TIPS FOR BETTER TEA

Many tea purists insist on china pots and cups.

Buy tea in small batches. Store it in a cool place in a tightly sealed container.

Tea bags tend to contain more powder than good-quality loose tea. Loose tea needs a little longer to brew, but the flavor is superior.

Start with cold, fresh water.

The flavor of water affects tea more than coffee, so you may wish to use bottled or filtered water if your tap water is heavily flavored.

Pre-warm the teapot by filling it with hot tap water; empty it just before adding the dry tea and water.

Use 2 or 3 tea bags or 2 to 3 teaspoons of loose tea per pot, depending on the size of the pot and how strong you like your tea.

Remove the kettle from the heat just as

the water comes to a full rolling boil and pour immediately over the tea.

Let the tea steep until it reaches the desired strength, then remove the tea bags before serving.

Do not squeeze the tea bags into the pot; squeezing releases tannin, which can make the brew bitter.

Keep tea warm with an authentic British-style "cozy" (an insulated or quilted fabric cover) or cover the pot with one or two kitchen towels.

Planning for Young Guests

If children are accompanying adults to your party, arrange a special play area with games and toys and, if possible, their own kid-sized table. Cover the table with butcher paper and set out crayons. For a large party, consider hiring a child care person (such as a neighborhood teenager or the teenage son or daughter of a party guest).

Don't be surprised if children are not interested in some of the fancy hors d'oeuvres that the adults love. Most children prefer familiar flavors, plainly served. Many kids will like the following appetizers:

- Toasted Mini-Sandwiches with Gouda and Tomato, page 199
- Petite Stuffed Pizza Snacks, page 201
- Pepperoni Pizza Snacks, page 201
- Sausage Snack Wraps (made with cocktail hot dogs), page 234
- Easy Italian Pinwheels, page 227
- Popcorn Munch Mix, page 250
- Seaside Snack Mix, page 258
- Cocktail Snack Kabobs, page 92

In addition, make sure you have plenty of other kid-friendly choices, such as:

- Cut-up vegetables
- Fruit cup or cut-up fruit
- Rolls or bread
- Peanut butter and jelly triangles
- Cheese slices or cubes and crackers

party menus

ITALIAN COUNTRYSIDE APPETIZER BUFFET
FOR 10 TO 12

Antipasto Platter, page 86

Bruschetta with Pears, Fontina and Pistachios, page 188

Mozzarella and Pesto Crescent Tarts, page 245

Country-Style Chicken Liver Pâté with Capers, page 75

Prosciutto-Wrapped Scallops, page 170

Rosemary and Garlic Marinated Olives, page 85

Tortellini and Roasted Bell Pepper Kabobs, page 94

Chianti wine

Espresso and/or cappuccino

WINE AND CHEESE SAMPLER
FOR 8 TO 10

Elegant Cheese and Fruit Platter, page 128

Baked Brie and Brandied Mushrooms, page 77

Goat Cheese Crostini, page 192

Caviar and Cream Cheese-Filled Endive, page 127

Selection of wine, such as:

White Zinfandel

Chardonnay

Merlot

Pinot Noir

(See Guide to Wine Selection on pages 18 to 20.)

NEW YEAR'S EVE CANDLELIGHT SOIREE
FOR 12

Pastry-Wrapped Jalapeño Brie with Fruit, page 76

Caviar and Cream Cheese-Filled Endive, page 127

Crostini with Beef and Caper Mayonnaise, page 109

Prosciutto-Wrapped Fruit, page 110

Salmon Canapés with Dilled Honey Mustard, page 99

Shrimp and Pineapple Kabobs, page 162

Spicy Honey Chicken Drummettes, page 157

Sun-Dried Tomato Cream Puffs, page 131

Strawberry Champagne Punch, page 271

A TASTE OF ENGLAND BUFFET
FOR 12

Stilton Cheese Puffs, page 242

Sharp Cheddar Cheesecake, page 73

Beef Tenderloin and Caramelized Onion Sandwiches, page 113

Fig-Filled Endive Leaves, page 128

Selection of pickled vegetables

Cranberry Wassail, page 276

English ale

MEXICAN FIESTA PATIO PARTY
FOR 6 TO 8

Acapulco Sunset Spread, page 68

Salsa Corn Dip, page 51

Green Chile and Cheese Half-Moons,
page 216

Guacamole Appetizer Squares, page 119

Strawberry Margarita Slush, page 273

Mock Margaritas, page 267

POTLUCK REUNION PICNIC
FOR 10 TO 12

Ranch Deviled Eggs, page 95

Cucumber-Shrimp Canapés, page 102

Turkey Club Tortilla Roll-Ups, page 114

Crunchy Broccoli Party Dip, page 34

Thinly sliced deli turkey or chicken
and roast beef

Selection of condiments for sandwiches

Watermelon wedges

Lemonade and/or iced tea

FIREWORKS CELEBRATION
FOR 8

Star-Studded Cheese Spread, page 63

Crabmeat Deviled Eggs, page 97

Veggie Wreath with Creamy Sun-Dried
Tomato Dip, page 58

Smoked Salmon and Caper Pizza, page 111

Spicy Honey Chicken Drummettes,
page 157

Orange-Ginger Iced Tea with Fruit Stirrers,
page 279

CHINESE SAMPLER
FOR 6 TO 8

Chinese Spare Riblets, page 153
or Chinese Glazed Chicken Wings, page 150

Cream Cheese Puffs, page 170

Light Shrimp Toast, page 175

Easy Egg Rolls, page 168

Mustard Dipping Sauce, page 178

Sweet Chili-Plum Sauce, page 178

Selection of sliced fresh fruit

Chinese tea

BACK TO THE 60S CASUAL CLASSICS
FOR 12

Appetizer Beer Cheese Fondue, page 57

Sweet and Zesty Meatballs with Peppers,
page 142

Bacon-Wrapped Rumaki, page 171

Sausage Snack Wraps, page 234

Deviled Ham and Eggs, page 95

Dilly Dip, page 30

Peachy Keen Slush, page 265

SURF AND TURF SAMPLER
FOR 8 TO 10

Light Crabmeat Spread, page 70

Salmon Fillet with Caviar Sauce, page 82

Beef Tenderloin Canapés with Mustard-
Caper Sauce, page 101

Shrimp Kabobs with Bacon-Wrapped
Water Chestnuts, page 163

Chutney-Glazed Meatballs, page 141

Manhattan Cocktails, page 262
and/or wine coolers

FRIDAY NIGHT VIDEO MARATHON
FOR 6 TO 8
Seven-Layer Pizza Dip, page 49

Ham and Swiss Appetizer Pizza, page 202

Petite Stuffed Pizza Snacks, page 201

Zesty Cheese Bread, page 247

Italian Snack Mix, page 251

Cantaloupe and honeydew melon wedges

Selection of soda pop

RESTAURANT REVIEW
FOR 10 TO 12
Boneless Buffalo Chicken Appetizers, page 158

Chili Potato Dippers with Cheddar Jalapeño Dip, page 185

Taquitos, page 214

Sun-Dried Tomato and Cheese Pizza, page 205

Crisp-Coated Mushrooms, page 179

Garden Fresh Salsa, page 50

Classic Guacamole, page 52

Beer and wine

HAWAIIAN BREEZE BUFFET FOR 10 TO 12
Orange-Pineapple Appetizer Meatballs, page 136

Mini Aloha Puff Pizzettes, page 206

Hot Macadamia Spread, page 59

Coconut Shrimp with Gingered Cocktail Sauce, page 159

Pork Tenderloin Canapés, page 99

Mango-Passion Fruit Slush, page 270

and/or Blue Hawaii Freeze, page 266

ELEGANT COCKTAILS
FOR 6 TO 8
Crescent-Wrapped Brie, page 76

Peppered Salmon with Dill-Caper Sauce, page 83

Crostini with Brie and Cherry Relish, page 192

Walnut-Blue Cheese Stuffed Mushrooms, page 182

Selection of olives

Martini Cocktails, page 260

and/or Gin and Tonic Cocktails, page 260

FANTASY FONDUE
FOR 6 TO 8
Party Pesto Squares, page 119

Cheese Fondue with Roasted Vegetable Dippers, page 55

Orange-Spiced Sugared Almonds, page 258

Wine and/or beer

SOUTHWESTERN SUNSET RECEPTION
FOR 12
Green Chile Cheesecake Spread, page 71

Mini Seafood Tostadas, page 122

Spinach and Jalapeño Roll-Ups, page 116

Fiesta Quesadillas, page 212

Assortment of seasonal fresh fruit

White Wine Sangría, page 268

or Golden Aztec Cooler, page 274

PARISIAN BISTRO FETE
FOR 8 TO 10

Apricot-Pecan Camembert, page 74

Olive and Roasted Garlic Canapés, page 103

Spinach Quiche Bites, page 218

Artichoke and Brie Pizzettes, page 206

Lemon-Garlic Skewered Shrimp, page 166

French wine, such as Beaujolais
or Chenin Blanc

(See Guide to Wine Selection on
pages 18 to 20.)

HOLIDAY TREE TRIMMING PARTY
FOR 8 TO 10

Spinach Dip Crescent Wreath, page 118

Cranberry-Glazed Appetizer Meatballs,
page 135

Sesame Chicken Drummies, page 157

Flaky Deli Slices, page 196

Blue Cheese Ball with Walnuts, page 67

Party Snack Mix, page 254

Rich and Creamy Eggnog, page 281

TV SPORTS REVIEW BASH
FOR 8 TO 10

Game-Time Nachos, page 208

Bacon Cheddar Dip, page 47

Sour Cream 'n Chive Twice-Baked Potato
Bites, page 186

Maple-Glazed BBQ Meatballs, page 143

Pastrami and Pepper Roll-Ups, page 114

Spicy Popcorn and Peanuts, page 250

Beer and a selection of soda pop

TROPICAL CRUISING
FOR 6 TO 8

Creamy Cilantro Dip, page 34

Crab Roll-Ups, page 116

Jerk Chicken Wings with Creamy Dipping
Sauce, page 160

Cilantro-Lime Shrimp with Chile Aïoli,
page 164

Bacon and Pineapple Yam Bites, page 194

Seaside Snack Mix, page 258

Tropical Rum Punch, page 271

GARDEN PATCH PATIO PARTY
FOR 8

Antipasto Spread, page 64

Fresh Tomato-Zucchini Salsa Crostini,
page 107

Roasted Vegetables with Spicy Aïoli Dip,
page 54

Salmon-Stuffed Cherry Tomatoes, page 125

Easy Vegetable Pizza, page 111

Mixed sliced strawberries, peaches
and blueberries

Frosty Raspberry Iced Tea, page 273

MEDITERRANEAN GETAWAY
FOR 6 TO 8

Sicilian Eggplant Caponata, page 66

Marinated Roasted Vegetable Antipasto,
page 88

Marinated Olive Kabobs, page 91

Mediterranean Dip with Pita Chips,
page 39

Marinara and Shrimp Canapés, page 195

Wild Mushroom-Stuffed Phyllo Bundles,
page 226

Retsina wine and/or Turkish coffee

WINTER SOLSTICE OPEN HOUSE
FOR 12

Creamy Cheese Spread with Brandied
Cranberries, page 79

Open-Faced Party Sandwiches, page 97

Stuffed Party Mushrooms, page 182

Baked Artichoke Squares, page 246

Sweet and Zesty Meatballs with Peppers,
page 142

Mixed nuts

Rosy Mulled Punches, page 281

EASY AFTER-WORK APPETIZER BUFFET FOR
10 TO 12

Beef Tenderloin Canapés with
Mustard-Caper Sauce, page 101

Triple Cheese Appetizer Cheesecake,
page 74

Lemon Yogurt Fruit Dip, page 37

Shrimp Cocktail, page 86

Sweet Orange-Glazed Chicken Wings,
page 148

Sherried Walnuts and Cashews, page 259

Wine coolers and coffee

MARDI GRAS MADNESS
FOR 8 TO 10

Spicy Cajun Dip, page 38

Mushroom Caps with Thyme-Cornbread
Stuffing, page 180

Shrimp-Stuffed Cherry Tomatoes, page 126

Crab Cakes Italiano, page 167

Party Punch, page 274

BIG SKY BASH FOR 8

Rustler Chili Fondue, page 54

Beer Cheese Spread, page 63

Bourbon Cocktail Meatballs, page 139

Boneless Buffalo Chicken Appetizers,
page 158

Spicy Cheesy Popcorn, page 254

Wine coolers and beer

APPETIZERS AT SUNRISE FOR 8

Maple Mustard Biscuit Bites, page 198

Mini Swiss Quiches, page 219

Smoked Salmon and Caper Pizza, page 111

Deviled Eggs, page 94

Lemon Yogurt Fruit Dip, page 37

Sunrise Mimosas, page 262

ALMOST-NO-PREP PARTY FOR 6 TO 8 PEOPLE

Twenty-Minute Party for 6 to 8 People,
page 130

dips & spreads

Dilly Dip

Finely chopped fresh parsley and dill may be substituted for the dried herbs in this rich, creamy dip. Garnish the serving bowl with a sprig of either herb. For suggestions on using this and other dishes in a party menu, see Back to the 60s Casual Classics for 12 (page 24).

PREP TIME: 10 MINUTES
(READY IN 2 HOURS 10 MINUTES)
MAKES 2 CUPS

1½ cups sour cream

⅔ cup mayonnaise

2 tablespoons instant minced onion

2 tablespoons dried parsley flakes

2 tablespoons dried dill weed

1 teaspoon celery salt or seasoned salt

4 drops green food color

1. In small bowl, combine all ingredients; mix well. Cover; refrigerate at least 2 hours to blend flavors.

2. Serve with assorted cut-up fresh vegetables.

make-ahead tip

Dip can be refrigerated up to 24 hours.

NUTRITION INFORMATION PER SERVING: SERVING SIZE: 2 Tablespoons • Calories 120 • Calories from Fat 110 • % Daily Value: Total Fat 12 g 18% • Saturated Fat 4 g 20% • Cholesterol 15 mg 5% • Sodium 180 mg 8% • Total Carbohydrate 2 g 1% • Dietary Fiber 0 g 0% • Sugars 2 g • Protein 1 g • Vitamin A 6% • Vitamin C 0% • Calcium 4% • Iron 2% • **Dietary Exchanges:** 2½ Fat

Spinach Dip

Hearty spinach and crisp water chestnuts in a rich, creamy base make this emerald-colored party dip a "most requested" dish.

PREP TIME: 20 MINUTES
(READY IN 4 HOURS 20 MINUTES)
MAKES 3 CUPS

3 cups frozen cut leaf spinach

1 (8-oz.) can water chestnuts, drained, finely chopped

2 tablespoons chopped green onions

1 (1.4-oz.) pkg. dry vegetable soup mix

1½ cups sour cream

½ cup mayonnaise

1. Cook spinach as directed on package; drain well.

2. In medium bowl, combine spinach and all remaining ingredients; mix well. Cover; refrigerate at least 4 hours to blend flavors.

3. Serve with assorted cut-up fresh vegetables or crackers.

make-ahead tip

Dip can be refrigerated up to 24 hours.

NUTRITION INFORMATION PER SERVING: SERVING SIZE: 2 Tablespoons • Calories 80 • Calories from Fat 60 • % Daily Value: Total Fat 7 g 11% • Saturated Fat 3 g 15% • Cholesterol 10 mg 3% • Sodium 150 mg 6% • Total Carbohydrate 4 g 1% • Dietary Fiber 1 g 4% • Sugars 1 g • Protein 1 g • Vitamin A 15% • Vitamin C 6% • Calcium 4% • Iron 0% • **Dietary Exchanges:** 1½ Fat

Creamy Spinach–Artichoke Dip

This dip is a good candidate for preparing early in the day of the party and then refrigerating until it's time to pop it in the oven.

PREP TIME: 10 MINUTES
(READY IN 35 MINUTES)
MAKES 2½ CUPS

1 (14-oz.) can artichoke hearts, drained, chopped

1 (9-oz.) pkg. frozen spinach in a pouch, thawed, squeezed to drain

4 oz. (1 cup) shredded mozzarella cheese

½ cup grated Parmesan cheese

½ cup mayonnaise

1 garlic clove, minced

Paprika

1. Heat oven to 325°F. In 1-quart casserole, combine all ingredients except paprika; mix well. Sprinkle with paprika.

2. Bake at 325°F. for 20 to 25 minutes or until bubbly and golden brown.

3. Serve with assorted crackers or cut-up fresh vegetables.

make-ahead tip

Combine all ingredients in casserole as directed in recipe. Cover; refrigerate up to 24 hours before baking. Uncover; sprinkle with paprika. Bake as directed in recipe.

NUTRITION INFORMATION PER SERVING: SERVING SIZE: 2 Tablespoons • Calories 80 • Calories from Fat 50 • % Daily Value: Total Fat 6 g 9% • Saturated Fat 2 g 10% • Cholesterol 10 mg 3% • Sodium 150 mg 6% • Total Carbohydrate 2 g 1% • Dietary Fiber 1 g 4% • Sugars 0 g • Protein 4 g • Vitamin A 10% • Vitamin C 4% • Calcium 10% • Iron 2% • **Dietary Exchanges:** ½ Medium-Fat Meat, 1 Fat

Hot Artichoke and Spinach Dip

Artichokes always add a special touch, as is the case in this warm, cheesy dip served with baguette slices.

PREP TIME: 15 MINUTES
(READY IN 2 HOURS 45 MINUTES)
MAKES 2½ CUPS

2 cups frozen cut leaf spinach

1 (14-oz.) can quartered artichoke hearts, drained, chopped

½ cup refrigerated Alfredo sauce (from 10-oz. container)

½ cup mayonnaise

¾ teaspoon garlic salt

¼ teaspoon pepper

4 oz. (1 cup) shredded Swiss cheese

1. Cook spinach as directed on package. Drain spinach, pressing with fork to remove excess liquid. Chop spinach finely.

2. In 1- to 3-quart slow cooker, combine spinach and all remaining ingredients; mix well.

3. Cover; cook on low setting for 1½ to 2½ hours. Serve with slices of baguette-style French bread.

NUTRITION INFORMATION PER SERVING: SERVING SIZE: 2 Tablespoons • Calories 90 • Calories from Fat 60 • % Daily Value: Total Fat 7 g 11% • Saturated Fat 2 g 10% • Cholesterol 10 mg 3% • Sodium 180 mg 8% • Total Carbohydrate 3 g 1% • Dietary Fiber 1 g 4% • Sugars 1 g • Protein 3 g • Vitamin A 10% • Vitamin C 4% • Calcium 8% • Iron 2% • **Dietary Exchanges:** ½ High-Fat Meat, 1 Fat

Hot Spinach Jalapeño Cheese Dip

Chunky and cheesy, rich with spinach and spiced with jalapeños, this dip also makes a good topping for baked potatoes, noodles or rice—something to keep in mind for leftovers.

PREP TIME: 30 MINUTES
MAKES 4 CUPS

1½ cups skim milk

2 tablespoons all-purpose flour

½ cup finely chopped onion

¼ teaspoon pepper

1 teaspoon Worcestershire sauce

1 8-oz. Mexican pasteurized prepared cheese product with jalapeño chiles, cut into small pieces

2 (9-oz.) pkg. frozen spinach in a pouch, thawed, squeezed to drain

1. Place 1¼ cups of the milk in large nonstick saucepan; place over medium-high heat. In small bowl, combine remaining ¼ cup milk and flour; blend with wire whisk until smooth. Add to milk in saucepan; cook about 5 minutes, stirring constantly, until thickened.

2. Add onion, pepper and Worcestershire sauce; mix well. Bring just to a boil. Reduce heat; simmer 10 minutes or until onion is tender, stirring occasionally.

3. Stir in cheese until melted. Add spinach; mix well. Cook until thoroughly heated. Serve with slices of baguette-style French bread or assorted cut-up fresh vegetables.

tip

To quickly thaw spinach, cut small slit in center of each pouch; microwave on HIGH for 2 to 3 minutes or until thawed. Remove spinach from pouch; squeeze dry with paper towels.

NUTRITION INFORMATION PER SERVING: SERVING SIZE: 2 Tablespoons • Calories 35 • Calories from Fat 20 • % Daily Value: Total Fat 2 g 3% • Saturated Fat 1 g 5% • Cholesterol 4 mg 1% • Sodium 140 mg 6% • Total Carbohydrate 2 g 1% • Dietary Fiber 0 g 0% • Sugars 1 g • Protein 2 g • Vitamin A 10% • Vitamin C 4% • Calcium 8% • Iron 0% • **Dietary Exchanges:** ½ Fat

Artichoke Dip

To trim a few calories from this popular dip, make it with reduced-fat mayonnaise instead of regular.

PREP TIME: 10 MINUTES
(READY IN 30 MINUTES)
MAKES 2 CUPS

1 (14-oz.) can artichoke hearts, drained, chopped

¾ cup mayonnaise

¼ cup grated Parmesan cheese

½ teaspoon lemon juice

Dash garlic powder

1. Heat oven to 375°F. In medium bowl, combine all ingredients; mix well. Spread in ungreased 9-inch quiche or pie pan or 1-quart shallow casserole.

2. Bake at 375°F. for 18 to 20 minutes or until thoroughly heated.

3. Serve warm with assorted crackers or cut-up fresh vegetables.

make-ahead tip

Combine all ingredients in quiche pan as directed in recipe. Cover; refrigerate up to 24 hours before baking. Uncover; bake as directed in recipe.

NUTRITION INFORMATION PER SERVING: SERVING SIZE: 2 Tablespoons • Calories 90 • Calories from Fat 80 • % Daily Value: Total Fat 9 g 14% • Saturated Fat 2 g 10% • Cholesterol 5 mg 2% • Sodium 105 mg 4% • Total Carbohydrate 2 g 1% • Dietary Fiber 1 g 4% • Sugars 0 g • Protein 1 g • Vitamin A 0% • Vitamin C 0% • Calcium 4% • Iron 0% • **Dietary Exchanges:** 2 Fat

Crunchy Broccoli Party Dip

You'll do the weight watchers a favor by setting out this low-calorie dip. Chopped fresh broccoli and water chestnuts provide plenty of satisfying crunch.

PREP TIME: 10 MINUTES
MAKES 3 CUPS

1/2 cup light mayonnaise or salad dressing

1 (8-oz.) container nonfat plain yogurt

1 teaspoon sugar

1/2 teaspoon salt

1/4 teaspoon garlic powder

1/4 teaspoon hot pepper sauce

2 cups finely chopped fresh broccoli

2 tablespoons finely chopped green onions

1 (8-oz.) can water chestnuts, drained, chopped

1 (2-oz.) jar diced pimientos, drained

1. In medium bowl, combine mayonnaise, yogurt, sugar, salt, garlic powder and hot pepper sauce; mix well. Stir in all remaining ingredients.

2. Serve with baked pita crisps or assorted cut-up fresh vegetables.

make-ahead tip

Dip can be refrigerated up to 24 hours.

NUTRITION INFORMATION PER SERVING: SERVING SIZE: 2 Tablespoons • Calories 30 • Calories from Fat 15 • % Daily Value: Total Fat 2 g 3% • Saturated Fat 0 g 0% • Cholesterol 5 mg 2% • Sodium 85 mg 4% • Total Carbohydrate 3 g 1% • Dietary Fiber 0 g 0% • Sugars 1 g • Protein 1 g • Vitamin A 4% • Vitamin C 15% • Calcium 2% • Iron 0% • **Dietary Exchanges:** 1 Vegetable

Creamy Cilantro Dip

Cilantro, widely used in Indian, Asian and Mexican cooking, has a sharp citrus-like tang that complements the lime in this cool dip. Save a sprig or two to garnish the bowl.

PREP TIME: 15 MINUTES
(READY IN 1 HOUR 15 MINUTES)
MAKES 1 1/2 CUPS

1 (8-oz.) container sour cream

1/3 cup mayonnaise

1/2 cup chopped fresh cilantro

1 tablespoon sugar

1 teaspoon grated lime peel

1/4 teaspoon cumin

1/8 teaspoon salt

2 tablespoons fresh lime juice

1. In medium bowl, combine all ingredients; mix well. Cover; refrigerate 1 to 2 hours to blend flavors.

2. Serve with assorted cut-up fresh vegetables.

make-ahead tip

Dip can be refrigerated up to 24 hours.

NUTRITION INFORMATION PER SERVING: SERVING SIZE: 2 Tablespoons • Calories 90 • Calories from Fat 80 • % Daily Value: Total Fat 9 g 14% • Saturated Fat 3 g 15% • Cholesterol 10 mg 3% • Sodium 70 mg 3% • Total Carbohydrate 2 g 1% • Dietary Fiber 0 g 0% • Sugars 2 g • Protein 1 g • Vitamin A 4% • Vitamin C 2% • Calcium 2% • Iron 0% • **Dietary Exchanges:** 2 Fat

Garden Patch Veggie Dip

At just 10 calories per tablespoon, this broccoli- and carrot-flecked blend couldn't get much leaner.

PREP TIME: 10 MINUTES
(READY IN 2 HOURS 10 MINUTES)
MAKES 1¼ CUPS

1 (8-oz.) container fat-free cream cheese

1 tablespoon skim milk

½ teaspoon salt-free onion-herb seasoning

½ cup finely chopped broccoli

½ cup shredded carrot

1. In small bowl, combine cream cheese, milk and herb seasoning; mix well. Stir in broccoli and carrot. Refrigerate at least 2 hours or until serving time.

2. Serve with assorted cut-up fresh vegetables.

make-ahead tip

Dip can be refrigerated up to 24 hours.

NUTRITION INFORMATION PER SERVING: SERVING SIZE: 2 Tablespoons • Calories 20 • Calories from Fat 0 • % Daily Value: Total Fat 0 g 0% • Saturated Fat 0 g 0% • Cholesterol 5 mg 2% • Sodium 140 mg 6% • Total Carbohydrate 2 g 1% • Dietary Fiber 0 g 0% • Sugars 1 g • Protein 3 g • Vitamin A 40% • Vitamin C 8% • Calcium 8% • Iron 0% • **Dietary Exchanges:** Free

Sweet 'n Creamy Dip for Fruit

Softening the cream cheese, by simply leaving it at room temperature for about an hour, is the key to a smooth, creamy-textured dip. Some good fruits to try are apples, pears, strawberries and grapes.

PREP TIME: 10 MINUTES
MAKES 1½ CUPS

1 (8-oz.) pkg. cream cheese, softened

½ cup frozen whipped topping, thawed

½ cup marshmallow creme

1. Beat cream cheese until fluffy in small bowl.

2. Add whipped topping and marshmallow creme; mix well. Serve immediately with cut-up fresh fruit or miniature cookies. Store any remaining dip in refrigerator.

NUTRITION INFORMATION PER SERVING: SERVING SIZE: 2 Tablespoons • Calories 90 • Calories from Fat 60 • % Daily Value: Total Fat 7 g 11% • Saturated Fat 5 g 25% • Cholesterol 20 mg 7% • Sodium 60 mg 3% • Total Carbohydrate 5 g 2% • Dietary Fiber 0 g 0% • Sugars 3 g • Protein 2 g • Vitamin A 6% • Vitamin C 0% • Calcium 0% • Iron 0% • **Dietary Exchanges:** ½ Starch, 1½ Fat **OR** ½ Carbohydrate, 1½ Fat

Fruit and Swiss Dip

This sweet dip makes a good counterpoint to the often salty selections on an appetizer table, and also rounds out a dessert buffet nicely. If you have trouble finding the sweetened dried cranberries, substitute chopped dried cherries or apricots.

PREP TIME: 5 MINUTES
(READY IN 25 MINUTES)
MAKES 1¾ CUPS

1 (8-oz.) container soft cream cheese with pineapple

6 oz. (1½ cups) shredded Swiss cheese

½ cup sweetened dried cranberries

1 tablespoon grated orange peel

2 tablespoons dry sherry or apple juice

1. Heat oven to 375°F. In medium bowl, combine all ingredients; mix well. Spread in ungreased 9-inch pie pan.

2. Bake at 375°F. for 14 to 16 minutes or until thoroughly heated.

3. Serve with apple or pear wedges and assorted crackers.

Combine all ingredients in pie pan as directed in recipe. Cover; refrigerate up to 24 hours before baking. Uncover; bake as directed in recipe.

NUTRITION INFORMATION PER SERVING: SERVING SIZE: 2 Tablespoons • Calories 120 • Calories from Fat 80 • % Daily Value: Total Fat 9 g 14% • Saturated Fat 6 g 30% • Cholesterol 30 mg 10% • Sodium 80 mg 3% • Total Carbohydrate 5 g 2% • Dietary Fiber 0 g 0% • Sugars 4 g • Protein 5 g • Vitamin A 6% • Vitamin C 0% • Calcium 15% • Iron 0% • **Dietary Exchanges:** ½ Fruit, ½ High-Fat Meat, 1 Fat **OR** ½ Carbohydrate, ½ High-Fat Meat, 1 Fat

Lemon Yogurt Fruit Dip

Granny Smith apple wedges or strawberries are especially good with this tangy-sweet dip. To garnish the serving bowl, sprinkle the surface of the dip with a little grated lemon or orange peel and top with a sprig of fresh mint.

PREP TIME: 5 MINUTES
(READY IN 1 HOUR 5 MINUTES)
MAKES 1¾ CUPS

1 (8-oz.) container lemon yogurt

1 (8-oz.) container sour cream

1 teaspoon ginger

1 tablespoon honey

½ teaspoon grated lemon peel

½ teaspoon lemon juice

1. In small bowl, combine all ingredients; blend well. Cover; refrigerate 1 to 2 hours before serving to blend flavors.

2. Serve with assorted fresh fruit.

Dip can be refrigerated up to 24 hours.

NUTRITION INFORMATION PER SERVING: SERVING SIZE: 2 Tablespoons • Calories 50 • Calories from Fat 35 • % Daily Value: Total Fat 4 g 6% • Saturated Fat 2 g 10% • Cholesterol 10 mg 3% • Sodium 20 mg 1% • Total Carbohydrate 3 g 1% • Dietary Fiber 0 g 0% • Sugars 3 g • Protein 1 g • Vitamin A 2% • Vitamin C 0% • Calcium 4% • Iron 0% • **Dietary Exchanges:** 1 Fat

Spicy Cajun Dip

After all the ingredients have been mixed, taste-test the dip. If you want more spice, add another dash of cayenne. If you want less spice, stir in a little more plain yogurt.

PREP TIME: 20 MINUTES
(READY IN 2 HOURS 20 MINUTES)
MAKES 2 CUPS

½ cup dry-pack sun-dried tomatoes

1 (8-oz.) pkg. ⅓-less-fat cream cheese (Neufchâtel), softened

½ cup nonfat plain yogurt

¼ cup chili sauce

¼ cup chopped green bell pepper

¼ cup chopped green onions

1 garlic clove, minced

½ teaspoon celery seed

⅛ teaspoon ground red pepper (cayenne)

1. In small bowl, pour 1 cup boiling water over tomatoes. Let stand at room temperature for 5 to 10 minutes. Drain and chop tomatoes.

2. Meanwhile, in another small bowl, combine cream cheese, yogurt and chili sauce; mix well. Add tomatoes and all remaining ingredients; mix well. Refrigerate at least 2 hours or until serving time.

3. Stir dip before serving. Serve with assorted cut-up fresh vegetables or garlic-flavored bagel crisps.

make-ahead tip

Dip can be refrigerated up to 24 hours.

NUTRITION INFORMATION PER SERVING: SERVING SIZE: 2 Tablespoons • Calories 45 • Calories from Fat 25 • % Daily Value: Total Fat 3 g 5% • Saturated Fat 2 g 10% • Cholesterol 10 mg 3% • Sodium 150 mg 6% • Total Carbohydrate 3 g 1% • Dietary Fiber 0 g 0% • Sugars 2 g • Protein 2 g • Vitamin A 6% • Vitamin C 4% • Calcium 2% • Iron 0% • **Dietary Exchanges:** ½ Vegetable, ½ Fat

Cuban Picadillo Dip

In larger portions, served over rice, the dip becomes a piquant entrée.

PREP TIME: 25 MINUTES
MAKES 4 CUPS

1 lb. lean ground turkey

1 teaspoon cumin

¼ teaspoon ground red pepper (cayenne)

1 garlic clove, minced

1 (14.5-oz.) can stewed tomatoes, undrained, cut up

½ cup raisins

¼ cup chopped pimiento-stuffed green olives

¼ cup water

2 tablespoons tomato paste

1. Heat medium nonstick skillet over medium-high heat until hot. Add turkey, cumin, ground red pepper and garlic; cook until liquid evaporates and turkey is lightly browned, stirring frequently to break up turkey.

2. Add all remaining ingredients; mix until well combined. Heat until bubbly. Reduce heat; cover and simmer 5 to 10 minutes to blend flavors.

3. Serve warm with pita bread wedges or baked tortilla chips.

NUTRITION INFORMATION PER SERVING: SERVING SIZE: 2 Tablespoons • Calories 35 • Calories from Fat 10 • % Daily Value: Total Fat 1 g 2% • Saturated Fat 0 g 0% • Cholesterol 10 mg 3% • Sodium 65 mg 3% • Total Carbohydrate 3 g 1% • Dietary Fiber 0 g 0% • Sugars 2 g • Protein 3 g • Vitamin A 2% • Vitamin C 2% • Calcium 0% • Iron 2% • **Dietary Exchanges:** 1 Vegetable

Mediterranean Eggplant Dip

Tahini, made from ground sesame seeds, gives a nutty nuance to this lemony eggplant dip/spread.

PREP TIME: 10 MINUTES
(READY IN 55 MINUTES)
MAKES 1¾ CUPS

1 medium eggplant

1 medium tomato, peeled, seeded and chopped

2 tablespoons chopped onion

2 garlic cloves, minced

3 tablespoons purchased tahini

2 tablespoons lemon juice

¾ teaspoon salt

1 tablespoon chopped fresh parsley

1. Heat oven to 400°F. Line 15x10x1-inch baking pan with foil; spray foil with nonstick cooking spray. Cut eggplant in half lengthwise; place cut side down in foil-lined pan.

2. Bake at 400°F. for 45 minutes or until eggplant is soft to the touch. Remove from oven; cool 5 minutes.

3. Scoop eggplant flesh from skin into food processor bowl with metal blade. Add tomato, onion and garlic; process with on/off pulses until pureed. Add tahini, lemon juice and salt; process until smooth. Spoon dip into serving bowl. Sprinkle with parsley.

4. Serve as a dip with assorted cut-up fresh vegetables or as a spread with toasted pita bread wedges, slices of baguette-style French bread or assorted crackers.

make-ahead tip

Dip can be refrigerated up to 24 hours.

NUTRITION INFORMATION PER SERVING: SERVING SIZE: 2 Tablespoons • Calories 40 • Calories from Fat 20 • % Daily Value: Total Fat 2 g 3% • Saturated Fat 0 g 0% • Cholesterol 0 mg 0% • Sodium 120 mg 5% • Total Carbohydrate 4 g 1% • Dietary Fiber 1 g 4% • Sugars 2 g • Protein 1 g • Vitamin A 0% • Vitamin C 6% • Calcium 0% • Iron 2% • **Dietary Exchanges:** ½ Fruit, ½ Fat **OR** ½ Carbohydrate, ½ Fat

Mediterranean Dip with Pita Chips

Hummus is a Middle Eastern dip made with ground chickpeas, tahini and lemon. Here, we add sour cream, feta cheese and vegetables for a more complex blend.

PREP TIME: 20 MINUTES
(READY IN 1 HOUR 20 MINUTES)
MAKES 32 SERVINGS

DIP

½ cup sour cream

1 (7-oz.) container hummus

½ cup sliced kalamata or ripe olives

4 oz. feta cheese, crumbled (1 cup)

1 (6-oz.) jar marinated artichoke hearts, drained and chopped, reserving marinade

¼ cup sliced green onions

1 medium carrot, shredded

CHIPS

4 (6-inch) pita (pocket) breads

1. In medium bowl, combine sour cream and hummus; mix well. Spread mixture on 10-inch serving plate. Sprinkle with olives, cheese, artichoke hearts, green onions and carrot. Drizzle with reserved artichoke marinade. Cover; refrigerate at least 1 hour or up to 12 hours.

2. Heat oven to 375°F. Split pita breads in half horizontally. Cut each round in half; cut each half crosswise into four 1½-inch-wide strips. Place on ungreased cookie sheets.

3. Bake at 375°F. for 8 to 10 minutes or until crisp.

4. Serve dip with warm or cool pita chips.

NUTRITION INFORMATION PER SERVING: SERVING SIZE: 1/32 of Recipe • Calories 70 • Calories from Fat 35 • % Daily Value: Total Fat 4 g 6% • Saturated Fat 1 g 5% • Cholesterol 5 mg 2% • Sodium 135 mg 6% • Total Carbohydrate 6 g 2% • Dietary Fiber 1 g 4% • Sugars 1 g • Protein 2 g • Vitamin A 15% • Vitamin C 0% • Calcium 4% • Iron 2% • **Dietary Exchanges:** ½ Starch, ½ Fat **OR** ½ Carbohydrate, ½ Fat

Smoky Bean Dip

Pinto beans make an earthy-flavored base for this hearty dip. Substitute great northern or cannellini beans, if you wish.

PREP TIME: 35 MINUTES
MAKES 2 CUPS

2 dried chipotle chiles

2 (15.5- or 15-oz.) cans pinto beans, drained, rinsed

⅛ teaspoon liquid smoke, if desired

1 large garlic clove, minced

2 tablespoons chopped fresh cilantro

½ each of green, yellow and red bell pepper

2 Italian plum tomatoes, chopped

4 oz. (1 cup) shredded Mexican cheese blend

1. Heat oven to 375°F. Place chiles in small bowl; cover with boiling water. Let stand 10 minutes or until soft.

2. Drain chiles, reserving 3 tablespoons of soaking water. Remove and discard seeds from chiles; coarsely chop chiles.

3. In food processor bowl with metal blade or blender container, combine beans, chiles, reserved 3 tablespoons soaking water, liquid smoke and garlic; process on high speed until well combined. Stir in cilantro. Place mixture in ungreased shallow 9-inch glass pie pan. Cover with foil.

4. Bake at 375°F. for 15 to 20 minutes or until mixture is thoroughly heated.

5. Meanwhile, cut bell peppers with cactus-, coyote- and moon-shaped cookie cutters. Set aside.

6. Uncover dip; sprinkle with tomatoes and cheese. Bake an additional 2 to 3 minutes or until cheese is melted.

7. To serve, garnish top of dip with bell pepper cutouts. Serve with tortilla chips.

make-ahead tip

Combine all ingredients in pie pan as directed in recipe. Cover; refrigerate up to 24 hours before baking. Bake at 375°F. for 15 to 20 minutes. Uncover; sprinkle with tomatoes and cheese. Bake an additional 2 to 3 minutes.

NUTRITION INFORMATION PER SERVING: SERVING SIZE: 2 Tablespoons • Calories 70 • Calories from Fat 20 • % Daily Value: Total Fat 2 g 3% • Saturated Fat 2 g 10% • Cholesterol 5 mg 2% • Sodium 125 mg 5% • Total Carbohydrate 9 g 3% • Dietary Fiber 2 g 8% • Sugars 1 g • Protein 4 g • Vitamin A 15% • Vitamin C 8% • Calcium 8% • Iron 2% • **Dietary Exchanges:** ½ Starch, ½ Very Lean Meat **OR** ½ Carbohydrate, ½ Very Lean Meat

Greek Layered Dip with Pita Crisps

(Pictured on page 28).

To prepare fragrant fresh oregano, strip the leaves from the stalks. The stalks can be used to flavor soup stock, but they're too tough for this dip.

PREP TIME: 20 MINUTES
MAKES 18 SERVINGS

PITA CRISPS

3 (6-inch) pita (pocket) breads

Nonstick cooking spray

1/2 teaspoon garlic powder

DIP

1 (8-oz.) container soft cream cheese with chives and onions

1 (8-oz.) container hummus

1 cucumber, peeled, seeded and chopped

3 Italian plum tomatoes, seeded, chopped

1 (2 1/4-oz.) can sliced ripe olives, drained

1 (4-oz.) container crumbled feta cheese

1/4 cup chopped green onions

1 tablespoon chopped fresh oregano

1. Heat oven to 350°F. Carefully split each pita bread into 2 rounds. Cut each round into 6 wedges; place on ungreased cookie sheets. Spray wedges lightly with nonstick cooking spray. Sprinkle with garlic powder.

2. Bake at 350°F. for 5 to 7 minutes or until crisp and golden brown. Cool.

3. Meanwhile, spread cream cheese in bottom of 10-inch plate or pie pan. Drop hummus by small spoonfuls evenly over cream cheese; spread evenly. Top with remaining ingredients in order listed. If desired, garnish with sprigs of fresh oregano. Serve with pita crisps.

make-ahead tip

Dip can be refrigerated up to 2 hours.

NUTRITION INFORMATION PER SERVING: SERVING SIZE: 1/18 of Recipe • Calories 120 • Calories from Fat 70 • % Daily Value: Total Fat 8 g 12% • Saturated Fat 4 g 20% • Cholesterol 20 mg 7% • Sodium 240 mg 10% • Total Carbohydrate 9 g 3% • Dietary Fiber 1 g 4% • Sugars 1 g • Protein 4 g • Vitamin A 6% • Vitamin C 2% • Calcium 6% • Iron 6% • **Dietary Exchanges:** 1/2 Starch, 1/2 Medium-Fat Meat, 1 Fat **OR** 1/2 Carbohydrate, 1/2 Medium-Fat Meat, 1 Fat

Mexican Olé Dip

Choose crisp, rather than tender-textured, lettuce for this dish. Shredded iceberg and romaine are excellent choices.

PREP TIME: 25 MINUTES
MAKES 12 SERVINGS

1 cup fat-free refried beans

1/3 cup finely chopped green onions

1 teaspoon chili powder

1/8 teaspoon salt

1/8 teaspoon garlic powder

1/8 teaspoon cumin

2 oz. (1/2 cup) shredded reduced-fat Cheddar cheese

1/2 cup chopped tomatoes

1/2 cup shredded lettuce

1. Heat oven to 425°F. In small bowl, combine refried beans, green onions, chili powder, salt, garlic powder and cumin; mix well. Spread mixture evenly in ungreased 9-inch glass pie pan. Sprinkle cheese evenly over top. Cover with sprayed foil, sprayed side down.

2. Bake at 425°F. for 8 to 12 minutes or until thoroughly heated and cheese is melted.

3. Sprinkle tomatoes evenly over cheese. Arrange lettuce around edge of pie pan. Serve warm with baked tortilla chips.

tip

To prepare in microwave, prepare bean mixture as directed above; spread evenly in 9-inch microwave-safe pie pan. Microwave on HIGH for 1 1/2 to 2 1/2 minutes or until thoroughly heated. Sprinkle cheese evenly over top. Microwave on HIGH for an additional minute or until cheese is melted. Continue as directed above.

make-ahead tip

Combine all ingredients except tomatoes and lettuce in pie pan as directed in recipe. Cover with sprayed foil; refrigerate up to 24 hours before baking. Bake at 425°F. for 8 to 12 minutes. Top with tomatoes and lettuce.

NUTRITION INFORMATION PER SERVING: SERVING SIZE: 1/12 of Recipe • Calories 40 • Calories from Fat 10 • % Daily Value: Total Fat 1 g 2% • Saturated Fat 1 g 5% • Cholesterol 3 mg 1% • Sodium 170 mg 7% • Total Carbohydrate 5 g 2% • Dietary Fiber 1 g 4% • Sugars 1 g • Protein 3 g • Vitamin A 4% • Vitamin C 2% • Calcium 4% • Iron 2% • **Dietary Exchanges:** 1/2 Starch **OR** 1/2 Carbohydrate

SPEEDWAY PUBLIC LIBRARY
SPEEDWAY, INDIANA

Light Taco Dip

Baked tortilla chips have excellent crispness and flavor, with a fraction of the calories found in regular fried chips. They're a thoughtful choice when your guest list includes people who are watching their weight.

PREP TIME: 20 MINUTES
MAKES 12 SERVINGS

2 (8-oz.) pkg. fat-free cream cheese, softened

1 (6-oz.) container frozen avocado dip, thawed

4 drops hot pepper sauce

2 cups shredded lettuce

1/3 cup chopped ripe olives

1 (4.5-oz.) can chopped green chiles

4 green onions, chopped

1 tomato, peeled, seeded and chopped

3 oz. (3/4 cup) shredded reduced-fat Cheddar cheese

1. In small bowl, combine cream cheese, avocado dip and hot pepper sauce; beat at low speed until well blended. Spread mixture on large serving plate. Top with all remaining ingredients.

2. Serve with baked tortilla chips.

Prepare cream cheese mixture up to 8 hours in advance. Just before serving, top with all remaining ingredients.

NUTRITION INFORMATION PER SERVING: SERVING SIZE: 1/12 of Recipe • Calories 100 • Calories from Fat 35 • % Daily Value: Total Fat 4 g 6% • Saturated Fat 2 g 10% • Cholesterol 10 mg 3% • Sodium 480 mg 20% • Total Carbohydrate 7 g 2% • Dietary Fiber 1 g 4% • Sugars 3 g • Protein 8 g • Vitamin A 15% • Vitamin C 10% • Calcium 25% • Iron 2% • **Dietary Exchanges:** 1 Vegetable, 1 Lean Meat, 1/2 Fat

Easy Cheesy Bean Dip

Served warm, this salsa-studded bean dip is casual party fare at its best. It's easy to put together on the spur of the moment, with just four ingredients.

PREP TIME: 15 MINUTES
MAKES 2 1/4 CUPS

1/4 cup chunky-style salsa

1 (8-oz.) can bean dip

1 (4.5-oz.) can chopped green chiles, drained

8 oz. (2 cups) shredded American cheese

1. In medium saucepan, combine all ingredients; mix well. Cook over low heat for 8 to 10 minutes or until cheese is melted, stirring constantly.

2. Serve warm with tortilla chips.

To prepare in microwave, combine salsa, bean dip and chiles in 1 1/2-quart microwave-safe bowl; mix well. Microwave on HIGH for 4 to 4 1/2 minutes or until mixture is hot, stirring once halfway through cooking. Stir in cheese. Microwave on HIGH for an additional minute or until cheese is melted. Stir before serving with tortilla chips.

NUTRITION INFORMATION PER SERVING: SERVING SIZE: 2 Tablespoons • Calories 60 • Calories from Fat 35 • % Daily Value: Total Fat 4 g 6% • Saturated Fat 2 g 10% • Cholesterol 10 mg 3% • Sodium 350 mg 15% • Total Carbohydrate 3 g 1% • Dietary Fiber 1 g 4% • Sugars 1 g • Protein 3 g • Vitamin A 4% • Vitamin C 2% • Calcium 10% • Iron 2% • **Dietary Exchanges:** 1/2 High-Fat Meat

Creamy Hot Black Bean Dip

Bean dips are very economical appetizers for a crowd. In this dip, the beans are smoothed with cream cheese and spiced up with cilantro and jalapeño chile.

PREP TIME: 25 MINUTES
MAKES 2 CUPS

1 (15-oz.) can black beans, drained, rinsed

1 (8-oz.) pkg. 1/3-less-fat cream cheese (Neufchâtel), softened

1/3 cup chopped red onion

2 tablespoons chopped fresh cilantro

1/2 teaspoon chili powder

1/4 teaspoon cumin

1/4 teaspoon dried oregano leaves

1/4 teaspoon hot pepper sauce

1 garlic clove, minced

1/2 jalapeño chile, chopped

2 tablespoons chopped fresh parsley or cilantro

1. Heat oven to 375°F. In food processor bowl with metal blade, combine all ingredients except parsley; process until well blended. Spread mixture in ungreased 9-inch pie pan.

2. Bake at 375°F. for 15 minutes or until hot.

3. Sprinkle with parsley. Serve with assorted cut-up fresh vegetables or baked tortilla chips.

make-ahead tip

Combine all ingredients except parsley in pie pan as directed in recipe. Cover; refrigerate up to 24 hours before baking. Uncover; bake at 375°F. for 15 minutes. Sprinkle with parsley.

NUTRITION INFORMATION PER SERVING: SERVING SIZE: 2 Tablespoons • Calories 60 • Calories from Fat 25 • % Daily Value: Total Fat 3 g 5% • Saturated Fat 2 g 10% • Cholesterol 10 mg 3% • Sodium 120 mg 5% • Total Carbohydrate 5 g 2% • Dietary Fiber 1 g 4% • Sugars 0 g • Protein 3 g • Vitamin A 4% • Vitamin C 0% • Calcium 2% • Iron 2% • **Dietary Exchanges:** 1/2 Starch, 1/2 Fat **OR** 1/2 Carbohydrate, 1/2 Fat

Slow-Cooked Hot Crab Dip

Heating the crab dip in a slow cooker preserves the texture of the sauce and gives you a head start on preparation.

PREP TIME: 10 MINUTES
(READY IN 2 HOURS 40 MINUTES)
MAKES 2 1/2 CUPS

1 (8-oz.) pkg. cream cheese, softened

1/2 cup mayonnaise

1/4 cup sour cream

1 teaspoon garlic salt

2 teaspoons white Worcestershire sauce

1 tablespoon dry sherry or apple juice

1/4 cup sliced green onions

2 (6-oz.) cans crabmeat, drained

1. In 1- to 3-quart slow cooker, combine cream cheese, mayonnaise, sour cream, garlic salt and Worcestershire sauce; mix well with fork. Add sherry, green onions and crabmeat; mix lightly.

2. Cover; cook on low setting for 1 1/2 to 2 1/2 hours. Serve with assorted crackers or cut-up fresh vegetables.

NUTRITION INFORMATION PER SERVING: SERVING SIZE: 2 Tablespoons • Calories 100 • Calories from Fat 80 • % Daily Value: Total Fat 9 g 14% • Saturated Fat 4 g 20% • Cholesterol 30 mg 10% • Sodium 210 mg 9% • Total Carbohydrate 1 g 1% • Dietary Fiber 0 g 0% • Sugars 1 g • Protein 4 g • Vitamin A 4% • Vitamin C 0% • Calcium 2% • Iron 0% • **Dietary Exchanges:** 1/2 Very Lean Meat, 2 Fat

Creamy Shrimp Dip

Leftover shrimp dip is delicious spread on a thick slice of whole-grain bread and topped with crisp lettuce and juicy tomato.

PREP TIME: 10 MINUTES
MAKES 1⅔ CUPS

1 (8-oz.) pkg. ⅓-less-fat cream cheese (Neufchâtel), softened

3 to 4 tablespoons skim milk

1 teaspoon salt-free lemon-herb seasoning

1 (4¼-oz.) can tiny shrimp, drained

1 tablespoon sliced green onions

1 tablespoon chopped green bell pepper

1. In small bowl, combine cream cheese, milk and lemon-herb seasoning; beat until smooth. Add shrimp, green onions and bell pepper; mix well.

2. Serve with assorted cut-up fresh vegetables or low-fat crackers. Store in refrigerator.

make-ahead tip

Dip can be refrigerated up to 8 hours.

NUTRITION INFORMATION PER SERVING: SERVING SIZE: 2 Tablespoons • Calories 60 • Calories from Fat 35 • % Daily Value: Total Fat 4 g 6% • Saturated Fat 3 g 15% • Cholesterol 25 mg 8% • Sodium 85 mg 4% • Total Carbohydrate 1 g 1% • Dietary Fiber 0 g 0% • Sugars 0 g • Protein 4 g • Vitamin A 4% • Vitamin C 0% • Calcium 2% • Iron 0% • **Dietary Exchanges:** ½ Very Lean Meat, ½ Fat

Bacon Cheddar Dip

Feature this smoky-salty mixture in a brunch buffet. It's good as a dip for fresh vegetables, as a spread for toasted bagels, or as a topping for scrambled eggs.

PREP TIME: 10 MINUTES
(READY IN 2 HOURS 10 MINUTES)
MAKES 1½ CUPS

1 cup sour cream

½ cup sharp Cheddar cold pack cheese food (from 8-oz. container), softened

3 tablespoons real bacon pieces

1 tablespoon chopped fresh parsley or 1 teaspoon dried parsley flakes

½ teaspoon instant minced onion

3 to 4 drops hot pepper sauce

1. In medium bowl, combine sour cream and cheese food; mix with wire whisk until well blended. Stir in all remaining ingredients. Refrigerate at least 2 hours to blend flavors.

2. Serve with assorted cut-up fresh vegetables.

make-ahead tip

Dip can be refrigerated up to 24 hours.

NUTRITION INFORMATION PER SERVING: SERVING SIZE: 2 Tablespoons • Calories 80 • Calories from Fat 60 • % Daily Value: Total Fat 7 g 11% • Saturated Fat 4 g 20% • Cholesterol 15 mg 5% • Sodium 160 mg 7% • Total Carbohydrate 2 g 1% • Dietary Fiber 0 g 0% • Sugars 2 g • Protein 3 g • Vitamin A 4% • Vitamin C 0% • Calcium 8% • Iron 0% • **Dietary Exchanges:** ½ High-Fat Meat, ½ Fat

Layered Pizza Dip

Assemble and refrigerate this dip ahead of time, then pop it into the preheated oven when the first guests arrive for a seemingly effortless hot dip.

PREP TIME: 25 MINUTES
MAKES 2 CUPS

1 (8-oz.) container soft cream cheese with chives and onions

½ cup chunky pizza sauce

½ cup chopped green bell pepper

⅓ cup finely chopped pepperoni

2 oz. (½ cup) shredded mozzarella cheese

2 oz. (½ cup) shredded Cheddar cheese

1. Heat oven to 350°F. In ungreased 9-inch pie pan or 1- to 1½-quart baking dish, layer all ingredients in order listed.

2. Bake at 350°F. for 10 to 15 minutes or until dip is hot and cheese is melted.

3. Serve warm with bagel crisps, bagel chips or assorted crackers.

make-ahead tip

Layer all ingredients in baking dish as directed in recipe. Cover; refrigerate up to 24 hours before baking. Uncover; bake as directed in recipe.

NUTRITION INFORMATION PER SERVING: SERVING SIZE: 2 Tablespoons • Calories 100 • Calories from Fat 70 • % Daily Value: Total Fat 8 g 12% • Saturated Fat 5 g 25% • Cholesterol 25 mg 8% • Sodium 160 mg 7% • Total Carbohydrate 2 g 1% • Dietary Fiber 0 g 0% • Sugars 1 g • Protein 4 g • Vitamin A 6% • Vitamin C 4% • Calcium 6% • Iron 0% • **Dietary Exchanges:** ½ High-Fat Meat, 1 Fat **OR** ½ High-Fat Meat, 1 Fat

Seven-Layer Pizza Dip

(Pictured on page 13.)

The pizza's all mixed up, with cheese on the bottom and sauce in the middle, but there's nothing confusing about the delicious layering of flavors.

PREP TIME: 30 MINUTES
MAKES 16 SERVINGS

1 (12-oz.) container (1½ cups) light cream cheese, softened

2 teaspoons dried Italian seasoning

3 tablespoons Italian-style dry bread crumbs

½ cup pizza sauce

1 (3.8-oz.) can sliced ripe olives, drained

2 tablespoons finely chopped green bell pepper

2 tablespoons finely chopped red bell pepper

1 oz. (¼ cup) shredded fresh Parmesan cheese

1. Heat oven to 400°F. In small bowl, combine cream cheese and Italian seasoning; blend well. Spread evenly in bottom of 9-inch shallow dish or glass pie pan.

2. Sprinkle bread crumbs over cream cheese mixture. Spoon pizza sauce over top. Sprinkle with olives, bell peppers and cheese.

3. Bake at 400°F. for 10 minutes or until cheese is melted.

4. Serve warm with assorted cut-up fresh vegetables and crisp breadsticks.

make-ahead tip

Layer all ingredients in dish as directed in recipe. Cover; refrigerate up to 24 hours before baking. Uncover; bake as directed in recipe.

NUTRITION INFORMATION PER SERVING: SERVING SIZE: 1/16 of Recipe • Calories 70 • Calories from Fat 45 • % Daily Value: Total Fat 5 g 8% • Saturated Fat 3 g 15% • Cholesterol 10 mg 3% • Sodium 230 mg 10% • Total Carbohydrate 4 g 1% • Dietary Fiber 0 g 0% • Sugars 2 g • Protein 3 g • Vitamin A 8% • Vitamin C 4% • Calcium 6% • Iron 2% • **Dietary Exchanges:** ½ Starch, 1 Fat **OR** ½ Carbohydrate, 1 Fat

Creamy Beef and Mushroom Dip

Madeira, a fortified wine from the island of the same name, has a natural affinity for meat and mushrooms that brings together the flavors of this cream cheese dip.

PREP TIME: 30 MINUTES
MAKES 3 CUPS

1 (8-oz.) pkg. 1/3-less-fat cream cheese (Neufchâtel), softened

1 tablespoon skim milk

1/2 cup chopped dried beef

1 (6-oz.) jar sliced mushrooms, drained

1/2 cup light sour cream

3 tablespoons chopped onion

2 to 3 tablespoons Madeira wine

1/2 teaspoon garlic powder

1/4 teaspoon pepper

1. Heat oven to 350°F. In medium bowl, beat cream cheese and milk on medium speed of electric mixer until light and fluffy. Stir in all remaining ingredients just until blended. Spoon mixture into ungreased 9-inch glass pie pan. Cover with foil.

2. Bake at 350°F. for 20 minutes or until thoroughly heated. Serve with toasted pita bread triangles and assorted cut-up fresh vegetables.

make-ahead tip

Combine all ingredients in pie pan as directed in recipe. Cover; refrigerate up to 24 hours before baking. Bake as directed in recipe.

NUTRITION INFORMATION PER SERVING: SERVING SIZE: 2 Tablespoons • Calories 40 • Calories from Fat 25 • % Daily Value: Total Fat 3 g 5% • Saturated Fat 2 g 10% • Cholesterol 10 mg 3% • Sodium 135 mg 6% • Total Carbohydrate 1 g 1% • Dietary Fiber 0 g 0% • Sugars 1 g • Protein 2 g • Vitamin A 4% • Vitamin C 0% • Calcium 0% • Iron 0% • **Dietary Exchanges:** 1/2 Medium-Fat Meat

Garden Fresh Salsa

This fresh, quick salsa closely resembles the Mexican original. For an added burst of citrus, grate some lime zest or peel (colored part of the rind) into the mixture before squeezing the lime juice.

PREP TIME: 15 MINUTES
MAKES 2 CUPS

2 large tomatoes, seeded, coarsely chopped

1 to 2 serrano chiles, seeded, chopped

1/3 cup chopped green onions

2 tablespoons chopped fresh cilantro

2 tablespoons fresh lime juice

1/4 teaspoon salt

1. In medium bowl, combine all ingredients; mix well.

2. Serve immediately, or cover and refrigerate until serving time. Salsa can be stored in refrigerator up to 1 week. Serve with tortilla chips.

NUTRITION INFORMATION PER SERVING: SERVING SIZE: 2 Tablespoons • Calories 10 • Calories from Fat 0 • % Daily Value: Total Fat 0 g 0% • Saturated Fat 0 g 0% • Cholesterol 0 mg 0% • Sodium 35 mg 1% • Total Carbohydrate 2 g 1% • Dietary Fiber 0 g 0% • Sugars 1 g • Protein 0 g • Vitamin A 4% • Vitamin C 35% • Calcium 0% • Iron 0% • **Dietary Exchanges:** Free

Pineapple Salsa

Use your nose to select a fresh pineapple. The sweeter the fragrance, the better the flavor is likely to be. To prepare fresh pineapple, chop off the spiky leaves from the top. Split the fruit lengthwise, then into lengthwise wedges. Cut away the hard core from the top length of each wedge, then run the knife between the skin and the fruit to loosen the golden flesh.

PREP TIME: 10 MINUTES
MAKES 2 CUPS

- 2 cups finely chopped fresh pineapple or 2 (8-oz.) cans crushed pineapple, drained
- ¼ cup orange marmalade
- 2 tablespoons chopped fresh cilantro
- 4 teaspoons chopped jalapeño chile
- 4 teaspoons diced pimientos
- 1 tablespoon lime juice
- ½ teaspoon salt

1. In medium bowl, combine all ingredients; mix well.

2. Serve immediately, or cover and refrigerate until serving time. Serve with chips or cooked shrimp.

NUTRITION INFORMATION PER SERVING: SERVING SIZE: 2 Tablespoons • Calories 25 • Calories from Fat 0 • % Daily Value: Total Fat 0 g 0% • Saturated Fat 0 g 0% • Cholesterol 0 mg 0% • Sodium 35 mg 1% • Total Carbohydrate 6 g 2% • Dietary Fiber 0 g 0% • Sugars 4 g • Protein 0 g • Vitamin A 0% • Vitamin C 10% • Calcium 0% • Iron 0% • **Dietary Exchanges:** ½ Fruit **OR** ½ Carbohydrate

Salsa Corn Dip

This warm and chunky dip is also delicious as a topping for grilled hamburgers.

PREP TIME: 10 MINUTES
MAKES 3 CUPS

- 1 (8-oz.) pkg. cream cheese, cut into cubes
- 1 (1.25-oz.) pkg. taco seasoning mix
- 1 cup chunky-style salsa
- 1 (11-oz.) can vacuum-packed whole kernel corn with red and green peppers

1. In medium saucepan, combine all ingredients; mix well. Cook over medium heat for 6 to 8 minutes or until thoroughly heated, stirring occasionally.

2. Serve warm with corn chips.

tip

To prepare in microwave, combine all ingredients in microwave-safe 1½-quart casserole; mix well. Cover. Microwave on HIGH for 2 to 3 minutes. Stir well. Microwave on HIGH for an additional 2 to 3 minutes or until thoroughly heated and cheese is melted. Stir before serving with corn chips.

NUTRITION INFORMATION PER SERVING: SERVING SIZE: 2 Tablespoons • Calories 50 • Calories from Fat 25 • % Daily Value: Total Fat 3 g 5% • Saturated Fat 2 g 10% • Cholesterol 10 mg 3% • Sodium 310 mg 13% • Total Carbohydrate 5 g 2% • Dietary Fiber 0 g 0% • Sugars 1 g • Protein 1 g • Vitamin A 4% • Vitamin C 0% • Calcium 0% • Iron 0% • **Dietary Exchanges:** ½ Starch, ½ Fat **OR** ½ Carbohydrate, ½ Fat

Classic Guacamole

The original avocado dip is still as delicious as ever. Use it as a dip, as a topping for tacos or nachos, or as a spread for a turkey or veggie sandwich.

PREP TIME: 15 MINUTES
(READY IN 45 MINUTES)
MAKES 3 CUPS

2 large ripe avocados, peeled, pitted and mashed

1/4 cup finely chopped onion

2 tablespoons lemon juice

2 to 5 drops hot pepper sauce, if desired

1/4 to 1/2 teaspoon garlic powder

1/4 teaspoon salt

Dash pepper

1 medium tomato, chopped

2 tablespoons finely chopped green chiles or 1 small fresh chile, chopped

1. In blender container or food processor bowl with metal blade, combine all ingredients except tomato and green chiles; cover and blend until smooth. Place in medium bowl.

2. Stir in tomato and green chiles. Cover; refrigerate at least 30 minutes before serving to blend flavors.

3. Serve with tortilla or corn chips.

NUTRITION INFORMATION PER SERVING: SERVING SIZE: 2 Tablespoons • Calories 35 • Calories from Fat 25 • % Daily Value: Total Fat 3 g 5% • Saturated Fat 0 g 0% • Cholesterol 0 mg 0% • Sodium 25 mg 1% • Total Carbohydrate 2 g 1% • Dietary Fiber 1 g 4% • Sugars 0 g • Protein 0 g • Vitamin A 2% • Vitamin C 8% • Calcium 0% • Iron 0% • **Dietary Exchanges:** 1/2 Fat

VARIATIONS
BACON GUACAMOLE

Stir in 2 slices crisply cooked bacon, crumbled, with the tomato and green chiles.

CREAMY GUACAMOLE

Add 1/4 cup mayonnaise or sour cream.

Guacamole Layered Dip

This impressive layered appetizer takes little effort, thanks to ready-made ingredients.

PREP TIME: 20 MINUTES
MAKES 3 1/4 CUPS

3/4 cup sour cream

1 (3-oz.) pkg. cream cheese, softened

3 oz. (3/4 cup) shredded hot pepper Monterey Jack cheese

3/4 cup purchased bean dip

1/2 cup chunky-style salsa

1 (8-oz.) container frozen or refrigerated guacamole, thawed

1/4 cup sliced ripe olives

1. In medium bowl, combine sour cream, cream cheese and Montery Jack cheese; mix well. Spread evenly on 10-inch serving plate. Refrigerate 5 to 10 minutes or until slightly set.

2. Carefully spread bean dip over sour cream mixture. Spread salsa over bean dip. Spoon guacamole onto salsa in ring 1 inch from edge. Sprinkle with olives.

3. Serve immediately, or cover loosely and refrigerate until serving time. Serve with tortilla chips.

NUTRITION INFORMATION PER SERVING: SERVING SIZE: 2 Tablespoons • Calories 70 • Calories from Fat 45 • % Daily Value: Total Fat 5 g 8% • Saturated Fat 3 g 15% • Cholesterol 10 mg 3% • Sodium 210 mg 9% • Total Carbohydrate 3 g 1% • Dietary Fiber 0 g 0% • Sugars 1 g • Protein 2 g • Vitamin A 4% • Vitamin C 0% • Calcium 4% • Iron 0% • **Dietary Exchanges:** 1/2 High-Fat Meat, 1/2 Fat

Roasted Vegetables with Spicy Aïoli Dip

This colorful assortment of crisp-tender roasted vegetables would also make a good side dish for roasted meat or poultry. If you wish, add a few sprigs of fresh thyme to the roasting pan.

PREP TIME: 20 MINUTES
(READY IN 40 MINUTES)
MAKES 8 SERVINGS

AÏOLI DIP

½ cup mayonnaise

¼ cup sour cream

2 tablespoons taco sauce

2 teaspoons chopped garlic in water (from 4.5-oz. jar)

VEGETABLES

1 medium red bell pepper, cut into 1½-inch squares

1 medium red onion, cut into wedges

1 medium yellow summer squash, cut into 1½-inch slices

12 fresh whole mushrooms

¼ lb. fresh whole green beans, trimmed

1 tablespoon olive or vegetable oil

1. In small bowl, combine all dip ingredients; mix well. Refrigerate at least 30 minutes to blend flavors.

2. Meanwhile, heat oven to 450°F. In large bowl, combine all vegetables with oil; toss to coat evenly. Arrange vegetables in ungreased 15x10x1-inch baking pan.

3. Bake at 450°F. for 15 to 20 minutes or until crisp-tender. Serve warm vegetables with dip.

NUTRITION INFORMATION PER SERVING: SERVING SIZE: ⅛ of Recipe • Calories 160 • Calories from Fat 130 • % Daily Value: Total Fat 14 g 22% • Saturated Fat 3 g 15% • Cholesterol 10 mg 3% • Sodium 110 mg 5% • Total Carbohydrate 7 g 2% • Dietary Fiber 2 g 8% • Sugars 4 g • Protein 2 g • Vitamin A 15% • Vitamin C 35% • Calcium 4% • Iron 4% • **Dietary Exchanges:** 1 Vegetable, 3 Fat

Rustler Chili Fondue

This spiced-up chili is versatile: Try it as a filling for tacos or sloppy Joe-style sandwiches, or as a topping for rice.

PREP TIME: 15 MINUTES
MAKES 5½ CUPS FONDUE; 22 SERVINGS

1 (16-oz.) can fat-free refried beans

1 (15-oz.) can spicy chili beans, undrained

1 (14-oz.) container refrigerated salsa

1 (4.5-oz.) can chopped green chiles, drained, rinsed

1 teaspoon cumin

3 teaspoons chili powder

3 oz. (¾ cup) shredded reduced-fat sharp Cheddar cheese

¼ cup sliced green onions

6 red or green bell peppers, cut into wedges

5 cups sourdough bread cubes or 7 oz. baked low-fat tortilla chips

1. In large saucepan, combine refried beans, chili beans, salsa, green chiles, cumin and chili powder; mix well. Bring to a boil over medium heat. Cook 4 to 5 minutes or until thoroughly heated, stirring frequently.

2. Spoon fondue into 9-inch shallow dish or glass pie pan. Sprinkle with cheese and green onions. Serve with pepper wedges and bread cubes for dipping.

NUTRITION INFORMATION PER SERVING: SERVING SIZE: 1/22 of Recipe • Calories 100 • Calories from Fat 20 • % Daily Value: Total Fat 2 g 3% • Saturated Fat 1 g 5% • Cholesterol 3 mg 1% • Sodium 460 mg 19% • Total Carbohydrate 16 g 5% • Dietary Fiber 3 g 12% • Sugars 3 g • Protein 4 g • Vitamin A 30% • Vitamin C 50% • Calcium 6% • Iron 6% • **Dietary Exchanges:** 1 Starch, 1 Vegetable **OR** 1 Carbohydrate, 1 Vegetable

Cheese Fondue with Roasted Vegetable Dippers

Roasting vegetables enhances their natural sugars, making them a good companion for bread in this cheesy, wine-spiked fondue.

PREP TIME: 30 MINUTES
MAKES 12 SERVINGS

DIPPERS

2 cups fresh cauliflower florets

1 medium green bell pepper, cut into 1 1/2-inch pieces

1 medium red bell pepper, cut into 1 1/2-inch pieces

1 medium yellow summer squash, cut into 1/2-inch slices

1 (8-oz.) pkg. fresh whole mushrooms

2 cups French bread cubes

1 tablespoon olive oil

FONDUE

4 oz. (1 cup) shredded sharp Cheddar cheese

4 oz. (1 cup) shredded Havarti cheese

4 oz. (1 cup) shredded American cheese

2 tablespoons all-purpose flour

1 cup dry white wine

1/4 teaspoon garlic powder

1. Heat oven to 450°F. In large bowl, combine all dippers with oil; toss to coat evenly. Arrange in ungreased 15x10x1-inch baking pan. Bake at 450°F. for 15 to 20 minutes or until vegetables are crisp-tender and bread cubes are toasted.

2. In medium bowl, combine all cheeses and flour; toss to mix. Place wine in medium saucepan; cook over medium heat about 1 minute or until very hot. DO NOT BOIL. Add cheese mixture 1/2 cup at a time, stirring each time until melted. Cook until very warm. Pour into fondue pot. Stir in garlic powder. Keep warm over medium-low heat.

3. To serve, skewer roasted vegetables and bread cubes with fondue forks or wooden skewers to be dipped into warm cheese.

NUTRITION INFORMATION PER SERVING: SERVING SIZE: 1/12 of Recipe • Calories 170 • Calories from Fat 100 • % Daily Value: Total Fat 11 g 17% • Saturated Fat 6 g 30% • Cholesterol 30 mg 10% • Sodium 300 mg 13% • Total Carbohydrate 9 g 3% • Dietary Fiber 2 g 8% • Sugars 2 g • Protein 9 g • Vitamin A 15% • Vitamin C 35% • Calcium 20% • Iron 4% • **Dietary Exchanges:** 1/2 Starch, 1 High-Fat Meat, 1/2 Fat **OR** 1/2 Carbohydrate, 1 High-Fat Meat, 1/2 Fat

Appetizer Beer Cheese Fondue

Fondue originates in Switzerland, where it serves as a casual meal enjoyed by friends who dip chunks of bread into a shared pot.

PREP TIME: 30 MINUTES
MAKES 6 SERVINGS

1 (1-lb.) round loaf sourdough bread

1 (8-oz.) pkg. pasteurized prepared cheese product, cubed

3/4 cup frozen cut broccoli, cooked, drained and chopped

2 tablespoons beer

2 tablespoons diced pimientos

1/2 teaspoon dry mustard

1. Heat oven to 350°F. Cut bread into bite-sized pieces. Place bread pieces in ungreased 15x10x1-inch baking pan.

2. Bake at 350°F. for 10 minutes or until lightly toasted, stirring twice. Transfer to serving bowl or basket.

3. Meanwhile, place cheese in large saucepan; cook over low heat until cheese is melted, stirring occasionally. Stir in broccoli, beer, pimientos and dry mustard. Cook until hot, stirring occasionally. Pour cheese mixture into ceramic fondue pot over low heat.

4. To serve, skewer toasted bread pieces with fondue forks or wooden skewers to be dipped into warm cheese mixture.

NUTRITION INFORMATION PER SERVING: SERVING SIZE: 1/6 of Recipe • Calories 310 • Calories from Fat 90 • % Daily Value: Total Fat 10 g 15% • Saturated Fat 6 g 30% • Cholesterol 20 mg 7% • Sodium 970 mg 40% • Total Carbohydrate 43 g 14% • Dietary Fiber 3 g 12% • Sugars 6 g • Protein 13 g • Vitamin A 10% • Vitamin C 15% • Calcium 25% • Iron 10% • **Dietary Exchanges:** 3 Starch, 1/2 High-Fat Meat, 1 Fat **OR** 3 Carbohydrate, 1/2 High-Fat Meat, 1 Fat

Holiday Mexican Spread

This appetizer looks like a candy cane, with snow-white sour cream and red bell pepper for stripes.

PREP TIME: 15 MINUTES
(READY IN 1 HOUR 15 MINUTES)
MAKES 3 CUPS

1 (8-oz.) pkg. cream cheese, softened

8 oz. (2 cups) shredded colby cheese

1 (4.5-oz.) can chopped green chiles, drained

1/3 cup sliced green onions

2/3 cup chopped red bell pepper

1/2 cup sour cream

Chopped fresh parsley

1. In large bowl, combine cream cheese and colby cheese; blend well. Stir in chiles, green onions and 1/3 cup of the bell pepper.

2. Place mixture on sheet of plastic wrap. Shape into 12-inch log. Bend upper third of log to form candy cane shape. With plastic wrap, transfer to serving plate; reshape if necessary. Cover; refrigerate at least 1 hour before serving.

3. To serve, spread candy cane with sour cream. Sprinkle remaining 1/3 cup bell pepper in stripes to resemble candy cane; sprinkle stripes with parsley. Serve with assorted crackers.

Cheese spread can be shaped and refrigerated up to 24 hours. Just before serving, spread with sour cream and decorate as directed in recipe.

NUTRITION INFORMATION PER SERVING: SERVING SIZE: 2 Tablespoons • Calories 80 • Calories from Fat 60 • % Daily Value: Total Fat 7 g 11% • Saturated Fat 5 g 25% • Cholesterol 20 mg 7% • Sodium 110 mg 5% • Total Carbohydrate 1 g 1% • Dietary Fiber 0 g 0% • Sugars 1 g • Protein 3 g • Vitamin A 10% • Vitamin C 10% • Calcium 8% • Iron 0% • **Dietary Exchanges:** 1/2 High-Fat Meat, 1/2 Fat

Veggie Wreath with Creamy Sun-Dried Tomato Dip

Deck the buffet table with this holiday-motif wreath. Look for napkins and paper plates imprinted with wreaths, too.

PREP TIME: 30 MINUTES
(READY IN 1 HOUR 30 MINUTES)
MAKES 12 SERVINGS

DIP

1 (8-oz.) container nonfat sour cream

¼ cup light mayonnaise

1 teaspoon sugar

1 teaspoon onion powder

½ teaspoon lemon-pepper seasoning

¼ teaspoon garlic powder

¼ cup finely chopped sun-dried tomatoes packed in olive oil and herbs (from 6.5-oz. jar)

WREATH

1 (16-oz.) pkg. fresh broccoli florets

1 (16-oz.) pkg. fresh cauliflower florets

⅓ cup drained roasted red bell peppers (from 7.25-oz. jar)

1. In medium bowl, combine all dip ingredients except sun-dried tomatoes; beat until smooth and creamy. Fold in tomatoes. Cover; refrigerate at least 1 hour to blend flavors.

2. Bring about 4 quarts (16 cups) water to a boil in Dutch oven. Add broccoli and cauliflower; cook 30 seconds. Drain; rinse with cold water. Cover; refrigerate 1 hour or until cool.

3. Drain broccoli and cauliflower again. Arrange in ring on large serving platter to form wreath shape, alternating stripes of broccoli and cauliflower. Decorate with red bell peppers cut into stars or long strips. Place small bowl of dip in center.

make-ahead tip

Prepare dip and cook vegetables as directed in recipe. Cover each separately; refrigerate up to 24 hours. Just before serving, shape wreath and decorate as directed in recipe.

NUTRITION INFORMATION PER SERVING: SERVING SIZE: 1/12 of Recipe • Calories 60 • Calories from Fat 20 • % Daily Value: Total Fat 2 g 3% • Saturated Fat 0 g 0% • Cholesterol 0 mg 0% • Sodium 120 mg 5% • Total Carbohydrate 7 g 2% • Dietary Fiber 2 g 8% • Sugars 3 g • Protein 3 g • Vitamin A 30% • Vitamin C 100% • Calcium 6% • Iron 4% • **Dietary Exchanges:** ½ Starch, ½ Fat **OR** ½ Carbohydrate, ½ Fat

Hot Macadamia Spread

Macadamia nuts are among the priciest—and tastiest—of nuts. It's an affordable luxury here. Just 1/3 cup gives flavor and crunch to this tempting hot dip.

PREP TIME: 10 MINUTES
(READY IN 30 MINUTES)
MAKES 2 1/3 CUPS

1/2 cup sour cream

1 (8-oz.) pkg. cream cheese, softened

1/4 cup chopped green bell pepper

1/4 cup sliced green onions

1 (8-oz.) can crushed pineapple, drained

1/2 teaspoon Chinese five-spice powder

1/3 cup chopped macadamia nuts

Chopped green bell pepper, if desired

1. Heat oven to 375°F. In medium bowl, combine sour cream and cream cheese; blend well. Add 1/4 cup bell pepper, green onions, pineapple and five-spice powder; mix well. Spread evenly in ungreased 1-quart baking dish. Sprinkle with nuts.

2. Bake at 375°F. for 15 to 20 minutes or until thoroughly heated.

3. Garnish with chopped bell pepper. Serve warm with assorted crackers.

make-ahead tip

Combine all ingredients in baking dish as directed in recipe. Cover; refrigerate up to 24 hours before baking. Uncover; bake as directed in recipe.

NUTRITION INFORMATION PER SERVING: SERVING SIZE: 2 Tablespoons • Calories 80 • Calories from Fat 60 • % Daily Value: Total Fat 7 g 11% • Saturated Fat 4 g 20% • Cholesterol 15 mg 5% • Sodium 40 mg 2% • Total Carbohydrate 2 g 1% • Dietary Fiber 0 g 0% • Sugars 2 g • Protein 1 g • Vitamin A 6% • Vitamin C 4% • Calcium 2% • Iron 0% • **Dietary Exchanges:** 1 1/2 Fat

Muenster Cheese Spread with Pumpernickel Toast

If you can't find cocktail bread, cut shapes from regular pumpernickel bread with a cookie cutter. Save the scraps for bread pudding or stuffing.

PREP TIME: 30 MINUTES
MAKES 3/4 CUP SPREAD; 8 SERVINGS

4 oz. cream cheese, softened

2 oz. (1/2 cup) shredded Muenster cheese

1 tablespoon chopped fresh dill

1/8 teaspoon coarse-ground black pepper

16 slices cocktail pumpernickel bread

4 teaspoons butter, softened

Paprika

Fresh dill sprigs

1. In small bowl, beat cream cheese until smooth. Add Muenster cheese, chopped dill and pepper; mix well. Spoon into small serving bowl. Cover; refrigerate until serving time.

2. Heat oven to 400°F. Spread bread slices with butter. Place slices on ungreased cookie sheet. Bake at 400°F. for 4 to 6 minutes or until lightly toasted.

3. Garnish cheese spread with paprika and dill sprigs. Serve with pumpernickel toast.

make-ahead tip

Cheese spread can be refrigerated up to 24 hours. Serve as directed in recipe.

NUTRITION INFORMATION PER SERVING: SERVING SIZE: 1/8 of Recipe • Calories 130 • Calories from Fat 80 • % Daily Value: Total Fat 9 g 14% • Saturated Fat 6 g 30% • Cholesterol 25 mg 8% • Sodium 200 mg 8% • Total Carbohydrate 7 g 2% • Dietary Fiber 1 g 4% • Sugars 1 g • Protein 4 g • Vitamin A 8% • Vitamin C 0% • Calcium 8% • Iron 4% • **Dietary Exchanges:** 1/2 Starch, 1/2 High-Fat Meat, 1 Fat **OR** 1/2 Carbohydrate, 1/2 High-Fat Meat, 1 Fat

Curried Gouda Spread

The finished product is spooned into the hollowed-out wax shell that originally held the Gouda cheese. If the wax is cracked, simply spoon the mixture into a small serving bowl instead.

PREP TIME: 20 MINUTES
(READY IN 4 HOURS 20 MINUTES)
MAKES 1¼ CUPS

1 (7-oz.) round Gouda cheese with red wax coating

1 (3-oz.) pkg. cream cheese, softened

1 tablespoon honey

2 teaspoons lemon juice

¼ teaspoon curry powder

1. With sharp knife, remove about 3-inch diameter slice from top of Gouda cheese. Carefully spoon out cheese, placing cheese in food processor bowl with metal blade and leaving wax coating intact to form shell.

2. Add all remaining ingredients to cheese; process until smooth and well blended. Spoon cheese mixture into shell, mounding in center. Cover; refrigerate at least 3 hours or overnight to blend flavors.

3. For easier spreading, let cheese spread stand at room temperature for 1 hour before serving. To serve, place cheese on serving tray; surround with wedges of fresh peaches, pears, apple or pineapple, grapes and/or assorted crackers. Spread cheese on fruit or crackers.

NUTRITION INFORMATION PER SERVING: SERVING SIZE: 2 Tablespoons • Calories 110 • Calories from Fat 70 • % Daily Value: Total Fat 8 g 12% • Saturated Fat 5 g 25% • Cholesterol 30 mg 10% • Sodium 190 mg 8% • Total Carbohydrate 3 g 1% • Dietary Fiber 0 g 0% • Sugars 2 g • Protein 6 g • Vitamin A 4% • Vitamin C 0% • Calcium 15% • Iron 0% • **Dietary Exchanges:** 1 High-Fat Meat

Herbed Cheese Ring with Apples

Celebrate the coming of fall and the season's crisp apples with this herb-spiked cheese ring. To blend the mixture smoothly, soften the cream cheese at room temperature for about an hour before beginning the recipe.

PREP TIME: 20 MINUTES
(READY IN 2 HOURS 20 MINUTES)
MAKES 8 SERVINGS

1 (12-oz.) container (1½ cups) fat-free cream cheese, softened

2 oz. feta cheese, crumbled (½ cup)

1 oz. blue cheese, crumbled (¼ cup)

½ teaspoon dried basil leaves

½ teaspoon dried rosemary leaves, crushed

1 tablespoon finely chopped fresh chives or green onion tops

2 red or green apples, cut into 16 slices each, or assorted fat-free crackers

1. Line 2-cup ring mold or small decorative mold with cheesecloth or plastic wrap.

2. In medium bowl, combine cream cheese, feta cheese, blue cheese, basil and rosemary; beat with electric mixer or spoon until well mixed.

3. Spoon cheese mixture into mold, spreading evenly. Cover with plastic wrap; refrigerate about 2 hours or until firm.

4. To serve, unmold onto serving platter. Sprinkle with chives. Serve with apple slices.

Cheese spread can be refrigerated up to 24 hours. Garnish just before serving.

NUTRITION INFORMATION PER SERVING: SERVING SIZE: ⅛ of Recipe • Calories 110 • Calories from Fat 25 • % Daily Value: Total Fat 3 g 5% • Saturated Fat 2 g 10% • Cholesterol 15 mg 5% • Sodium 400 mg 17% • Total Carbohydrate 12 g 4% • Dietary Fiber 1 g 4% • Sugars 10 g • Protein 8 g • Vitamin A 15% • Vitamin C 25% • Calcium 6% • Iron 0% • **Dietary Exchanges:** 1 Fruit, 1 Lean Meat **OR** 1 Carbohydrate, 1 Lean Meat

Smoky Cheese Ring

Fill the center of the cheese ring with sprigs of fresh parsley.

PREP TIME: 20 MINUTES
(READY IN 3 HOURS 20 MINUTES)
MAKES 2¼ CUPS

1 (8-oz.) pkg. cream cheese, softened

1 (7-oz.) round smoky Gouda cheese, shredded

¼ cup mayonnaise

1 (2.25-oz.) jar sliced dried beef, rinsed, dried and finely chopped

¼ cup thinly sliced green onions

¼ cup chopped fresh parsley

1 tablespoon pimiento pieces, well drained

1. Line 8-inch pie pan with plastic wrap. Set 6-oz. custard cup upside down in center.

2. In medium bowl, combine cream cheese, Gouda cheese and mayonnaise; mix until well blended. Stir in dried beef and green onions. Spoon cheese mixture into pie pan around custard cup, smoothing and packing firmly with rubber scraper. Cover tightly with plastic wrap; refrigerate at least 3 hours or until firm.

3. To serve, uncover ring; turn upside down onto serving plate. Remove plastic wrap and custard cup. Cover top of ring with parsley, pressing in lightly. Garnish with pimiento pieces. Serve with assorted crackers.

make-ahead tip

Cheese ring can be refrigerated up to 24 hours. Just before serving, cover with parsley and garnish with pimiento as directed in recipe.

NUTRITION INFORMATION PER SERVING: SERVING SIZE: 2 Tablespoons • Calories 110 • Calories from Fat 90 • % Daily Value: Total Fat 10 g 15% • Saturated Fat 5 g 25% • Cholesterol 30 mg 10% • Sodium 270 mg 11% • Total Carbohydrate 1 g 1% • Dietary Fiber 0 g 0% • Sugars 1 g • Protein 5 g • Vitamin A 6% • Vitamin C 2% • Calcium 8% • Iron 2% • **Dietary Exchanges:** ½ High-Fat Meat, 1 Fat

Herbed Cheese Spread

To vary the flavor, mix the cheese with fresh chopped basil or rosemary instead of thyme.

PREP TIME: 15 MINUTES
MAKES 1½ CUPS

1 (8-oz.) pkg. cream cheese, softened

3 oz. (¾ cup) crumbled feta cheese

2 tablespoons chopped fresh parsley

2 tablespoons cut (1-inch) fresh chives

1 tablespoon fresh thyme leaves

Dash coarse-ground black pepper

1 small garlic clove

¼ cup finely chopped ripe olives

1. In food processor bowl with metal blade, combine all ingredients except olives; process until well blended. Stir in olives.

2. Spoon into serving bowl. Serve with assorted crackers.

NUTRITION INFORMATION PER SERVING: SERVING SIZE: 2 Tablespoons • Calories 90 • Calories from Fat 70 • % Daily Value: Total Fat 8 g 12% • Saturated Fat 5 g 25% • Cholesterol 25 mg 8% • Sodium 160 mg 7% • Total Carbohydrate 1 g 1% • Dietary Fiber 0 g 0% • Sugars 1 g • Protein 3 g • Vitamin A 8% • Vitamin C 2% • Calcium 6% • Iron 2% • **Dietary Exchanges:** ½ High-Fat Meat, 1 Fat

Star-Studded Cheese Spread

If you invite friends over to watch the Academy Awards, set out this festive cheese spread. Garnish the platter with slices of golden star fruit, and offer star-shaped crackers on the side.

PREP TIME: 15 MINUTES
MAKES 2½ CUPS

- 1 (7-oz.) pkg. round Gouda cheese with red wax coating
- 1 (3-oz.) pkg. cream cheese, softened
- 3 tablespoons purchased mango chutney
- ¼ cup chopped green onions

1. With 3-inch star-shaped cookie cutter or paper pattern as a guide and a small sharp knife, cut opening in top of red wax coating of Gouda cheese. Carefully spoon out cheese, placing cheese in food processor bowl with metal blade and leaving wax coating intact to form shell.

2. Add cream cheese and chutney to cheese; process until smooth. Stir in green onions. Spoon half of mixture into wax shell, mounding in center. Refrigerate remaining cheese mixture; refill wax shell as needed.

3. Serve with assorted crackers.

NUTRITION INFORMATION PER SERVING: SERVING SIZE: 2 Tablespoons • Calories 60 • Calories from Fat 35 • % Daily Value: Total Fat 4 g 6% • Saturated Fat 3 g 15% • Cholesterol 15 mg 5% • Sodium 120 mg 5% • Total Carbohydrate 3 g 1% • Dietary Fiber 0 g 0% • Sugars 2 g • Protein 3 g • Vitamin A 2% • Vitamin C 0% • Calcium 8% • Iron 0% • **Dietary Exchanges:** ½ High-Fat Meat

Beer Cheese Spread

The alcohol in the beer boils away, but the flavor remains to work its magic in this sharp-flavored cheese spread.

PREP TIME: 10 MINUTES
(READY IN 1 HOUR 40 MINUTES)
MAKES 1¼ CUPS

- 8 oz. (2 cups) finely shredded sharp Cheddar cheese
- 1 teaspoon Worcestershire sauce
- ½ teaspoon hot honey mustard or Dijon mustard
- ⅛ teaspoon ground red pepper (cayenne)
- 1 garlic clove, minced
- ⅓ cup beer
- 2 tablespoons margarine or butter, softened

1. In food processor bowl with metal blade, combine cheese, Worcestershire sauce, mustard, ground red pepper and garlic.

2. Bring beer just to a boil in small saucepan. Pour over cheese mixture in processor; process 1 to 1½ minutes or just until smooth. Add margarine; process until blended. Spoon into serving bowl. Cover; refrigerate at least 1 hour to blend flavors.

3. For easier spreading, let cheese spread stand at room temperature for at least 30 minutes before serving. Serve with assorted crackers.

NUTRITION INFORMATION PER SERVING: SERVING SIZE: 2 Tablespoons • Calories 120 • Calories from Fat 90 • % Daily Value: Total Fat 10 g 15% • Saturated Fat 5 g 25% • Cholesterol 25 mg 8% • Sodium 180 mg 8% • Total Carbohydrate 1 g 1% • Dietary Fiber 0 g 0% • Sugars 0 g • Protein 6 g • Vitamin A 8% • Vitamin C 0% • Calcium 15% • Iron 0% • **Dietary Exchanges:** 1 High-Fat Meat, ½ Fat

Cherry Cheese Spread

Smoky Swiss cheese lends intriguing character to a spread made with three other cheeses, nuts and dried cherries.

PREP TIME: 15 MINUTES
(READY IN 25 HOURS 15 MINUTES)
MAKES 2¼ CUPS

1 (8-oz.) pkg. cream cheese, cubed

4 oz. Havarti cheese, cubed

4 oz. smoky Swiss cheese, shredded (1 cup)

1 oz. (¼ cup) crumbled blue cheese

¼ cup slivered almonds

3 tablespoons cherry-flavored liqueur

1 teaspoon chopped shallot

¼ cup dried cherries, chopped

1. Let all cheeses stand at room temperature for at least 30 minutes to soften. Meanwhile, heat oven to 350°F. Spread almonds on ungreased cookie sheet. Bake at 350°F. for 5 to 7 minutes or until golden brown, stirring occasionally. Cool.

2. In food processor bowl with metal blade, combine all cheeses, liqueur and shallot; process until smooth. Add cherries and almonds; process with on/off pulses until almonds are chopped. Spoon into crock or other container; cover. Refrigerate at least 24 hours to blend flavors.

3. Let cheese spread stand at room temperature for 30 minutes before serving. Serve with thin slices of baguette-style French bread, assorted crackers, celery sticks or fresh pea pods.

NUTRITION INFORMATION PER SERVING: SERVING SIZE: 2 Tablespoons • Calories 120 • Calories from Fat 80 • % Daily Value: Total Fat 9 g 14% • Saturated Fat 5 g 25% • Cholesterol 25 mg 8% • Sodium 115 mg 5% • Total Carbohydrate 4 g 1% • Dietary Fiber 0 g 0% • Sugars 2 g • Protein 5 g • Vitamin A 8% • Vitamin C 0% • Calcium 15% • Iron 0% • **Dietary Exchanges:** ½ Fruit, ½ High-Fat Meat, 1 Fat **OR** ½ Carbohydrate, ½ High-Fat Meat, 1 Fat

Antipasto Spread

Zucchini does not need to be peeled if the skin is tender and unwaxed. Grating the skin into the vegetable mixture adds deep green flecks to the spread.

PREP TIME: 15 MINUTES
(READY IN 2 HOURS 15 MINUTES)
MAKES 4 CUPS

1 cup sliced fresh mushrooms

1 medium zucchini, shredded (1 cup)

1 medium carrot, shredded (¾ cup)

2 tablespoons sliced green onions

1 (2¼-oz.) can sliced ripe olives, drained

⅓ cup purchased Italian salad dressing

2 (4- to 5-oz.) containers gourmet spreadable cheese with garlic and herbs

1. In medium bowl, combine mushrooms, zucchini, carrot, green onions, olives and dressing; mix well. Cover; refrigerate at least 2 hours or overnight.

2. To serve, spread cheese on 10-inch serving plate. Drain vegetables; spoon onto cheese. Serve with assorted crackers.

NUTRITION INFORMATION PER SERVING: SERVING SIZE: 2 Tablespoons • Calories 45 • Calories from Fat 35 • % Daily Value: Total Fat 4 g 6% • Saturated Fat 2 g 10% • Cholesterol 10 mg 3% • Sodium 90 mg 4% • Total Carbohydrate 1 g 1% • Dietary Fiber 0 g 0% • Sugars 1 g • Protein 1 g • Vitamin A 15% • Vitamin C 0% • Calcium 0% • Iron 0% • **Dietary Exchanges:** 1 Fat

Sicilian Eggplant Caponata

Serve caponata warm or cool on slices of baguette. It's also good as a chunky sauce for pasta, with plenty of freshly grated Parmesan.

PREP TIME: 35 MINUTES
(READY IN 50 MINUTES)
MAKES 2 CUPS

½ lb. tomatoes (1 large or 2 small)

½ lb. baby eggplants or ½ medium eggplant, unpeeled, cut into ½-inch cubes (2 cups)

2 teaspoons olive oil

⅓ cup chopped onion

1 to 2 garlic cloves, minced

¼ cup chopped fresh basil

½ teaspoon sugar

¼ teaspoon salt

2 teaspoons white wine vinegar

1. Bring 4 cups water to a boil in large saucepan over high heat. Place tomatoes in water for 10 seconds. With slotted spoon, remove tomatoes from water; set aside to cool.

2. Place eggplant cubes in water in saucepan; cover and simmer 10 minutes. Drain; set eggplant aside.

3. Wipe saucepan dry with paper towels. Heat oil in saucepan over medium heat until hot. Add onion; cook 5 minutes, stirring frequently.

4. Meanwhile, remove and discard skins from tomatoes; coarsely chop tomatoes.

5. Add tomatoes, eggplant, garlic, basil, sugar, salt and vinegar to onion in saucepan; mix well. Cook over medium heat for 10 minutes, stirring occasionally. Cool 2 hours or until room temperature, or refrigerate until serving time.

6. Serve caponata on slices of baguette-style French bread.

make-ahead tip

Dip can be refrigerated up to 2 days.

NUTRITION INFORMATION PER SERVING: SERVING SIZE: ¼ Cup • Calories 30 • Calories from Fat 10 • % Daily Value: Total Fat 1 g 2% • Saturated Fat 0 g 0% • Cholesterol 0 mg 0% • Sodium 70 mg 3% • Total Carbohydrate 4 g 1% • Dietary Fiber 1 g 4% • Sugars 2 g • Protein 1 g • Vitamin A 6% • Vitamin C 8% • Calcium 0% • Iron 0% • **Dietary Exchanges:** 1 Vegetable

Mixed Olive Spread

Process the ingredients with on/off pulses to yield a spread that is smooth enough to hold together, yet retains an interesting texture.

PREP TIME: 5 MINUTES
MAKES 1 1/4 CUPS

1/2 cup pitted kalamata olives, drained

1/2 cup pitted ripe olives, drained

1/2 cup pimiento-stuffed green olives, drained

2 garlic cloves, chopped

3 tablespoons olive oil

2 tablespoons balsamic vinegar

1. In food processor bowl with metal blade, combine all ingredients; process with on/off pulses until finely chopped.

2. Serve with small, thin slices of Italian bread or baguette-style French bread.

NUTRITION INFORMATION PER SERVING: SERVING SIZE: 2 Tablespoons • Calories 70 • Calories from Fat 60 • % Daily Value: Total Fat 7 g 11% • Saturated Fat 1 g 5% • Cholesterol 0 mg 0% • Sodium 330 mg 14% • Total Carbohydrate 1 g 1% • Dietary Fiber 0 g 0% • Sugars 0 g • Protein 0 g • Vitamin A 0% • Vitamin C 0% • Calcium 0% • Iron 0% • **Dietary Exchanges:** 1 1/2 Fat

Blue Cheese Ball with Walnuts

The blue cheese-walnut combo also suits slices of crisp apple or ripe pear.

PREP TIME: 15 MINUTES
MAKES 1 1/2 CUPS

1 (8-oz.) pkg. cream cheese, softened

1 (4-oz.) pkg. blue cheese, room temperature

2 tablespoons chopped green onions

2/3 cup chopped walnuts

1. Beat cream cheese in medium bowl until smooth and creamy. Add blue cheese and green onions; blend well. Shape mixture into ball. Roll in walnuts.

2. Serve immediately, or cover loosely and refrigerate until serving time. Serve with assorted crackers.

make-ahead tip

Cheese ball can be refrigerated up to 24 hours.

NUTRITION INFORMATION PER SERVING: SERVING SIZE: 2 Tablespoons • Calories 150 • Calories from Fat 130 • % Daily Value: Total Fat 14 g 22% • Saturated Fat 6 g 30% • Cholesterol 30 mg 10% • Sodium 190 mg 8% • Total Carbohydrate 2 g 1% • Dietary Fiber 0 g 0% • Sugars 1 g • Protein 4 g • Vitamin A 6% • Vitamin C 0% • Calcium 8% • Iron 2% • **Dietary Exchanges:** 1/2 High-Fat Meat, 2 Fat

Three-Cheese Ball

This sesame-coated appetizer, made with cream cheese, chèvre and Parmesan, looks great on a holiday buffet table and makes a good hostess gift, too. For neatest shaping, use the seed-sprinkled waxed paper rather than your bare hands. You could also use minced almonds or walnuts instead of sesame seeds.

PREP TIME: 15 MINUTES
(READY IN 2 HOURS 15 MINUTES)
MAKES 2¼ CUPS

1 (8-oz.) pkg. cream cheese

1 (6-oz.) pkg. chèvre (goat) cheese

4 oz. (1 cup) shredded fresh Parmesan cheese

⅓ cup chopped fresh basil

¼ cup diced red bell pepper

¼ cup toasted sesame seed

1. Place cheeses in food processor bowl with metal blade; process until well blended.

2. Add basil and bell pepper; process with on/off pulses 2 or 3 times or until finely chopped and well blended. Cover; refrigerate at least 2 hours or until firm.

3. Spread sesame seed evenly over waxed paper. Spoon cheese mixture in mound over seed. Gently shape cheese mixture into ball, rolling in seed to coat.

4. Serve immediately, or cover loosely and refrigerate until serving time. Serve with assorted crackers or cocktail sourdough bread slices.

make-ahead tip

Cheese mixture can be refrigerated up to 24 hours. Prepare cheese ball and serve as directed in recipe.

NUTRITION INFORMATION PER SERVING: SERVING SIZE: 2 Tablespoons • Calories 120 • Calories from Fat 90 • % Daily Value: Total Fat 10 g 15% • Saturated Fat 6 g 30% • Cholesterol 25 mg 8% • Sodium 190 mg 8% • Total Carbohydrate 1 g 1% • Dietary Fiber 0 g 0% • Sugars 1 g • Protein 6 g • Vitamin A 10% • Vitamin C 4% • Calcium 10% • Iron 2% • **Dietary Exchanges:** 1 High-Fat Meat, ½ Fat

Acapulco Sunset Spread

Shrimp-topped avocado, beans and salsa make a winning combination for a Mexican Fiesta Patio Party. Turn to page 24 for the complete menu.

PREP TIME: 20 MINUTES
MAKES 4 CUPS

1 (16-oz.) can refried beans

½ cup chunky-style salsa

1 (8-oz.) pkg. ⅓-less-fat cream cheese (Neufchâtel), softened

1 avocado, pitted, peeled and chopped

1 tablespoon fresh lime juice

½ lb. frozen shelled deveined cooked small shrimp, thawed

1 tomato, chopped

Fresh cilantro, if desired

1. In medium bowl, combine beans and salsa; mix well. Spread bean mixture onto large serving plate.

2. In food processor bowl with metal blade or blender container, combine cream cheese, avocado and lime juice; process until well blended. Spread cream cheese mixture over bean mixture.

3. Top with shrimp and tomato. Garnish or sprinkle with cilantro. Serve with tortilla chips.

NUTRITION INFORMATION PER SERVING: SERVING SIZE: 2 Tablespoons • Calories 50 • Calories from Fat 25 • % Daily Value: Total Fat 3 g 5% • Saturated Fat 1 g 5% • Cholesterol 20 mg 7% • Sodium 140 mg 6% • Total Carbohydrate 3 g 1% • Dietary Fiber 1 g 4% • Sugars 0 g • Protein 3 g • Vitamin A 4% • Vitamin C 4% • Calcium 0% • Iron 4% • **Dietary Exchanges:** ½ Lean Meat, ½ Fat

Light Crabmeat Spread

(Pictured on page 12.)

This simple spread often lures guests to linger near the bowl.

PREP TIME: 10 MINUTES
MAKES 1½ CUPS

1 (8-oz.) pkg. fat-free cream cheese, softened

1 tablespoon butter, melted

¼ teaspoon garlic salt

2 tablespoons skim milk

1 tablespoon lemon juice

3 small green onions, sliced

1 (6-oz.) can crabmeat, drained, flaked

1. In medium bowl, beat cream cheese with fork. Add butter; beat until blended. Add all remaining ingredients; mix well. Serve immediately, or cover and refrigerate until serving time.

2. If refrigerated, let spread stand at room temperature for 1 hour before serving. If desired, sprinkle with paprika. Serve with assorted fat-free crackers or cut-up fresh vegetables.

make-ahead tip

Spread can be refrigerated up to 8 hours. Serve as directed in recipe.

NUTRITION INFORMATION PER SERVING: SERVING SIZE: 2 Tablespoons • Calories 35 • Calories from Fat 10 • % Daily Value: Total Fat 1 g 2% • Saturated Fat 1 g 5% • Cholesterol 15 mg 5% • Sodium 190 mg 8% • Total Carbohydrate 2 g 1% • Dietary Fiber 0 g 0% • Sugars 1 g • Protein 5 g • Vitamin A 6% • Vitamin C 0% • Calcium 10% • Iron 0% • **Dietary Exchanges:** 1 Lean Meat

Warm Roasted Pepper and Artichoke Spread

To roast your own red bell peppers, broil them, turning occasionally, until the surface is evenly blackened all the way around. When the peppers have cooled, it's easy to peel off the charred skin and reveal the beautifully roasted pepper beneath. However, pre-roasted peppers in a jar or from the deli may actually be more economical than starting from scratch.

PREP TIME: 15 MINUTES
(READY IN 40 MINUTES)
MAKES 3¼ CUPS

1 cup grated Parmesan cheese

½ cup fat-free mayonnaise or salad dressing

1 (8-oz.) pkg. cream cheese, softened

1 small garlic clove

1 (14-oz.) can artichoke hearts, drained, finely chopped

⅓ cup finely chopped roasted red bell peppers (from 7.25-oz. jar)

1. Heat oven to 350°F. In food processor bowl with metal blade, combine Parmesan cheese, mayonnaise, cream cheese and garlic; process until smooth.

2. Place mixture in large bowl. Add artichoke hearts and roasted peppers; mix well. Spread in ungreased 9-inch quiche dish or glass pie pan.

3. Bake at 350°F. for 20 to 25 minutes or until thoroughly heated.

4. Serve warm with assorted crackers, cocktail bread slices or cut-up fresh vegetables.

make-ahead tip

Combine all ingredients in quiche dish as directed in recipe. Cover; refrigerate up to 24 hours before baking. Uncover; bake as directed in recipe.

NUTRITION INFORMATION PER SERVING: SERVING SIZE: 2 Tablespoons • Calories 60 • Calories from Fat 35 • % Daily Value: Total Fat 4 g 6% • Saturated Fat 3 g 15% • Cholesterol 15 mg 5% • Sodium 140 mg 6% • Total Carbohydrate 2 g 1% • Dietary Fiber 1 g 4% • Sugars 1 g • Protein 3 g • Vitamin A 4% • Vitamin C 4% • Calcium 6% • Iron 0% • **Dietary Exchanges:** ½ High-Fat Meat

Hot Reuben Spread

This spread blends all the characteristic flavors of the New York deli sandwich into a luscious warm dip that essentially makes itself once you mix the ingredients in the slow cooker. Brighten the finished dip with a garnish of curly parsley.

PREP TIME: 10 MINUTES
(READY IN 2 HOURS 40 MINUTES)
MAKES 4 CUPS

½ lb. sliced cooked corned beef, coarsely chopped

1 (16-oz.) can sauerkraut, rinsed, well drained

¾ cup purchased Thousand Island salad dressing

8 oz. (2 cups) shredded Swiss cheese

1 (3-oz.) pkg. cream cheese, cubed

1. In 1½- to 3-quart slow cooker, combine all ingredients; mix well.

2. Cover; cook on low setting for 1½ to 2½ hours. Stir spread. Serve with toasted cocktail rye bread slices.

NUTRITION INFORMATION PER SERVING: SERVING SIZE: 2 Tablespoons • Calories 70 • Calories from Fat 50 • % Daily Value: Total Fat 6 g 9% • Saturated Fat 3 g 15% • Cholesterol 15 mg 5% • Sodium 150 mg 6% • Total Carbohydrate 2 g 1% • Dietary Fiber 0 g 0% • Sugars 1 g • Protein 3 g • Vitamin A 2% • Vitamin C 0% • Calcium 8% • Iron 0% • **Dietary Exchanges:** ½ High-Fat Meat, ½ Fat

Green Chile Cheesecake Spread

To decorate this spread, use minced red, yellow and green bell peppers to make a spiral pattern or concentric circles on top.

PREP TIME: 15 MINUTES
(READY IN 1 HOUR 50 MINUTES)
MAKES 4 CUPS

¼ cup unseasoned dry bread crumbs

½ cup sour cream

2 (8-oz.) pkg. cream cheese, softened

1 (5-oz.) jar pasteurized process cheese spread

1 (1.25-oz.) pkg. taco seasoning mix

2 eggs

1 (4.5-oz.) can chopped green chiles

1 (2-oz.) jar diced pimientos, drained

1. Heat oven to 350°F. Grease bottom and 1 inch up sides of 10-inch springform pan. Sprinkle bread crumbs in bottom of greased pan; tilt pan to coat sides with crumbs. Shake pan to coat bottom with crumbs.

2. In large bowl, combine sour cream, cream cheese, cheese spread, taco seasoning mix and eggs; beat until smooth. Fold in chiles and pimientos until well blended. Spoon into crumb-lined pan; spread evenly.

3. Bake at 350°F. for 30 to 35 minutes or until center is set. Cool about 1 hour or until completely cooled.

4. To serve, carefully remove sides of pan; place base of pan and cheesecake on serving plate. Serve with tortilla chips for dipping or crackers for spreading. Store in refrigerator.

make-ahead tip

Cheesecake can be refrigerated up to 24 hours.

NUTRITION INFORMATION PER SERVING: SERVING SIZE: 2 Tablespoons • Calories 80 • Calories from Fat 60 • % Daily Value: Total Fat 7 g 11% • Saturated Fat 4 g 20% • Cholesterol 35 mg 12% • Sodium 230 mg 10% • Total Carbohydrate 2 g 1% • Dietary Fiber 0 g 0% • Sugars 1 g • Protein 3 g • Vitamin A 8% • Vitamin C 4% • Calcium 4% • Iron 2% • **Dietary Exchanges:** ½ High-Fat Meat, ½ Fat

Sharp Cheddar Cheesecake

Don't skimp on the required cooling time. It's necessary for neat slicing. Even better, make the cheesecake a full day ahead of the party.

PREP TIME: 20 MINUTES
(READY IN 4 HOURS)
MAKES 16 SERVINGS

CHEESECAKE

⅔ cup crushed crisp rye or pumpernickel crackers

3 tablespoons butter, melted

2 (8-oz.) pkg. cream cheese, softened

¼ cup whipping cream

1 tablespoon Worcestershire sauce

½ teaspoon dry mustard

2 eggs

8 oz. (2 cups) shredded sharp Cheddar cheese

½ cup chopped roasted red bell peppers (from 7.25-oz. jar)

¼ cup sliced green onions

GARNISH

Green onion curls, if desired

Roasted red bell peppers, cut into shapes with cutters, if desired

1. Heat oven to 350°F. In medium bowl, combine crushed crackers and butter; mix well. Press evenly in bottom of ungreased 9-inch springform pan. Bake at 350°F. for 8 to 10 minutes or until golden brown.

2. Beat cream cheese in medium bowl until light and fluffy. Add cream, Worcestershire sauce, mustard and eggs; beat until smooth and well blended. Stir in shredded cheese, roasted peppers and ¼ cup green onions; mix well. Spread over partially baked crust.

3. Bake at 350°F. for 35 to 40 minutes or until center is set. Cool 30 minutes.

4. Loosen edges of cheesecake with small metal spatula or knife. Cool an additional 30 minutes. Refrigerate at least 2 hours before serving.

5. To serve, carefully remove sides of pan. Place cheesecake on serving platter. Garnish with green onion curls and roasted pepper cutouts. Surround cheesecake with apple and pear slices or assorted crackers.

Cheesecake can be refrigerated up to 24 hours.

NUTRITION INFORMATION PER SERVING: SERVING SIZE: ¹⁄₁₆ of Recipe • Calories 220 • Calories from Fat 170 • % Daily Value: Total Fat 19 g 29% • Saturated Fat 12 g 60% • Cholesterol 85 mg 28% • Sodium 220 mg 9% • Total Carbohydrate 5 g 2% • Dietary Fiber 1 g 4% • Sugars 1 g • Protein 7 g • Vitamin A 20% • Vitamin C 15% • Calcium 15% • Iron 4% • **Dietary Exchanges:** ½ Starch, 1 High-Fat Meat, 2 Fat **OR** ½ Carbohydrate, 1 High-Fat Meat, 2 Fat

Triple Cheese Appetizer Cheesecake

This three-cheese pie is not at all complicated to make, yet the finished product looks—and tastes—as if it came from a gourmet caterer.

PREP TIME: 15 MINUTES
(READY IN 5 HOURS 55 MINUTES)
MAKES 24 SERVINGS

1 cup crushed sesame crackers

3 tablespoons margarine or butter, melted

1 cup ricotta cheese

4 oz. feta cheese, finely crumbled (1 cup)

1 (8-oz.) pkg. cream cheese, softened

2 eggs

½ cup chopped roasted red bell peppers
    (from 7.25-oz. jar)

⅓ cup sour cream

2 tablespoons chopped fresh basil

¼ teaspoon garlic powder

1. Heat oven to 350°F. In medium bowl, combine crushed crackers and margarine; mix well. Press in bottom and 1½ inches up sides of ungreased 9-inch springform pan.

2. In large bowl, combine ricotta, feta and cream cheese; beat until creamy. Add eggs 1 at a time, beating well after each addition. Stir in all remaining ingredients. Pour mixture into crust-lined pan.

3. Bake at 350°F. for 35 to 40 minutes or until center is just about set. Cool 30 minutes.

4. Loosen edges of cheesecake with small metal spatula or knife; cool 30 minutes or until completely cooled. Refrigerate at least 4 hours before serving.

5. To serve, carefully remove sides of pan; place base of pan and cheesecake on serving plate. Cut into thin wedges. Serve with assorted crackers. Store in refrigerator.

make-ahead tip

Cheesecake can be refrigerated up to 24 hours.

NUTRITION INFORMATION PER SERVING: SERVING SIZE: ½₄ of Recipe • Calories 100 • Calories from Fat 70 • % Daily Value: Total Fat 8 g 12% • Saturated Fat 4 g 20% • Cholesterol 35 mg 12% • Sodium 150 mg 6% • Total Carbohydrate 4 g 1% • Dietary Fiber 0 g 0% • Sugars 1 g • Protein 3 g • Vitamin A 8% • Vitamin C 6% • Calcium 6% • Iron 2% • **Dietary Exchanges:** ½ Starch, 1½ Fat **OR** ½ Carbohydrate, 1½ Fat

Apricot-Pecan Camembert

Camembert, a soft cheese even before it's melted, makes a smooth, creamy base for the apricot-pecan topping.

PREP TIME: 25 MINUTES
MAKES 8 SERVINGS

1 (8-oz.) round Camembert cheese

¼ cup apricot preserves

1 tablespoon finely chopped pecans

1. Heat oven to 350°F. Place cheese in shallow ovenproof serving dish.

2. Bake at 350°F. for 20 minutes or until cheese is soft.

3. Remove from oven. Top cheese with preserves and pecans. Return to oven; bake an additional 3 minutes or until preserves are warm.

4. Serve with crackers or cocktail bread slices.

NUTRITION INFORMATION PER SERVING: SERVING SIZE: ⅛ of Recipe • Calories 120 • Calories from Fat 70 • % Daily Value: Total Fat 8 g 12% • Saturated Fat 4 g 20% • Cholesterol 20 mg 7% • Sodium 240 mg 10% • Total Carbohydrate 7 g 2% • Dietary Fiber 0 g 0% • Sugars 5 g • Protein 6 g • Vitamin A 6% • Vitamin C 0% • Calcium 10% • Iron 0% • **Dietary Exchanges:** ½ Fruit, 1 High-Fat Meat **OR** ½ Carbohydrate, 1 High-Fat Meat

Country-Style Chicken Liver Pâté with Capers

To make quick canapés, spread the pâté on thin slices of baguette or cocktail bread and top each with a bit of chopped hard-cooked egg.

PREP TIME: 35 MINUTES
(READY IN 1 HOUR 50 MINUTES)
MAKES 2¼ CUPS

4 tablespoons butter

½ cup sliced green onions

2 garlic cloves, minced

¾ to 1 lb. chicken livers, drained

¼ teaspoon salt

⅛ teaspoon coarse-ground black pepper

2 tablespoons dry white wine

2 tablespoons drained capers

¼ cup sour cream

2 tablespoons Dijon mustard

2 tablespoons chopped roasted red bell peppers
(from 7.25-oz. jar)

Chopped fresh parsley

1. Melt 2 tablespoons of the butter in large skillet over medium heat. Add green onions and garlic; cook and stir 2 to 3 minutes or until tender. Add remaining 2 tablespoons butter, chicken livers, salt and pepper; cook 8 to 10 minutes or until thoroughly cooked, stirring occasionally.

2. Add wine; cook an additional 2 minutes. Cool 15 minutes.

3. In food processor bowl with metal blade, combine chicken liver mixture and capers; process with on/off pulses until slightly chunky. Stir in sour cream, mustard and roasted peppers. Spoon into small serving bowl. Cover; refrigerate at least 1 hour to blend flavors.

4. To serve, sprinkle pâté with parsley. Serve with thin slices of baguette-style French bread.

make-ahead tip

Pâté can be refrigerated up to 24 hours. Garnish just before serving.

NUTRITION INFORMATION PER SERVING: SERVING SIZE: 2 Tablespoons • Calories 70 • Calories from Fat 45 • % Daily Value: Total Fat 5 g 8% • Saturated Fat 3 g 15% • Cholesterol 170 mg 57% • Sodium 140 mg 6% • Total Carbohydrate 1 g 1% • Dietary Fiber 0 g 0% • Sugars 0 g • Protein 6 g • Vitamin A 90% • Vitamin C 8% • Calcium 0% • Iron 15% • **Dietary Exchanges:** 1 Lean Meat, ½ Fat

Pastry-Wrapped Jalapeño Brie with Fruit

Cut the apple and pear just before serving to preserve their creamy color. Set out a small knife or cheese server alongside the baked Brie.

PREP TIME: 15 MINUTES
(READY IN 1 HOUR)
MAKES 12 SERVINGS

1 (8-oz.) can refrigerated crescent dinner rolls

1 (8-oz.) round Brie cheese

2 tablespoons green or red jalapeño jelly or hot pepper jelly

2 tablespoons chopped fresh cilantro

1 egg, beaten

8 small seedless red or green grape clusters

1 pear, unpeeled, sliced

1 apple, unpeeled, sliced

½ cup fresh strawberry halves

Fresh cilantro or rosemary sprigs

1. Heat oven to 350°F. Spray cookie sheet with nonstick cooking spray. Unroll dough. Separate dough crosswise into 2 sections. Press dough to form 2 squares, firmly pressing per-forations to seal. Place 1 square on sprayed cookie sheet.

2. Cut cheese crosswise into 2 equal layers. Place bottom half of cheese on center of dough square on cookie sheet. Spread jelly over cheese. Sprinkle with chopped cilantro. Top with remaining cheese half.

3. With small cookie or canapé cutter, cut 1 shape from each corner of remaining square of dough and roll 3 small pieces of dough to form 3 balls; set aside. Place square of dough on top of cheese round. Press dough evenly around cheese. Fold bottom edges of dough up over top edges; press to seal. Brush dough with beaten egg. Top with cutouts and dough balls; brush with additional beaten egg.

4. Bake at 350°F. for 20 to 30 minutes or until deep golden brown. Cool 15 minutes before serving.

5. To serve, place warm pastry-wrapped cheese on platter. Arrange fruit around cheese. Garnish with cilantro sprigs.

NUTRITION INFORMATION PER SERVING: SERVING SIZE: ½ of Recipe • Calories 180 • Calories from Fat 90 • % Daily Value: Total Fat 10 g 15% • Saturated Fat 4 g 20% • Cholesterol 35 mg 12% • Sodium 270 mg 11% • Total Carbohydrate 17 g 6% • Dietary Fiber 1 g 4% • Sugars 9 g • Protein 6 g • Vitamin A 4% • Vitamin C 8% • Calcium 4% • Iron 4% • **Dietary Exchanges:** 1 Starch, ½ High-Fat Meat, 1 Fat **OR** 1 Carbohydrate, ½ High-Fat Meat, 1 Fat

Crescent-Wrapped Brie

A flaky crust encloses the melted filling of creamy, full-flavored Brie cheese.

PREP TIME: 20 MINUTES
(READY IN 1 HOUR)
MAKES 12 SERVINGS

1 (8-oz.) can refrigerated crescent dinner rolls

1 (8-oz.) round natural Brie cheese

1 egg, beaten

1. Heat oven to 350°F. Unroll dough; separate crosswise into 2 sections. Pat dough and firmly press perforations to seal, forming 2 squares. Place 1 square on ungreased cookie sheet. Place cheese on center of dough.

2. With small cookie or canapé cutter, cut 1 shape from each corner of remaining square; set cutouts aside.

3. Place remaining square on top of cheese round. Press dough evenly around cheese; fold bottom edges over top edges. Gently stretch dough evenly around cheese; press to seal completely. Brush with beaten egg. Top with cutouts; brush with additional beaten egg.

4. Bake at 350°F. for 20 to 24 minutes or until golden brown. Cool 15 minutes before serving.

NUTRITION INFORMATION PER SERVING: SERVING SIZE: ½ of Recipe • Calories 130 • Calories from Fat 80 • % Daily Value: Total Fat 9 g 14% • Saturated Fat 4 g 20% • Cholesterol 35 mg 12% • Sodium 270 mg 11% • Total Carbohydrate 7 g 2% • Dietary Fiber 0 g 0% • Sugars 1 g • Protein 6 g • Vitamin A 4% • Vitamin C 0% • Calcium 4% • Iron 4% • Dietary Exchanges: ½ Starch, ½ High-Fat Meat, 1 Fat OR ½ Carbohydrate, ½ High-Fat Meat, 1 Fat

Baked Brie and Brandied Mushrooms

Tarragon has a pleasant, almost licorice-like flavor that complements the almond-mushroom combination beautifully.

PREP TIME: 20 MINUTES
MAKES 16 SERVINGS

1 tablespoon margarine or butter

2 tablespoons slivered almonds

1 cup chopped fresh mushrooms

2 garlic cloves, minced

1 tablespoon brandy

1 teaspoon chopped fresh tarragon
    or ¼ teaspoon dried tarragon leaves

⅛ teaspoon pepper

1 (8-oz.) round Brie cheese

2 sprigs fresh tarragon, if desired

1. Heat oven to 375°F. Melt margarine in medium skillet over medium heat. Add almonds; cook and stir 2 to 3 minutes or until almonds are browned. Stir in mushrooms, garlic, brandy, tarragon and pepper. Cook and stir 1 to 2 minutes or until mushrooms are tender. Remove from heat.

2. Place cheese in ungreased decorative shallow baking dish or 8- or 9-inch pie pan. Spoon mushrooms over top.

3. Bake at 375°F. for 10 to 12 minutes or until cheese is soft.

4. Garnish with tarragon sprigs. Serve as a spread or dip with Melba toast rounds or crackers.

To make mushroom mixture ahead, prepare as directed in recipe; cool. Cover; refrigerate up to 24 hours before topping cheese. Top cheese as directed; bake as directed in recipe.

NUTRITION INFORMATION PER SERVING: SERVING SIZE: ⅟₁₆ of Recipe • Calories 60 • Calories from Fat 45 • % Daily Value: Total Fat 5 g 8% • Saturated Fat 3 g 15% • Cholesterol 15 mg 5% • Sodium 100 mg 4% • Total Carbohydrate 1 g 1% • Dietary Fiber 0 g 0% • Sugars 0 g • Protein 3 g • Vitamin A 2% • Vitamin C 0% • Calcium 4% • Iron 0% • Dietary Exchanges: ½ High-Fat Meat

Camembert with Cranberry Caramelized Onions

Water crackers or other plain biscuits are ideal accompaniments for this rich mixture. The cranberry-onion mixture is also good spooned over roasted pork or chicken.

PREP TIME: 35 MINUTES
MAKES 12 SERVINGS

1 tablespoon butter

1 small sweet onion, halved, thinly sliced

1 (8-oz.) round Camembert cheese

¼ cup sweetened dried cranberries

2 teaspoons brown sugar

¼ teaspoon salt

2 tablespoons sweet or dry sherry

2 tablespoons chopped fresh marjoram
   or 1 teaspoon dried marjoram leaves

1. Heat oven to 350°F. Melt butter in large nonstick skillet over medium heat. Add onion; cook 8 to 10 minutes or until very tender, stirring frequently.

2. Meanwhile, place cheese in ungreased decorative ovenproof shallow baking dish or plate. Bake at 350°F. for 10 to 12 minutes or until cheese is soft.

3. Add cranberries, brown sugar, salt and sherry to onion; mix well. Cook 5 minutes or until sugar is dissolved, stirring frequently. Stir in marjoram; cook and stir 1 minute.

4. To serve, spoon warm onion mixture over cheese. Serve with assorted crackers and small cocktail bread slices.

NUTRITION INFORMATION PER SERVING: SERVING SIZE: ¹⁄₁₂ of Recipe • Calories 90 • Calories from Fat 50 • % Daily Value: Total Fat 6 g 9% • Saturated Fat 3 g 15% • Cholesterol 15 mg 5% • Sodium 210 mg 9% • Total Carbohydrate 4 g 1% • Dietary Fiber 0 g 0% • Sugars 3 g • Protein 4 g • Vitamin A 4% • Vitamin C 0% • Calcium 8% • Iron 0% • **Dietary Exchanges:** ½ Fruit, ½ High-Fat Meat **OR** ½ Carbohydrate, ½ High-Fat Meat

Appetizer Pie

This warm pie tastes incredibly rich, yet the use of nonfat dairy products makes it low in calories and virtually fat-free.

PREP TIME: 25 MINUTES
MAKES 2 CUPS

1 (8-oz.) pkg. fat-free cream cheese, softened

2 tablespoons skim milk

½ cup nonfat sour cream

2 tablespoons sliced green onions

2 tablespoons chopped green bell pepper

⅛ teaspoon pepper

1 (2½-oz.) jar sliced dried beef, rinsed, drained and finely chopped

¼ cup chopped fresh parsley

1. Heat oven to 350°F. In medium bowl, combine cream cheese and milk; beat until smooth. Stir in all remaining ingredients except parsley; mix well. Spoon and spread mixture in ungreased 9-inch pie pan or small shallow baking dish.

2. Bake at 350°F. for 15 minutes or until thoroughly heated. Sprinkle with parsley. Serve immediately with slices of cocktail bread or baguette-style French bread.

make-ahead tip

Combine all ingredients in pie pan as directed. Cover; refrigerate up to 24 hours before baking. Uncover; bake at 350°F. for 15 minutes. Sprinkle with parsley.

NUTRITION INFORMATION PER SERVING: SERVING SIZE: 2 Tablespoons • Calories 25 • Calories from Fat 0 • % Daily Value: Total Fat 0 g 0% • Saturated Fat 0 g 0% • Cholesterol 4 mg 1% • Sodium 240 mg 10% • Total Carbohydrate 2 g 1% • Dietary Fiber 0 g 0% • Sugars 1 g • Protein 4 g • Vitamin A 4% • Vitamin C 2% • Calcium 4% • Iron 0% • **Dietary Exchanges:** ½ Medium-Fat Meat

Creamy Cheese Spread with Brandied Cranberries

Cranberries have just the right acidity to balance the richness of the three cheeses. The salty-sweet-sharp flavor combination is fantastic.

PREP TIME: 30 MINUTES
(READY IN 1 HOUR 30 MINUTES)
MAKES 12 SERVINGS

1 (8-oz.) pkg. 1/3-less-fat cream cheese (Neufchâtel), softened

1 oz. (1/4 cup) crumbled blue cheese

4 oz. (1 cup) shredded white Cheddar cheese

1 tablespoon chopped onion

1 cup fresh or frozen cranberries, thawed

1/4 cup sugar

3 tablespoons frozen apple juice concentrate, thawed

3 tablespoons brandy

1. Line flat shallow 1½-cup dish with plastic wrap. In food processor bowl with metal blade or mixer bowl, combine cream cheese, blue cheese, Cheddar cheese and onion; process until well blended. Spoon cheese mixture into lined dish; smooth top. Cover; refrigerate.

2. In small saucepan, combine cranberries, sugar and apple juice concentrate. Cook over low heat until juices flow and cranberries pop, stirring frequently. Cook 3 minutes or until slightly thickened. Remove from heat; cool 5 minutes. Stir in brandy. Cover; refrigerate 30 minutes or until cooled.

3. About 30 minutes before serving time, remove cover from cheese; invert onto small serving plate. Remove plastic wrap. Let stand at room temperature for 30 minutes for best flavor. Before serving, spoon cranberry mixture over cheese. Serve with assorted crackers.

make-ahead tip

Prepare cheese spread and cranberries. Cover each separately; refrigerate up to 24 hours. Serve as directed in recipe.

NUTRITION INFORMATION PER SERVING: SERVING SIZE: 2 Tablespoons • Calories 290 • Calories from Fat 140 • % Daily Value: Total Fat 16 g 25% • Saturated Fat 7 g 35% • Cholesterol 25 mg 8% • Sodium 430 mg 18% • Total Carbohydrate 27 g 9% • Dietary Fiber 1 g 4% • Sugars 7 g • Protein 7 g • Vitamin A 6% • Vitamin C 0% • Calcium 15% • Iron 8% • **Dietary Exchanges:** 1 Starch, 1 Fruit, ½ High-Fat Meat, 2 Fat **OR** 2 Carbohydrate, ½ High-Fat Meat, 2 Fat

cold appetizers

SHRIMP COCKTAIL, PAGE 86;
RANCH DEVILED EGGS, PAGE 95

LF (low-fat) = recipes that have 5 grams of fat or less per serving.

Salmon Fillet with Caviar Sauce

Salmon caviar is an affordable luxury. Its bright orange color and burst of juicy saltiness contrast with the cool sour cream sauce.

PREP TIME: 25 MINUTES
(READY IN 55 MINUTES)
MAKES 8 SERVINGS

SALMON

2 tablespoons chopped fresh basil

2 tablespoons chopped fresh parsley

2 tablespoons fresh lemon juice

1/2 teaspoon garlic salt

1/4 teaspoon coarse-ground black pepper

1 (1-lb.) salmon fillet with skin

SAUCE

1 cup sour cream

2 tablespoons finely chopped red onion

1 teaspoon grated lemon peel

1 tablespoon fresh lemon juice

1 teaspoon honey

1 teaspoon Dijon mustard

GARNISH AND BREAD

Fresh basil

Lemon slices or wedges

1/4 cup caviar (2 colors if desired)

24 slices small cocktail bread, halved if desired

1. In large skillet, combine 4 cups water, 2 tablespoons basil, parsley, 2 tablespoons lemon juice, garlic salt and pepper. Bring to a boil. Add salmon, skin side down. Reduce heat to medium; cover and cook 6 to 10 minutes or until fish flakes easily with fork.

2. Remove salmon from skillet. Cool 30 minutes or until completely cooled.

3. In small serving bowl, combine all sauce ingredients; mix well. Cover loosely; refrigerate until serving time.

4. To serve, place salmon on serving plate. (If desired, carefully remove skin.) Garnish plate with basil and lemon slices. Place caviar on paper towel to drain; sprinkle caviar over sauce and salmon. Serve salmon with sauce and bread slices.

make-ahead tip

Cook salmon and prepare sauce as directed in recipe. Cover each separately; refrigerate up to 24 hours. Serve as directed in recipe.

NUTRITION INFORMATION PER SERVING: SERVING SIZE: 1/8 of Recipe • Calories 220 • Calories from Fat 110 • % Daily Value: Total Fat 12 g 18% • Saturated Fat 5 g 25% • Cholesterol 55 mg 18% • Sodium 180 mg 8% • Total Carbohydrate 13 g 4% • Dietary Fiber 1 g 4% • Sugars 3 g • Protein 16 g • Vitamin A 8% • Vitamin C 4% • Calcium 6% • Iron 6% • **Dietary Exchanges:** 1 Starch, 2 Lean Meat, 1 Fat **OR** 1 Carbohydrate, 2 Lean Meat, 1 Fat

Peppered Salmon with Dill-Caper Sauce

Feathery fresh dill is a perfect partner for salmon. Before grilling the salmon, gently run your fingers over the fillet to locate any remaining bones.

PREP TIME: 25 MINUTES
(READY IN 1 HOUR 25 MINUTES)
MAKES 12 SERVINGS

SALMON

½ lb. salmon fillet

¼ teaspoon Dijon mustard

¾ teaspoon coarse-ground pepper

½ teaspoon mustard seed

Fresh dill sprigs, if desired

SAUCE

1 tablespoon drained capers

1 teaspoon chopped fresh dill or ¼ teaspoon dried dill weed

2 tablespoons sour cream

2 teaspoons mayonnaise

1 teaspoon milk

2 or 3 drops hot pepper sauce

BREAD

24 slices cocktail rye or sourdough bread

1. Heat grill. Place salmon, skin side down, on work surface; spread top with mustard. In small bowl, combine pepper and mustard seed; mix well. Sprinkle over mustard; press into salmon.

2. When ready to grill, place salmon, skin side down, on gas grill over medium heat or on charcoal grill 4 to 6 inches from medium coals. Cover grill or tent with foil. Cook 10 minutes or until fish flakes easily with fork. Refrigerate salmon for at least 1 hour or until cold.

3. Meanwhile, in small bowl, combine all sauce ingredients; blend well.

4. Carefully remove skin from salmon, leaving salmon in one piece. Place on serving plate, mustard side up. Garnish plate with fresh dill. Serve with sauce and bread slices.

tip

To broil salmon, place, skin side down, on broiler pan; broil 4 to 6 inches from heat using times above as a guide.

make-ahead tip

Cook salmon and prepare sauce as directed in recipe. Cover each separately; refrigerate up to 24 hours. Serve as directed in recipe.

NUTRITION INFORMATION PER SERVING: SERVING SIZE: ¹⁄₁₂ of Recipe • Calories 80 • Calories from Fat 25 • % Daily Value: Total Fat 3 g 5% • Saturated Fat 1 g 5% • Cholesterol 15 mg 5% • Sodium 135 mg 6% • Total Carbohydrate 7 g 2% • Dietary Fiber 1 g 4% • Sugars 1 g • Protein 6 g • Vitamin A 0% • Vitamin C 0% • Calcium 0% • Iron 4% • **Dietary Exchanges:** ½ Starch, ½ Lean Meat **OR** ½ Carbohydrate, ½ Lean Meat

Honey-Mustard Marinated Vegetables

Here's a colorful alternative to ordinary veggies with dip. You can substitute green or yellow bell pepper for the red, and cut-up regular carrots for the baby carrots.

PREP TIME: 30 MINUTES
(READY IN 1 HOUR)
MAKES 8 SERVINGS

1/2 lb. fresh whole green beans

1 1/2 cups fresh baby carrots

1 1/2 cups fresh cauliflower florets

1/3 cup purchased fat-free honey mustard salad dressing

1/4 teaspoon dried dill weed

1/8 teaspoon salt

1 cup fresh small whole mushrooms

1 red bell pepper, cut lengthwise into thin strips

Lettuce leaves

1. Bring about 5 cups water to a boil in large saucepan. Add green beans; cook 3 minutes. Add carrots and cauliflower. Return to a boil; boil 2 to 3 minutes or just until blanched. Drain; rinse with cold water to cool.

2. In small bowl, combine salad dressing, dill and salt; blend well.

3. In large nonmetal bowl, combine blanched vegetables, mushrooms and bell pepper. Add dressing mixture; toss to coat. Cover; refrigerate at least 30 minutes or until serving time.

4. To serve, line platter with lettuce leaves. Arrange vegetables over lettuce. Serve with cocktail forks.

NUTRITION INFORMATION PER SERVING: SERVING SIZE: 1/8 of Recipe • Calories 45 • Calories from Fat 0 • % Daily Value: Total Fat 0 g 0% • Saturated Fat 0 g 0% • Cholesterol 0 mg 0% • Sodium 170 mg 7% • Total Carbohydrate 10 g 3% • Dietary Fiber 3 g 12% • Sugars 5 g • Protein 1 g • Vitamin A 140% • Vitamin C 40% • Calcium 2% • Iron 4% • **Dietary Exchanges:** 1/2 Fruit, 1 Vegetable **OR** 1/2 Carbohydrate, 1 Vegetable

Rosemary and Garlic Marinated Olives

Olives, a favorite cocktail party nibble, become even tastier after soaking in a flavorful vinaigrette.

PREP TIME: 10 MINUTES
(READY IN 24 HOURS 10 MINUTES)
MAKES 16 SERVINGS

1/2 cup olive oil

1/4 cup balsamic vinegar

1 teaspoon grated lemon peel

4 garlic cloves, thinly sliced

4 sprigs fresh rosemary, cut up

1/2 cup coarsely chopped red onion

1/2 cup pitted green olives

1 (6-oz.) can pitted ripe olives, drained

1 (6-oz.) jar pitted kalamata olives, drained

1. In medium nonmetal bowl or resealable food storage plastic bag, combine oil, vinegar, lemon peel, garlic and rosemary; mix well. Add onion and olives; stir gently to mix. Cover bowl or seal bag. Refrigerate at least 24 hours.

2. To serve, remove olives from marinade with slotted spoon; place in serving bowl. Reserve marinade for later storage of olives. Serve with decorative toothpicks or cocktail forks.

NUTRITION INFORMATION PER SERVING: SERVING SIZE: 1/16 of Recipe • Calories 60 • Calories from Fat 50 • % Daily Value: Total Fat 6 g 9% • Saturated Fat 0 g 0% • Cholesterol 0 mg 0% • Sodium 360 mg 15% • Total Carbohydrate 1 g 1% • Dietary Fiber 0 g 0% • Sugars 0 g • Protein 0 g • Vitamin A 0% • Vitamin C 0% • Calcium 0% • Iron 2% • **Dietary Exchanges:** 1 Fat

Shrimp Cocktail

(Pictured on page 80.)

For an attractive presentation, set the sauce dish in the middle of the tray, surrounded by lemon wedges and sprigs of curly parsley.

PREP TIME: 5 MINUTES
MAKES 16 SERVINGS

COCKTAIL SAUCE

½ cup ketchup

½ cup chili sauce

2 to 3 teaspoons prepared horseradish

1 teaspoon Worcestershire sauce

SHRIMP

1 lb. shelled deveined cooked medium shrimp

1. In small bowl, combine all cocktail sauce ingredients; mix well.

2. Arrange shrimp on serving tray. Serve shrimp with sauce immediately, or cover and refrigerate separately until serving time.

make-ahead tip

Cocktail can be refrigerated up to 24 hours.

NUTRITION INFORMATION PER SERVING: SERVING SIZE: ⅟₁₆ of Recipe • Calories 50 • Calories from Fat 10 • % Daily Value: Total Fat 1 g 2% • Saturated Fat 0 g 0% • Cholesterol 55 mg 18% • Sodium 270 mg 11% • Total Carbohydrate 4 g 1% • Dietary Fiber 0 g 0% • Sugars 2 g • Protein 6 g • Vitamin A 6% • Vitamin C 6% • Calcium 0% • Iron 6% • **Dietary Exchanges:** ½ Fruit, 1 Very Lean Meat **OR** ½ Carbohydrate, 1 Very Lean Meat

Antipasto Platter

Prosciutto, an Italian-style ham, often costs much more than regular boiled or baked ham, but it's typically sold in paper-thin slices so a little goes a long way. It lends authenticity to the antipasto, but you could easily substitute regular ham or another cold cut.

PREP TIME: 20 MINUTES
MAKES 8 SERVINGS

DRESSING

⅓ cup olive oil

¼ cup white balsamic vinegar

1 teaspoon sugar

1 tablespoon chopped fresh basil

½ teaspoon salt

ANTIPASTO

3 to 4 large leaves leaf lettuce

4 oz. thinly sliced Genoa salami

4 oz. thinly sliced prosciutto

¾ cup fresh cauliflower florets

¾ cup fresh baby carrots, halved lengthwise

½ medium green bell pepper, cut into thin strips

½ medium red bell pepper, cut into thin strips

¼ honeydew melon, cut into thin wedges

¼ cantaloupe, cut into thin wedges

1 oz. (¼ cup) crumbled Gorgonzola cheese

1. In small bowl, combine all dressing ingredients; blend well.

2. Arrange lettuce on large serving platter. Roll up salami and proscuitto slices. Arrange salami and prosciutto rolls, and all remaining antipasto ingredients except cheese over lettuce. Drizzle dressing over all. Sprinkle with cheese.

NUTRITION INFORMATION PER SERVING: SERVING SIZE: ⅛ of Recipe • Calories 220 • Calories from Fat 140 • % Daily Value: Total Fat 16 g 25% • Saturated Fat 4 g 20% • Cholesterol 20 mg 7% • Sodium 660 mg 28% • Total Carbohydrate 10 g 3% • Dietary Fiber 1 g 4% • Sugars 8 g • Protein 8 g • Vitamin A 90% • Vitamin C 70% • Calcium 4% • Iron 4% • **Dietary Exchanges:** ½ Starch, 1 High-Fat Meat, 1½ Fat **OR** ½ Carbohydrate, 1 High-Fat Meat, 1½ Fat

Marinated Antipasto Tray

Provolone, an Italian cheese that comes either mild or sharp, would be a fine addition. You can buy a chunk and cut it into cubes, or buy it sliced and roll the cheese into cone shapes to match the salami.

PREP TIME: 25 MINUTES
(READY IN 2 HOURS 25 MINUTES)
MAKES 12 SERVINGS

2 cups fresh baby carrots

½ cup oil

⅓ cup tarragon vinegar

1 tablespoon sugar

2 tablespoons water

3 garlic cloves, minced

6 drops hot pepper sauce

1 (.7-oz.) envelope Italian salad dressing mix

2 medium onions, thinly sliced, separated into rings

2 (4.5-oz.) jars whole mushrooms, drained

1 medium zucchini, halved lengthwise, cut into ½-inch slices

Leaf lettuce

5 oz. thinly sliced salami

Assorted cheeses, if desired

1. In medium saucepan, bring ½ cup water to a boil. Add carrots; cover and cook over medium heat for 5 minutes or until carrots are crisp-tender. Drain; rinse with cold water to cool.

2. In small bowl or jar with tight-fitting lid, combine oil, vinegar, sugar, water, garlic, hot pepper sauce and salad dressing mix; mix or shake well.

3. In large bowl, combine carrots, onions, mushrooms and zucchini. Pour dressing over vegetables; toss gently. Cover; refrigerate at least 2 hours or overnight.

4. To serve, arrange drained marinated vegetables on lettuce-lined serving tray. Cut salami slices in half; roll into cones. Insert salami cones and assorted cheeses around base of vegetables.

NUTRITION INFORMATION PER SERVING: SERVING SIZE: ¹⁄₁₂ of Recipe • Calories 250 • Calories from Fat 180 • % Daily Value: Total Fat 20 g 31% • Saturated Fat 7 g 35% • Cholesterol 30 mg 10% • Sodium 610 mg 25% • Total Carbohydrate 8 g 3% • Dietary Fiber 2 g 8% • Sugars 5 g • Protein 10 g • Vitamin A 110% • Vitamin C 8% • Calcium 20% • Iron 4% • **Dietary Exchanges:** 1½ Vegetable, 1 High-Fat Meat, 2½ Fat

Marinated Roasted Vegetable Antipasto

Oven roasting brings out the sweetness of onion, eggplant, peppers and mushrooms, making them a delightful partner for the white wine/balsamic marinade. To reduce the fat content of this dish slightly, spritz the vegetables with nonfat cooking spray before roasting instead of drizzling them with oil.

PREP TIME: 45 MINUTES
(READY IN 1 HOUR 45 MINUTES)
MAKES 12 SERVINGS

ROASTED VEGETABLES

1/2 large onion, cut into 3/8-inch-thick wedges

4 tablespoons extra-virgin olive oil

1/2 small eggplant (cut lengthwise)

1 small red bell pepper

1 small yellow bell pepper

4 oz. portobello mushrooms, cut into 3/8-inch-thick slices

MARINADE

1/4 cup white wine or chicken broth

2 tablespoons balsamic vinegar

1 teaspoon dried basil leaves

1/2 teaspoon dried oregano leaves

1/2 teaspoon salt

1/4 teaspoon pepper

2 garlic cloves, minced

1. Heat oven to 400°F. Arrange onion wedges in ungreased 15x10x1-inch baking pan. Drizzle with 1 tablespoon of the oil. Bake at 400°F. for 5 minutes.

2. Meanwhile, cut eggplant half crosswise into 3/8-inch-thick slices. Cut top and bottom from red and yellow bell peppers; reserve for another use. Remove seeds and membranes from bell peppers. Cut into 2x1-inch strips.

3. Remove onion from oven. Arrange eggplant, bell peppers and mushrooms in pan. Drizzle with remaining 3 tablespoons oil.

4. Return to oven; bake an additional 10 minutes. Turn vegetables; bake an additional 5 to 10 minutes or until vegetables are crisp-tender.

5. In medium bowl, combine all marinade ingredients; mix well. Add roasted vegetables; toss to coat. Cover; refrigerate 1 hour or until cool.

6. To serve, drain vegetables; arrange on serving platter. Discard marinade.

make-ahead tip

Vegetables can be refrigerated up to 24 hours.

NUTRITION INFORMATION PER SERVING: SERVING SIZE: 1/12 of Recipe • Calories 50 • Calories from Fat 45 • % Daily Value: Total Fat 5 g 8% • Saturated Fat 1 g 5% • Cholesterol 0 mg 0% • Sodium 25 mg 1% • Total Carbohydrate 2 g 1% • Dietary Fiber 1 g 4% • Sugars 1 g • Protein 0 g • Vitamin A 4% • Vitamin C 20% • Calcium 0% • Iron 0% • **Dietary Exchanges:** 1 Fat

Marinated Antipasto Platter

Lemon leaves can be ordered through a florist. If you don't have them, garnish the platter with washed and dried lettuce or spinach leaves.

PREP TIME: 25 MINUTES
(READY IN 12 HOURS 25 MINUTES)
MAKES 24 SERVINGS

MARINADE

¼ cup red wine vinegar

2 tablespoons orange juice

1 teaspoon grated orange peel

1 teaspoon dried rosemary leaves

1 teaspoon dried tarragon leaves

¼ cup olive oil

ANTIPASTO

2 cups assorted olives, drained

1 (6-oz.) jar whole mushrooms, drained

1 (8-oz.) block whole-milk mozzarella cheese, cut into ½-inch cubes

½ lb. sliced hard salami (about ⅛ inch thick)

Cocktail toothpicks

Lemon leaves

1. In small nonmetal bowl, combine all marinade ingredients except oil; mix well. Slowly add oil, beating with wire whisk until marinade is thick and well blended. In nonmetal container or resealable food storage plastic bag, combine olives, mushrooms and cheese. Add marinade; cover and refrigerate at least 12 hours or overnight to blend flavors.

2. When ready to serve, cut salami slices in half. Roll slices into small cone shapes; spear with cocktail toothpicks. Line outside edge of large serving platter with lemon leaves. Arrange salami around edge of platter.

3. Drain marinated olives, mushrooms and cheese, reserving marinade; arrange in center of platter. Drizzle 1 to 2 tablespoons of reserved marinade over salami. (Discard remaining marinade.) Tuck several lemon leaves among olives, mushrooms and cheese.

NUTRITION INFORMATION PER SERVING: SERVING SIZE: ¹⁄₂₄ of Recipe • Calories 120 • Calories from Fat 90 • % Daily Value: Total Fat 10 g 15% • Saturated Fat 3 g 15% • Cholesterol 15 mg 5% • Sodium 500 mg 21% • Total Carbohydrate 2 g 1% • Dietary Fiber 0 g 0% • Sugars 0 g • Protein 5 g • Vitamin A 2% • Vitamin C 0% • Calcium 8% • Iron 2% • **Dietary Exchanges:** ½ High-Fat Meat, 1½ Fat

Pickled Carrot Kabobs

For a change of pace, make the recipe with dill seed instead of dill weed. Monterey Jack, another mild cheese, can substitute for the Muenster.

PREP TIME: 30 MINUTES
(READY IN 8 HOURS 30 MINUTES)
MAKES 24 KABOBS

- **24 fresh baby carrots**
- **½ cup water**
- **½ cup white vinegar**
- **¼ cup sugar**
- **1 tablespoon chopped fresh dill or 1 teaspoon dried dill weed**
- **½ teaspoon salt**
- **24 pitted ripe olives**
- **6 oz. Muenster cheese, cut into 24 cubes**
- **24 toothpicks**

1. In small saucepan, combine carrots, water, vinegar, sugar, dill and salt; mix well. Cook over high heat until mixture comes to a boil. Reduce heat; simmer 7 to 8 minutes or until carrots can be easily pierced with sharp knife.

2. Remove saucepan from heat; cool 10 minutes. Place in food storage plastic bag or nonmetal container. Seal bag or cover container. Refrigerate at least 8 hours or overnight.

3. To serve, spear 1 olive, 1 carrot and 1 cheese cube onto each toothpick.

NUTRITION INFORMATION PER SERVING: Not possible to calculate because of recipe variables.

Marinated Olive Kabobs

Once the olives have been removed from the marinade, discard the lemon slices and garlic pieces. The marinade makes a fine salad dressing for tossed greens or coleslaw blend. These need at least a couple of days to marinate.

PREP TIME: 15 MINUTES
(READY IN 2 DAYS)
MAKES 36 KABOBS

MARINADE

- **½ cup olive oil**
- **¼ cup balsamic vinegar**
- **½ teaspoon dried oregano leaves**
- **2 thin slices lemon, quartered**
- **2 garlic cloves, quartered**

KABOBS

- **1 (6-oz.) can pitted large ripe olives, drained**
- **1 red bell pepper, cut into ½-inch squares**
- **36 toothpicks**
- **4 oz. feta cheese, cut into ½-inch cubes**

1. In food storage plastic container or plastic bag set in bowl, combine all marinade ingredients; mix well.

2. Add olives; seal container or bag. Turn to coat olives well with marinade. Refrigerate 2 to 4 days, occasionally turning container or bag to coat with marinade.

3. To serve, remove olives from marinade; discard marinade or save for a later use. For each kabob, thread 1 olive and 1 bell pepper square onto toothpick. Gently spear 1 cheese cube onto point of toothpick.

NUTRITION INFORMATION PER SERVING: SERVING SIZE: 1 Kabob • Calories 20 • Calories from Fat 20 • % Daily Value: Total Fat 2 g 3% • Saturated Fat 1 g 5% • Cholesterol 3 mg 1% • Sodium 75 mg 3% • Total Carbohydrate 1 g 1% • Dietary Fiber 0 g 0% • Sugars 0 g • Protein 1 g • Vitamin A 4% • Vitamin C 6% • Calcium 0% • Iron 0% • **Dietary Exchanges:** ½ Fat

Italian Tortellini Kabobs

To serve the tortellini as a first course instead of a cocktail appetizer, omit the skewers and toss the marinated tortellini with the tomatoes and olives. Serve the salad on a bed of shredded lettuce on individual plates.

PREP TIME: 35 MINUTES
(READY IN 2 HOURS 35 MINUTES)
MAKES 28 KABOBS

1 (9-oz.) pkg. refrigerated uncooked cheese tortellini

28 pitted kalamata or large ripe olives

½ cup purchased Italian salad dressing

14 cherry tomatoes, halved

28 cocktail toothpicks or 6-inch skewers

1. Cook tortellini to desired doneness as directed on package. Drain; rinse with cold water.

2. In medium nonmetal bowl, combine cooked tortellini, olives and salad dressing. Refrigerate 2 hours to marinate, stirring occasionally.

3. Add tomatoes to tortellini mixture; toss to coat. On each toothpick, alternately thread 3 tortellini, 1 olive and 1 tomato half.

4. Serve immediately, or cover loosely and refrigerate until serving time.

Tortellini mixture can be refrigerated up to 24 hours. Just before serving, prepare kabobs as directed in recipe.

NUTRITION INFORMATION PER SERVING: SERVING SIZE: 1 Kabob • Calories 40 • Calories from Fat 20 • % Daily Value: Total Fat 2 g 3% • Saturated Fat 0 g 0% • Cholesterol 5 mg 2% • Sodium 85 mg 4% • Total Carbohydrate 5 g 2% • Dietary Fiber 1 g 4% • Sugars 0 g • Protein 1 g • Vitamin A 0% • Vitamin C 0% • Calcium 2% • Iron 2% • **Dietary Exchanges:** ½ Starch **OR** ½ Carbohydrate

Cocktail Snack Kabobs

When assembling the kabobs, choose trios of ingredients with pleasing contrast of color and texture. If you use apple or pear cubes, dip them into water with a squirt of lemon or into apple juice to prevent them from browning.

PREP TIME: 15 MINUTES

Cocktail toothpicks

Pitted olives (pimiento-stuffed green, ripe or kalamata)

Pickled vegetables (mushrooms, hot peppers, cauliflower florets or assorted pickled vegetables)

Cheese cubes (Swiss, Monterey Jack or Cheddar)

Meat cubes (cooked ham, smoked cooked turkey, cooked corned beef or salami)

Seafood (cooked shrimp or scallops)

Vegetable pieces (cucumbers, bell peppers, red or sweet onion or cherry tomatoes)

Fruit (pineapple chunks, apple or pear cubes, melon balls or strawberries)

On each toothpick, thread your choice of 3 of the above suggested ingredients.

NUTRITION INFORMATION PER SERVING: Not possible to calculate because of recipe variables.

Tortellini and Roasted Bell Pepper Kabobs

If you have fresh basil on hand, use 1 1/2 teaspoons minced fresh basil instead of dried; garnish the platter with an extra sprig or two.

PREP TIME: 50 MINUTES
(READY IN 1 HOUR 10 MINUTES)
MAKES 20 KABOBS

1 (9-oz.) pkg. refrigerated cheese-filled tortellini

1 large red bell pepper, cut into 20 pieces

1 large green bell pepper, cut into 20 pieces

1 large yellow bell pepper, cut into 20 pieces

1 to 2 tablespoons olive oil

1/2 teaspoon dried basil leaves

1/4 teaspoon salt

20 (6-inch) bamboo skewers

1. Cook tortellini as directed on package. Drain; rinse with cold water to cool.

2. Meanwhile, heat oven to 450°F. Combine bell peppers in medium bowl. Add oil, basil and salt; toss to coat. Spread bell peppers in ungreased 15x10x1-inch baking pan. Bake at 450°F. for 15 to 20 minutes or until crisp-tender.

3. Add cooked tortellini to pan; toss to coat slightly with any remaining oil mixture. Cool 5 minutes.

4. Thread 2 tortellini and 3 bell pepper pieces on each skewer. Serve immediately, or cover and refrigerate until serving time.

NUTRITION INFORMATION PER SERVING: SERVING SIZE: 1 Kabob • Calories 50 • Calories from Fat 20 • % Daily Value: Total Fat 2 g 3% • Saturated Fat 1 g 5% • Cholesterol 5 mg 2% • Sodium 70 mg 3% • Total Carbohydrate 7 g 2% • Dietary Fiber 1 g 4% • Sugars 1 g • Protein 2 g • Vitamin A 6% • Vitamin C 30% • Calcium 0% • Iron 0% • **Dietary Exchanges:** 1/2 Starch OR 1/2 Carbohydrate

Deviled Eggs

A party classic, with good reason. To reduce the fat slightly, use low-fat or nonfat mayonnaise or nonfat plain yogurt in place of the regular mayonnaise.

PREP TIME: 50 MINUTES
MAKES 24 DEVILED EGGS

12 eggs

1 teaspoon dry mustard or 2 teaspoons prepared mustard

Dash pepper

1/3 cup mayonnaise, salad dressing or sour cream

1 tablespoon vinegar

1 teaspoon Worcestershire sauce

Paprika or chopped fresh parsley

1. Place eggs in single layer in large saucepan. Add enough water to cover eggs by 1 inch. Bring to a boil. Immediately remove from heat; cover and let stand 15 minutes. Drain; rinse with cold water. Place eggs in bowl of ice water; let stand 10 minutes.

2. Peel eggs; cut in half lengthwise. Remove yolks; place in small bowl. Mash yolks with fork.

3. Add all remaining ingredients except paprika; mix until fluffy. Spoon or pipe mixture into egg white halves. Sprinkle with paprika.

make-ahead tip

Prepare eggs as directed in recipe. Place in covered container; refrigerate up to 24 hours. Garnish just before serving.

NUTRITION INFORMATION PER SERVING: SERVING SIZE: 1 Deviled Egg • Calories 60 • Calories from Fat 45 • % Daily Value: Total Fat 5 g 8% • Saturated Fat 1 g 5% • Cholesterol 110 mg 37% • Sodium 50 mg 2% • Total Carbohydrate 0 g 0% • Dietary Fiber 0 g 0% • Sugars 0 g • Protein 3 g • Vitamin A 4% • Vitamin C 0% • Calcium 0% • Iron 0% • **Dietary Exchanges:** 1/2 Medium-Fat Meat, 1/2 Fat

Ranch Deviled Eggs

(Pictured on page 80.)

These may look like the classic Deviled Eggs, but their secret is a touch of ranch dressing.

PREP TIME: 40 MINUTES
(READY IN 1 HOUR 10 MINUTES)
MAKES 12 DEVILED EGGS

6 eggs

1½ teaspoons dry ranch salad dressing mix (from 2-oz. envelope)

3 tablespoons mayonnaise

½ teaspoon Dijon mustard

Paprika

1. Place eggs in single layer in medium saucepan. Add enough water to cover eggs by 1 inch. Bring to a boil. Immediately remove from heat; cover and let stand 15 minutes. Drain; rinse with cold water. Place eggs in bowl of ice water; let stand 10 minutes.

2. Peel eggs; cut in half lengthwise. With tip of knife, carefully lift out yolks; place in medium bowl. Mash yolks with fork. Add salad dressing mix, mayonnaise and mustard; mix well.

3. Spoon or pipe yolk mixture into egg white halves. Sprinkle with paprika. Refrigerate at least 30 minutes before serving.

make-ahead tip

Prepare eggs as directed in recipe. Place in covered container; refrigerate up to 24 hours. Garnish just before serving.

NUTRITION INFORMATION PER SERVING: SERVING SIZE: 1 Deviled Egg • Calories 60 • Calories from Fat 45 • % Daily Value: Total Fat 5 g 8% • Saturated Fat 1 g 5% • Cholesterol 110 mg 37% • Sodium 55 mg 2% • Total Carbohydrate 0 g 0% • Dietary Fiber 0 g 0% • Sugars 0 g • Protein 3 g • Vitamin A 4% • Vitamin C 0% • Calcium 0% • Iron 2% • **Dietary Exchanges:** ½ Meat, ½ Fat

Deviled Ham and Eggs

If you're lucky enough to have leftovers, chop them up and spread the mixture on whole-grain bread with tomato slices and lettuce for a delicious sandwich.

PREP TIME: 40 MINUTES
MAKES 12 DEVILED EGGS

6 eggs

¼ cup mayonnaise

2 teaspoons prepared mustard

1 teaspoon vinegar

1 cup finely chopped cooked ham

2 teaspoons sweet pickle relish

1 tablespoon chopped fresh chives

1. Place eggs in single layer in medium saucepan. Add enough water to cover eggs by 1 inch. Bring to a boil. Immediately remove from heat; cover and let stand 15 minutes.

2. Drain eggs; rinse with cold water. Place eggs in bowl of ice water; let stand 10 minutes.

3. Peel eggs; cut in half lengthwise. Remove yolks; place in medium bowl. Mash yolks with fork. Add all remaining ingredients except chives; mix well. Spoon or pipe yolk mixture into egg white halves. Sprinkle with chives.

make-ahead tip

Prepare eggs as directed in recipe. Place in covered container; refrigerate up to 24 hours. Garnish just before serving.

NUTRITION INFORMATION PER SERVING: SERVING SIZE: 1 Deviled Egg • Calories 90 • Calories from Fat 60 • % Daily Value: Total Fat 7 g 11% • Saturated Fat 2 g 10% • Cholesterol 115 mg 38% • Sodium 240 mg 10% • Total Carbohydrate 1 g 1% • Dietary Fiber 0 g 0% • Sugars 1 g • Protein 5 g • Vitamin A 4% • Vitamin C 0% • Calcium 0% • Iron 2% • **Dietary Exchanges:** ½ Medium-Fat Meat, 1 Fat

Open-Faced Party Sandwiches

Arrange these tiny, colorful sandwiches in a pattern, or mix them randomly like a crazy quilt. The "pullman" sandwich bread bakes in a covered loaf pan, giving it a squared-off shape.

PREP TIME: 15 MINUTES
MAKES 48 SANDWICHES

3 (½-inch-thick) lengthwise slices whole wheat, rye or white unsliced pullman sandwich bread (from 1½-lb. loaf)

½ cup purchased ham spread

½ cup purchased chicken spread

¼ cup sharp Cheddar cold pack cheese food (from 8-oz. container), softened

GARNISH CHOICES

Cooked small shrimp

Cooked tuna or salmon pieces

Hard-cooked egg slices

Small broccoli or cauliflower florets

Small tomato slices or cherry tomato wedges

Green onion fans

Roasted bell peppers, cut with decorative cutters

Small zucchini or cucumber pieces

Olive slices

Radish slices

Pear or apple slices

Strawberry or pineapple slices

Grape slices

Edible flowers

Fresh herb sprigs, such as parsley, basil or rosemary

Caviar

1. Spread 1 slice of bread with ham spread, 1 slice with chicken spread and 1 slice with cheese spread. Cut each into 1½-inch squares, diamonds or rectangles. Garnish as desired.

2. Serve immediately, or cover loosely and refrigerate until serving time.

NUTRITION INFORMATION PER SERVING: Not possible to calculate because of recipe variables.

Crabmeat Deviled Eggs

Rich crabmeat turns the simple egg into a gourmet treat. Whenever you use crabmeat, it's a good idea to gently run your fingers through the meat to check for bits of shell.

PREP TIME: 50 MINUTES
(READY IN 1 HOUR 50 MINUTES)
MAKES 16 DEVILED EGGS

8 eggs

1 (6-oz.) can crabmeat, drained, flaked

¼ cup mayonnaise

½ teaspoon dry mustard

¼ teaspoon ground red pepper (cayenne)

16 sprigs parsley

1. Place eggs in single layer in medium saucepan. Add enough water to cover eggs by 1 inch. Bring to a boil. Immediately remove from heat; cover and let stand 15 minutes. Drain; rinse with cold water. Place eggs in bowl of ice water; let stand 10 minutes.

2. Peel eggs; cut in half lengthwise. Scoop yolks from 4 eggs into medium bowl. Remove remaining yolks; reserve for another use.

3. Add crabmeat, mayonnaise, dry mustard and ground red pepper to yolks in bowl; mix and mash with fork until well blended. Mound yolk mixture into center of each egg white half. Garnish each with parsley sprig. Cover; refrigerate at least 1 hour or until serving time.

make-ahead tip

Prepare eggs as directed in recipe. Place in covered container; refrigerate up to 24 hours. Garnish just before serving.

NUTRITION INFORMATION PER SERVING: SERVING SIZE: 1 Deviled Egg • Calories 70 • Calories from Fat 45 • % Daily Value: Total Fat 5 g 8% • Saturated Fat 1 g 5% • Cholesterol 115 mg 38% • Sodium 80 mg 3% • Total Carbohydrate 0 g 0% • Dietary Fiber 0 g 0% • Sugars 0 g • Protein 5 g • Vitamin A 4% • Vitamin C 0% • Calcium 2% • Iron 2% • **Dietary Exchanges:** ½ Medium-Fat Meat, ½ Fat

Puff Pastry with Cranberry Turkey Salad

Invite friends over the day after Thanksgiving and treat them to these puff pastry appetizers.

PREP TIME: 20 MINUTES
(READY IN 55 MINUTES)
MAKES 24 APPETIZERS

1 sheet frozen ready-to-bake puff pastry (from 17 1/4-oz. pkg.), thawed

1 cup chopped cooked turkey

1/4 cup chopped green onions

1/4 cup mayonnaise

2 tablespoons jellied cranberry sauce

1/4 teaspoon ginger

1/4 teaspoon dry mustard

GARNISH

1 to 2 teaspoons jellied cranberry sauce

1. Heat oven to 375°F. Place pastry sheet on lightly floured surface. Cut 12 (2-inch) rounds from pastry; place on ungreased cookie sheet. Bake at 375°F. for 20 to 25 minutes or until puffed and golden brown.

2. Remove warm pastry rounds from cookie sheet; place on wire rack. While still warm, split each round into 2 layers to form 24 rounds. Cool completely.

3. Meanwhile, in small bowl, combine turkey, green onions, mayonnaise, 2 tablespoons cranberry sauce, ginger and dry mustard; mix well. Refrigerate until serving time.

4. To serve, spoon about 1 teaspoon turkey mixture on split side of each round. Garnish appetizers with small dots of cranberry sauce.

make-ahead tip

Prepare puff pastry and filling as directed in recipe. Store cooled puff pastry loosely covered at room temperature up to 12 hours. Cover filling; refrigerate up to 24 hours. Serve as directed in recipe.

NUTRITION INFORMATION PER SERVING: SERVING SIZE: 1 Appetizer • Calories 90 • Calories from Fat 50 • % Daily Value: Total Fat 6 g 9% • Saturated Fat 1 g 5% • Cholesterol 5 mg 2% • Sodium 45 mg 2% • Total Carbohydrate 6 g 2% • Dietary Fiber 0 g 0% • Sugars 1 g • Protein 3 g • Vitamin A 0% • Vitamin C 0% • Calcium 0% • Iron 2% • **Dietary Exchanges:** 1/2 Starch, 1 Fat **OR** 1/2 Carbohydrate, 1 Fat

Pork Tenderloin Canapés

Pork tenderloin cooks quickly and has a lovely fork-tender texture. These canapés show off pork's natural affinity for apples.

PREP TIME: 15 MINUTES
(READY IN 45 MINUTES)
MAKES 24 APPETIZERS

1 (½-lb.) pork tenderloin

¼ teaspoon salt

¼ teaspoon pepper

¼ cup soft cream cheese with chives and onion (from 8-oz. tub)

24 (¼-inch-thick) slices French bread

24 thin slices red or green apple

1 tablespoon apple juice

Chopped fresh chives

1. Heat oven to 425°F. Line cookie sheet with foil. Place pork tenderloin on foil-lined cookie sheet, tucking small end under to prevent overcooking. Sprinkle all sides with salt and pepper.

2. Bake at 425°F. for 20 to 30 minutes or until no longer pink in center and juices run clear. Remove from oven; cover with foil. Let stand 10 minutes.

3. Meanwhile, spread ½ teaspoon cream cheese on each slice of bread.

4. Cut pork into 24 thin slices; place 1 slice on each slice of bread. Toss apple slices with apple juice to prevent browning. Arrange apple slices over pork. Sprinkle with fresh chives.

5. Serve immediately, or cover and refrigerate until serving time.

NUTRITION INFORMATION PER SERVING: SERVING SIZE: 1 Appetizer • Calories 90 • Calories from Fat 20 • % Daily Value: Total Fat 2 g 3% • Saturated Fat 1 g 5% • Cholesterol 10 mg 3% • Sodium 190 mg 8% • Total Carbohydrate 14 g 5% • Dietary Fiber 1 g 4% • Sugars 1 g • Protein 4 g • Vitamin A 0% • Vitamin C 0% • Calcium 2% • Iron 4% • **Dietary Exchanges:** 1 Starch **OR** 1 Carbohydrate

Salmon Canapés with Dilled Honey Mustard

This combination of smoky salmon, cream cheese and fresh dill also works well as a topping for cucumber slices.

PREP TIME: 25 MINUTES
MAKES 24 APPETIZERS

1 tablespoon finely chopped red onion

3 tablespoons Dijon mustard

1 tablespoon honey

2 teaspoons chopped fresh dill

12 slices cocktail pumpernickel or rye bread

2 to 3 tablespoons soft cream cheese (from 8-oz. tub)

¼ lb. smoked salmon (lox), cut into 24 pieces

24 sprigs fresh dill

1. In small bowl, combine onion, mustard, honey and chopped dill; mix well.

2. Spread each bread slice with cream cheese. Top each with mustard mixture. Cut each bread slice in half diagonally. Top each bread triangle with salmon and dill sprig.

make-ahead tip

Combine onion, mustard, honey and chopped dill as directed in recipe. Cover; refrigerate up to 24 hours. Just before serving, top bread slices as directed in recipe.

NUTRITION INFORMATION PER SERVING: SERVING SIZE: 1 Appetizer • Calories 25 • Calories from Fat 10 • % Daily Value: Total Fat 1 g 2% • Saturated Fat 0 g 0% • Cholesterol 2 mg 1% • Sodium 110 mg 5% • Total Carbohydrate 3 g 1% • Dietary Fiber 0 g 0% • Sugars 1 g • Protein 1 g • Vitamin A 0% • Vitamin C 0% • Calcium 0% • Iron 0% • **Dietary Exchanges:** ½ Starch **OR** ½ Carbohydrate

Beef Tenderloin Canapés with Mustard-Caper Sauce

If you prepare the beef and sauce ahead of time (refrigerating them separately), you should assemble the canapés shortly before serving so the bread maintains its texture.

PREP TIME: 30 MINUTES
(READY IN 1 HOUR 30 MINUTES)
MAKES 36 APPETIZERS

BEEF

1 (2 to 2½-lb.) beef tenderloin

1 tablespoon olive oil

½ teaspoon salt

½ teaspoon cracked black pepper

SAUCE AND BREAD

½ cup mayonnaise

5 tablespoons finely chopped green onions

2 tablespoons drained capers

2 tablespoons Dijon mustard

1 tablespoon purchased creamy horseradish sauce

36 slices baguette-style or small French bread

Radicchio and/or watercress leaves

1. Heat oven to 450°F. Place beef tenderloin in ungreased shallow metal roasting pan or ovenproof skillet. Rub beef with oil. Sprinkle with salt and pepper. Place pan over medium-high heat; cook until beef is browned on all sides.

2. Place beef in 450°F. oven. Immediately reduce oven temperature to 375°F.; bake 30 to 35 minutes or until meat thermometer inserted in center registers 140°F.

3. Remove beef from oven. Cool 30 minutes or until completely cooled. If desired, wrap tightly; refrigerate until serving time.

4. Meanwhile, in small bowl, combine mayonnaise, green onions, capers, mustard and horseradish sauce; mix well. Cover; refrigerate until serving time.

5. To serve, thinly slice beef. Spread bread slices with sauce. Top each with small piece of radicchio, beef slice and watercress. Serve immediately, or cover loosely and refrigerate until serving time.

Bake beef tenderloin and prepare sauce as directed in recipe. Wrap beef and cover sauce; refrigerate up to 24 hours. Serve as directed in recipe.

NUTRITION INFORMATION PER SERVING: SERVING SIZE: 1 Appetizer • Calories 80 • Calories from Fat 45 • % Daily Value: Total Fat 5 g 8% • Saturated Fat 1 g 5% • Cholesterol 15 mg 5% • Sodium 125 mg 5% • Total Carbohydrate 3 g 1% • Dietary Fiber 0 g 0% • Sugars 0 g • Protein 5 g • Vitamin A 0% • Vitamin C 0% • Calcium 0% • Iron 4% • **Dietary Exchanges:** 1 Very Lean Meat, 1 Fat

Cucumber-Shrimp Canapés

Scoring the cucumber lengthwise with the tines of a fork gives the slices a striped border. Cucumbers from the farmer's market or your garden need no peeling, but those sold in the grocery store are often coated with wax and are best pared.

PREP TIME: 20 MINUTES
MAKES 36 APPETIZERS

2 medium cucumbers, chilled

1 (3-oz.) pkg. cream cheese, softened

2 tablespoons finely chopped fresh parsley

2 tablespoons finely chopped chives

1 tablespoon sour cream or mayonnaise

1 teaspoon prepared horseradish

1/2 teaspoon lemon juice

1/2 cup finely chopped cooked shrimp

1. Draw tines of fork lengthwise through cucumber peel to score; cut into 1/4-inch-thick slices. Place on paper towels to drain.

2. In small bowl, combine cream cheese, parsley, chives, sour cream, horseradish and lemon juice; beat until smooth. Stir in shrimp.

3. Spread or pipe 1 teaspoon cream cheese mixture onto each cucumber slice. Garnish as desired.

4. Serve immediately, or cover loosely and refrigerate up to 2 hours before serving.

NUTRITION INFORMATION PER SERVING: SERVING SIZE: 1 Appetizer • Calories 10 • Calories from Fat 10 • % Daily Value: Total Fat 1 g 2% • Saturated Fat 1 g 5% • Cholesterol 5 mg 2% • Sodium 10 mg 0% • Total Carbohydrate 0 g 0% • Dietary Fiber 0 g 0% • Sugars 0 g • Protein 1 g • Vitamin A 0% • Vitamin C 0% • Calcium 0% • Iron 0% • **Dietary Exchanges:** Free

Caponata and Shrimp Canapés

For easy seeding, cut the cucumbers in half lengthwise. Scrape the seeds out with a spoon —a serrated grapefruit spoon works very well. If you have the time, you can make your own caponata from scratch (see page 66).

PREP TIME: 40 MINUTES
MAKES 24 APPETIZERS

1 egg

1/2 cup purchased caponata (eggplant appetizer spread)

24 (1/4-inch-thick) slices baguette-style or small French bread

1/4 cup chopped seeded cucumber

24 shelled deveined cooked medium shrimp

1. Place egg in small saucepan. Add enough water to cover egg by 1 inch. Bring to a boil. Immediately remove from heat; cover and let stand 15 minutes. Drain; rinse with cold water. Place egg in bowl of ice water; let stand 10 minutes.

2. Meanwhile, spread caponata on bread slices.

3. Peel egg; chop. Top each appetizer with cucumber, egg and 1 shrimp.

4. Serve immediately, or cover loosely and refrigerate until serving time.

NUTRITION INFORMATION PER SERVING: SERVING SIZE: 1 Appetizer • Calories 40 • Calories from Fat 10 • % Daily Value: Total Fat 1 g 2% • Saturated Fat 0 g 0% • Cholesterol 20 mg 7% • Sodium 105 mg 4% • Total Carbohydrate 6 g 2% • Dietary Fiber 1 g 4% • Sugars 1 g • Protein 2 g • Vitamin A 0% • Vitamin C 0% • Calcium 0% • Iron 2% • **Dietary Exchanges:** 1/2 Starch **OR** 1/2 Carbohydrate

Tomato-Cheese Canapés

These canapés also translate easily to a first course for a sit-down dinner; simply spread the pesto and cheese on larger tomato slices, and eat with forks and knives.

PREP TIME: 55 MINUTES
MAKES 20 APPETIZERS

4 oz. soft cream cheese with garden vegetables (from 8-oz. tub)

1 large yellow bell pepper

4 Italian plum tomatoes, each cut into 5 slices

Fresh chives, cut into 1- to 2-inch lengths, if desired

1. Allow cream cheese spread to stand at room temperature for 30 minutes. Meanwhile, using 1-inch star canapé cutter, cut 20 stars from yellow pepper.

2. Pipe or spoon about 2 teaspoons cream cheese spread onto each tomato slice. Top each with pepper star and several chive pieces. Serve immediately, or cover loosely and refrigerate until serving time.

NUTRITION INFORMATION PER SERVING: SERVING SIZE: 1 Appetizer • Calories 25 • Calories from Fat 20 • % Daily Value: Total Fat 2 g 3% • Saturated Fat 1 g 5% • Cholesterol 5 mg 2% • Sodium 20 mg 1% • Total Carbohydrate 1 g 1% • Dietary Fiber 0 g 0% • Sugars 0 g • Protein 1 g • Vitamin A 4% • Vitamin C 15% • Calcium 0% • Iron 0% • **Dietary Exchanges:** ½ Fat

Olive and Roasted Garlic Canapés

The same qualities that make plum tomatoes a good choice for spaghetti sauce—thicker flesh, fewer seeds—make them ideal for canapés, too. They give just the right balance to the garlicky cream cheese spread.

PREP TIME: 10 MINUTES
MAKES 36 APPETIZERS

½ cup light cream cheese with roasted garlic (from 8-oz. tub)

2 tablespoons mayonnaise

⅔ cup chopped pimiento-stuffed green olives

¼ cup chopped celery

2 tablespoons chopped fresh parsley

36 thin slices French bread

2 to 3 Italian plum tomatoes, cut into 36 thin slices

36 sprigs fresh parsley

1. In small bowl, stir cream cheese until smooth. Add mayonnaise; stir to combine. Add olives, celery and parsley; mix well.

2. Spread about 1 teaspoon cream cheese mixture onto each slice of bread. Top each with tomato and sprig of parsley. Serve immediately, or cover and refrigerate until serving time.

NUTRITION INFORMATION PER SERVING: SERVING SIZE: 1 Appetizer • Calories 35 • Calories from Fat 20 • % Daily Value: Total Fat 2 g 3% • Saturated Fat 1 g 5% • Cholesterol 0 mg 0% • Sodium 110 mg 5% • Total Carbohydrate 3 g 1% • Dietary Fiber 0 g 0% • Sugars 1 g • Protein 1 g • Vitamin A 2% • Vitamin C 2% • Calcium 0% • Iron 0% • **Dietary Exchanges:** ½ Fat

Corn Cakes with Shrimp and Guacamole

Southwest essentials—corn, pepper, cilantro, avocado, lime, chile—are a perfect backdrop for juicy shrimp.

PREP TIME: 40 MINUTES
MAKES 24 APPETIZERS

CORN CAKES

½ cup fresh corn kernels or frozen whole kernel corn, thawed

1 cup buttermilk complete pancake and waffle mix

¾ cup water

2 tablespoons finely chopped red bell pepper

2 tablespoons finely chopped green onions

2 tablespoons grated Parmesan cheese

1 tablespoon chopped fresh cilantro

⅛ teaspoon hot pepper sauce

GUACAMOLE

1 ripe avocado

1½ tablespoons lime juice

2 tablespoons finely chopped sweet onion

1 tablespoon finely chopped jalapeño chile, seeded, membranes removed

⅛ teaspoon salt

TOPPING

24 shelled deveined cooked medium shrimp, tails removed

Fresh cilantro sprigs, if desired

1. Bring ½ cup water to a boil in small saucepan. Add corn; cook 4 to 6 minutes or until tender. Drain.

2. In medium bowl, combine pancake mix and water; stir just until large lumps disappear. Stir in cooked corn and all remaining corn cake ingredients.

3. Heat large nonstick skillet or griddle to medium-high heat (375°F.). For each cake, spoon scant 1 tablespoon batter into skillet, forming 24 cakes. Cook 4 to 6 minutes or until golden brown, turning once. Place on wire racks to cool.

4. Remove pit and peel avocado. In small bowl, coarsely mash avocado flesh with fork. Stir in lime juice, onion, chile and salt.

5. Just before serving, place corn cakes on serving platter. Top each with about 1 teaspoon guacamole, 1 shrimp and cilantro sprig.

NUTRITION INFORMATION PER SERVING: SERVING SIZE: 1 Appetizer • Calories 50 • Calories from Fat 20 • % Daily Value: Total Fat 2 g 3% • Saturated Fat 0 g 0% • Cholesterol 10 mg 3% • Sodium 100 mg 4% • Total Carbohydrate 6 g 2% • Dietary Fiber 1 g 4% • Sugars 1 g • Protein 2 g • Vitamin A 4% • Vitamin C 4% • Calcium 2% • Iron 2% • **Dietary Exchanges:** ½ Starch, ½ Fat **OR** ½ Carbohydrate, ½ Fat

Greek Feta Spread on Vegetables and Toast Rounds

Spreading the feta-vegetable mixture on Melba toast, cherry tomatoes and cucumber slices gives nice diversity of color, texture and flavor to these quick hors d'oeuvres.

PREP TIME: 15 MINUTES
MAKES 24 APPETIZERS; 8 SERVINGS

2 oz. (½ cup) crumbled tomato-basil feta cheese

2 oz. fat-free cream cheese

Dash ground red pepper (cayenne)

3 tablespoons chopped fresh parsley

8 (¼-inch-thick) unpeeled cucumber slices

4 cherry tomatoes, halved, seeded

8 Melba toast rounds

Paprika, if desired

1. In small bowl, combine feta cheese, cream cheese and ground red pepper; mix until well blended. Stir in 2 tablespoons of the parsley.

2. Just before serving, spoon or pipe 1 teaspoon cheese mixture onto each cucumber slice, tomato half and toast round. Top each with remaining parsley. If desired, sprinkle with paprika.

NUTRITION INFORMATION PER SERVING: SERVING SIZE: ⅛ of Recipe • Calories 50 • Calories from Fat 20 • % Daily Value: Total Fat 2 g 3% • Saturated Fat 1 g 5% • Cholesterol 5 mg 2% • Sodium 170 mg 7% • Total Carbohydrate 5 g 2% • Dietary Fiber 0 g 0% • Sugars 1 g • Protein 3 g • Vitamin A 6% • Vitamin C 6% • Calcium 8% • Iron 0% • **Dietary Exchanges:** 1 Vegetable, ½ Fat

Herbed Cheese Spread on Toast

Extra-virgin olive oil, made from the first pressing of the olives, lends its fruity flavor to this herb-flecked spread.

PREP TIME: 15 MINUTES
MAKES 16 APPETIZERS

1 (8-oz.) pkg. fat-free or ⅓-less-fat cream cheese (Neufchâtel), softened

1 tablespoon finely chopped fresh oregano or marjoram

1 tablespoon finely chopped fresh rosemary

2 teaspoons finely chopped fresh thyme

½ teaspoon garlic-pepper blend

1 teaspoon extra-virgin olive oil

16 (¼-inch-thick) slices baguette-style French bread or cocktail rye bread, toasted

1. In medium bowl, combine all ingredients except bread slices; blend until smooth.

2. Just before serving, spread about 2 teaspoons cream cheese mixture onto each toasted slice of bread.

NUTRITION INFORMATION PER SERVING: SERVING SIZE: 1 Appetizer • Calories 50 • Calories from Fat 10 • % Daily Value: Total Fat 1 g 2% • Saturated Fat 0 g 0% • Cholesterol 2 mg 1% • Sodium 150 mg 6% • Total Carbohydrate 7 g 2% • Dietary Fiber 0 g 0% • Sugars 1 g • Protein 3 g • Vitamin A 4% • Vitamin C 0% • Calcium 6% • Iron 0% • **Dietary Exchanges:** ½ Starch **OR** ½ Carbohydrate

Strawberries and Watercress on Wheat Crackers

Plump red berries don't need to wait for dessert. Showcase them with sweetened cream cheese and peppery watercress on crisp crackers.

PREP TIME: 15 MINUTES
MAKES 18 APPETIZERS

4 oz. cream cheese, softened

1 tablespoon orange marmalade

½ cup coarsely chopped fresh watercress

9 medium fresh strawberries

18 (2- to 2½-inch) round wheat crackers

1. In small bowl, combine cream cheese, marmalade and watercress; mix well. Cover; refrigerate until serving time.

2. Cut each strawberry in half lengthwise. Refrigerate berries until serving time.

3. Just before serving, spoon rounded teaspoonful cheese mixture onto each cracker. Top each with strawberry half, cut side down; press gently into cheese mixture.

NUTRITION INFORMATION PER SERVING: SERVING SIZE: 1 Appetizer • Calories 40 • Calories from Fat 25 • % Daily Value: Total Fat 3 g 5% • Saturated Fat 1 g 5% • Cholesterol 5 mg 2% • Sodium 45 mg 2% • Total Carbohydrate 3 g 1% • Dietary Fiber 0 g 0% • Sugars 1 g • Protein 1 g • Vitamin A 2% • Vitamin C 8% • Calcium 0% • Iron 0% • **Dietary Exchanges:** ½ Fruit, ½ Fat **OR** ½ Carbohydrate, ½ Fat

Fresh Tomato-Zucchini Salsa Crostini

A medley of chopped red and green vegetables tops baguette slices with fresh-from-the-garden flavor.

PREP TIME: 10 MINUTES
MAKES 24 APPETIZERS

2 medium tomatoes, chopped (1 cup)

½ cup finely chopped zucchini

¼ cup finely chopped green bell pepper

¼ cup sliced ripe olives

2 tablespoons chopped fresh basil

¼ teaspoon garlic powder

⅛ teaspoon salt

24 (¼-inch-thick) diagonal slices baguette-style French bread

1 tablespoon olive oil

1. In medium bowl, combine all ingredients except bread and oil; mix well.

2. Place bread slices on ungreased cookie sheet. Drizzle each bread slice with oil. Broil 4 to 6 inches from heat for 30 to 45 seconds or until lightly toasted.

3. Just before serving, top each toasted bread slice with about 1 tablespoon vegetable mixture.

NUTRITION INFORMATION PER SERVING: SERVING SIZE: 1 Appetizer • Calories 15 • Calories from Fat 10 • % Daily Value: Total Fat 1 g 2% • Saturated Fat 0 g 0% • Cholesterol 0 mg 0% • Sodium 40 mg 2% • Total Carbohydrate 2 g 1% • Dietary Fiber 0 g 0% • Sugars 0 g • Protein 0 g • Vitamin A 0% • Vitamin C 4% • Calcium 0% • Iron 0% • **Dietary Exchanges:** Free

2. Meanwhile, place bread slices on ungreased cookie sheet. Spray bread lightly with non-stick cooking spray. Broil 4 to 6 inches from heat for 1 to 2 minutes or until golden brown.

3. Drain tomatoes. Coarsely chop tomatoes and roasted peppers with knife or in food processor; place in medium bowl. Add oil, garlic, basil and salt; mix well.

4. Just before serving, spoon about 2 teaspoons tomato-pepper mixture onto toasted side of each bread slice; spread evenly. Garnish with fresh basil.

NUTRITION INFORMATION PER SERVING: SERVING SIZE: ⅛ of Recipe • Calories 60 • Calories from Fat 20 • % Daily Value: Total Fat 2 g 3% • Saturated Fat 0 g 0% • Cholesterol 0 mg 0% • Sodium 150 mg 6% • Total Carbohydrate 9 g 3% • Dietary Fiber 1 g 4% • Sugars 2 g • Protein 2 g • Vitamin A 15% • Vitamin C 60% • Calcium 0% • Iron 4% • **Dietary Exchanges:** ½ Starch, 1 Vegetable **OR** ½ Carbohydrate, 1 Vegetable

Tomato-Red Pepper Crostini

Sun-dried tomatoes hold the concentrated essence of the tomato, combined here with roasted peppers, garlic and herbs.

PREP TIME: 25 MINUTES
MAKES 16 APPETIZERS; 8 SERVINGS

½ cup dried sun-dried tomatoes

16 (¼-inch-thick) slices French bread

Olive oil nonstick cooking spray

1 (7.25-oz.) jar roasted red bell peppers, drained

1 teaspoon olive oil

¼ teaspoon minced garlic

¼ teaspoon dried basil leaves

Dash salt

Fresh basil or parsley leaves, if desired

1. Place sun-dried tomatoes in medium bowl; cover with boiling water. Let stand 3 minutes or until soft.

Savory Cucumber Sandwiches

Set out the cucumber sandwiches with some scones and perhaps some shortbread cookies for an English-style teatime.

PREP TIME: 10 MINUTES
MAKES 12 APPETIZERS

⅓ cup soft cream cheese with herbs and garlic (from 8-oz. tub)

12 slices pumpernickel cocktail bread

12 thin slices cucumber (about ¼ medium)

1 tablespoon diced pimiento, well drained

1. Spread about 1½ teaspoons cream cheese onto each slice of bread. Top each with cucumber slice. Sprinkle each with small amount of pimiento.

2. Serve immediately, or cover loosely and refrigerate until serving time.

NUTRITION INFORMATION PER SERVING: SERVING SIZE: 1 Appetizer • Calories 40 • Calories from Fat 20 • % Daily Value: Total Fat 2 g 3% • Saturated Fat 1 g 5% • Cholesterol 5 mg 2% • Sodium 75 mg 3% • Total Carbohydrate 4 g 1% • Dietary Fiber 0 g 0% • Sugars 0 g • Protein 2 g • Vitamin A 0% • Vitamin C 2% • Calcium 0% • Iron 0% • **Dietary Exchanges:** 1 Vegetable, ½ Fat

Crostini with Beef and Caper Mayonnaise

If you're a real garlic lover, add a clove of chopped garlic to the olive oil and heat the mixture in the microwave for 10 to 20 seconds before brushing it onto the bread.

PREP TIME: 30 MINUTES
MAKES 24 APPETIZERS

24 (¼- to ½-inch-thick) slices baguette-style or small French bread

2 tablespoons olive oil

½ cup mayonnaise

¼ cup grated Parmesan cheese

2 tablespoons chopped fresh chives

2 to 4 tablespoons drained capers

¼ teaspoon garlic powder

½ lb. thinly sliced cooked roast beef, cut into 24 pieces

2 Italian plum tomatoes, cut into 24 thin slices

Chopped fresh chives, if desired

1. Heat oven to 350°F. Place bread slices on ungreased cookie sheet; brush lightly with oil. Bake at 350°F. for 8 to 10 minutes or until crisp. Cool 5 minutes or until completely cooled.

2. Meanwhile, in small bowl, combine mayonnaise, cheese, 2 tablespoons chives, capers and garlic powder; mix well.

3. Spread mayonnaise mixture on bread slices. Top each with roast beef and tomato slice. Garnish with chives. Serve immediately, or cover loosely and refrigerate up to 2 hours before serving.

NUTRITION INFORMATION PER SERVING: SERVING SIZE: 1 Appetizer • Calories 90 • Calories from Fat 50 • % Daily Value: Total Fat 6 g 9% • Saturated Fat 1 g 5% • Cholesterol 10 mg 3% • Sodium 250 mg 10% • Total Carbohydrate 6 g 2% • Dietary Fiber 0 g 0% • Sugars 1 g • Protein 4 g • Vitamin A 0% • Vitamin C 0% • Calcium 2% • Iron 4% • **Dietary Exchanges:** ½ Starch, ½ Lean Meat, ½ Fat **OR** ½ Carbohydrate, ½ Lean Meat, ½ Fat

CROSTINI WITH BEEF AND CAPER MAYONNAISE

Tomato-Basil Bruschetta

Bring Mediterranean flavors—garlic, olive oil, tomato, basil—to the appetizer table with this simple, delicious bruschetta.

PREP TIME: 15 MINUTES
MAKES 8 APPETIZERS

8 (½-inch-thick) slices Italian or French bread

2 garlic cloves, peeled, halved

4 teaspoons olive oil

1 teaspoon salt

½ teaspoon cracked black pepper

2 small tomatoes, thinly sliced

2 tablespoons chopped fresh basil

1. Grill, broil or toast bread slices on both sides until light golden brown. While hot, rub cut side of garlic over one side of each bread slice.

2. Just before serving, brush ½ teaspoon oil over garlic side of each slice; sprinkle with salt and pepper. Top each with tomato slices. Sprinkle with basil.

NUTRITION INFORMATION PER SERVING: SERVING SIZE: 1 Appetizer • Calories 110 • Calories from Fat 25 • % Daily Value: Total Fat 3 g 5% • Saturated Fat 1 g 5% • Cholesterol 0 mg 0% • Sodium 440 mg 18% • Total Carbohydrate 17 g 6% • Dietary Fiber 1 g 4% • Sugars 2 g • Protein 3 g • Vitamin A 2% • Vitamin C 6% • Calcium 4% • Iron 8% • **Dietary Exchanges:** 1 Starch, ½ Fat **OR** 1 Carbohydrate, ½ Fat

Prosciutto-Wrapped Fruit

In Italy, salty prosciutto is often paired with juicy summer melon. This variation substitutes ripe pear and crisp apple.

PREP TIME: 25 MINUTES
MAKES 42 APPETIZERS

⅔ cup mascarpone cheese

½ lb. thinly sliced prosciutto ham

1 pear, unpeeled, cut into ½-inch wedges

1 red-skinned apple, unpeeled, cut into ½-inch wedges

1. Spread cheese evenly on prosciutto slices. Place pear or apple wedge on shortest side of each slice; roll up.

2. Serve immediately, or cover loosely and refrigerate until serving time. To serve, cut each roll into 3 pieces. Secure each with cocktail toothpick.

NUTRITION INFORMATION PER SERVING: SERVING SIZE: 1 Appetizer • Calories 30 • Calories from Fat 20 • % Daily Value: Total Fat 2 g 3% • Saturated Fat 1 g 5% • Cholesterol 5 mg 2% • Sodium 135 mg 6% • Total Carbohydrate 1 g 1% • Dietary Fiber 0 g 0% • Sugars 1 g • Protein 2 g • Vitamin A 0% • Vitamin C 0% • Calcium 0% • Iron 0% • **Dietary Exchanges:** ½ Fat

Smoked Salmon and Caper Pizza

This tasty, elegant pizza uses a prebaked crust that you crisp in the oven, then cool and top.

PREP TIME: 25 MINUTES
MAKES 24 APPETIZERS

1 (10-oz.) prebaked thin-crust Italian pizza crust

½ cup soft cream cheese with chives and onions (from 8-oz. tub)

2 tablespoons Dijon mustard

1 tablespoon honey

8 oz. thinly sliced smoked salmon

2 tablespoons finely chopped red onion

2 tablespoons drained capers

1 tablespoon chopped fresh dill

1. Heat oven to 425°F. Place pizza crust on ungreased cookie sheet. Bake at 425°F. for 6 to 8 minutes or just until crisp. Cool at least 15 minutes or until completely cooled.

2. Meanwhile, in small bowl, combine cream cheese, mustard and honey; mix until well blended.

3. Spread cream cheese mixture over cooled crust. Arrange salmon over top. Sprinkle with onion, capers and dill. Cut into wedges.

4. Serve immediately, or cover and refrigerate until serving time.

NUTRITION INFORMATION PER SERVING: SERVING SIZE: 1 Appetizer • Calories 70 • Calories from Fat 25 • % Daily Value: Total Fat 3 g 5% • Saturated Fat 1 g 5% • Cholesterol 10 mg 3% • Sodium 210 mg 9% • Total Carbohydrate 6 g 2% • Dietary Fiber 0 g 0% • Sugars 1 g • Protein 5 g • Vitamin A 0% • Vitamin C 0% • Calcium 0% • Iron 2% • **Dietary Exchanges:** ½ Starch, ½ Lean Meat, ½ Fat **OR** ½ Carbohydrate, ½ Lean Meat, ½ Fat

Easy Vegetable Pizza

Refrigerated crescent rolls make a convenient base for this cool pizza garnished with cherry tomatoes, broccoli florets and cucumber slices.

PREP TIME: 20 MINUTES
(READY IN 1 HOUR 55 MINUTES)
MAKES 60 APPETIZERS

2 (8-oz.) cans refrigerated crescent dinner rolls

1 (8-oz.) pkg. cream cheese, softened

½ cup sour cream

1 teaspoon dried dill weed

⅛ teaspoon garlic powder

20 small fresh broccoli florets

20 cucumber or zucchini slices

10 cherry tomatoes, halved

2 tablespoons tiny fresh parsley sprigs, if desired

1. Heat oven to 375°F. Unroll dough into 4 long rectangles. Place crosswise in ungreased 15x10x1-inch baking pan; press over bottom and 1 inch up sides to form crust. Firmly press perforations to seal.

2. Bake at 375°F. for 13 to 17 minutes or until golden brown. Cool 15 minutes or until completely cooled.

3. In small bowl, combine cream cheese, sour cream, dill and garlic powder; blend until smooth. Spread evenly over cooled crust. Cover; refrigerate 1 to 2 hours.

4. Just before serving, cut into 1½-inch squares. Top each square with broccoli floret, cucumber slice or tomato half. Garnish each with parsley.

NUTRITION INFORMATION PER SERVING: SERVING SIZE: 1 Appetizer • Calories 45 • Calories from Fat 25 • % Daily Value: Total Fat 3 g 5% • Saturated Fat 1 g 5% • Cholesterol 5 mg 2% • Sodium 70 mg 3% • Total Carbohydrate 3 g 1% • Dietary Fiber 0 g 0% • Sugars 1 g • Protein 1 g • Vitamin A 4% • Vitamin C 4% • Calcium 0% • Iron 0% • **Dietary Exchanges:** ½ Vegetable, ½ Fat

Beef Tenderloin and Caramelized Onion Sandwiches

Cooked slowly with butter and accented with brown sugar, onions become a sweet "marmalade" to pair with beef tenderloin. The caramelized onions are also good with roasted or grilled pork.

PREP TIME: 30 MINUTES
(READY IN 1 HOUR)
MAKES 36 SANDWICHES

TENDERLOIN

1/2 teaspoon salt

1/4 teaspoon garlic powder

1/4 teaspoon paprika

1/4 teaspoon coarse-ground black pepper

1 lb. beef tenderloin, trimmed

CARAMELIZED ONIONS

3 tablespoons butter

1 tablespoon oil

2 tablespoons brown sugar

3 medium onions, cut into 1/4-inch-thick slices

2 tablespoons red wine or water

SAUCE

1/2 cup sour cream

1 tablespoon purchased horseradish sauce

1/2 teaspoon salt

SANDWICH

1 (10-inch) round loaf focaccia (Italian flat bread)

1 1/2 cups firmly packed baby spinach leaves

Cocktail toothpicks

1. Heat oven to 450°F. In small bowl, combine 1/2 teaspoon salt, garlic powder, paprika and pepper; mix well. Rub mixture on all surfaces of beef tenderloin. Place beef in small shallow roasting pan; tuck thin end under.

2. Bake at 450°F. for 20 to 25 minutes or until meat thermometer inserted in center registers 140°F. for rare. Remove from oven.

Cool 30 minutes or until completely cooled. If desired, wrap tightly; refrigerate until serving time.

3. Meanwhile, in large skillet, heat butter and oil over medium heat until butter melts. Add brown sugar and onions; stir to coat. Cook over medium heat for 10 minutes or until onions begin to soften, stirring occasionally. Add wine. Reduce heat to medium-low; cover and cook 10 to 15 minutes or until onions are very tender. Cover; refrigerate until serving time.

4. When ready to serve, combine all sauce ingredients in small bowl; mix well. Heat focaccia as directed on package; cut in half horizontally. Spread both cut sides with sauce. Arrange spinach leaves over sauce on bottom half of focaccia.

5. Slice beef very thin; layer over spinach. Top with onions and top half of focaccia; press down. Insert cocktail toothpicks through all layers at 1 1/4- to 1 1/2-inch intervals. Cut between toothpicks to form tiny sandwich squares.

make-ahead tip

Bake tenderloin and cook onions as directed in recipe. Wrap tenderloin and place onions in covered container; refrigerate up to 24 hours. Just before serving, prepare sauce and assemble sandwiches as directed in recipe.

NUTRITION INFORMATION PER SERVING: SERVING SIZE: 1 Sandwich • Calories 60 • Calories from Fat 25 • % Daily Value: Total Fat 3 g 5% • Saturated Fat 1 g 5% • Cholesterol 10 mg 3% • Sodium 110 mg 5% • Total Carbohydrate 5 g 2% • Dietary Fiber 0 g 0% • Sugars 2 g • Protein 3 g • Vitamin A 4% • Vitamin C 0% • Calcium 2% • Iron 2% • **Dietary Exchanges:** 1/2 Starch, 1/2 Lean Meat **OR** 1/2 Carbohydrate, 1/2 Lean Meat

Pastrami and Pepper Roll-Ups

With just three ingredients, these simple roll-ups take little effort to assemble and can be made up to a day ahead.

PREP TIME: 25 MINUTES
(READY IN 2 HOURS 25 MINUTES)
MAKES 40 APPETIZERS

½ lb. thinly sliced pastrami (from deli)

⅓ cup soft cream cheese with chives and onions (from 8-oz. tub)

½ cup purchased roasted red bell peppers, drained, cut into ¾-inch-wide strips

1. Spread each pastrami slice with cream cheese. Top each with roasted pepper piece at one edge. Starting at roasted pepper edge, roll up each tightly. Refrigerate at least 2 hours or until firm.

2. To serve, cut each roll into 1-inch-thick pieces. Secure each with cocktail toothpick.

make-ahead tip
Roll-ups can be refrigerated up to 24 hours. Just before serving, cut into slices.

NUTRITION INFORMATION PER SERVING: SERVING SIZE: 1 Appetizer • Calories 20 • Calories from Fat 20 • % Daily Value: Total Fat 2 g 3% • Saturated Fat 1 g 5% • Cholesterol 5 mg 2% • Sodium 75 mg 3% • Total Carbohydrate 0 g 0% • Dietary Fiber 0 g 0% • Sugars 0 g • Protein 1 g • Vitamin A 0% • Vitamin C 6% • Calcium 0% • Iron 0% • **Dietary Exchanges:** ½ Fat

Turkey Club Tortilla Roll-Ups

A touch of cilantro and a tortilla wrap give a Southwestern twist to the classic bacon-turkey combo.

PREP TIME: 50 MINUTES
MAKES 48 APPETIZERS

4 slices bacon

6 (7- or 8-inch) flour tortillas

½ cup mayonnaise or salad dressing

4 oz. cream cheese, softened

½ cup chopped drained pepperoncini

2 tablespoons chopped fresh cilantro

½ cup chopped tomato

½ lb. thinly sliced cooked turkey

6 leaves leaf lettuce

1. Cook bacon until crisp. Drain on paper towel. Crumble bacon; set aside. Warm tortillas as directed on package.

2. Meanwhile, in small bowl, combine mayonnaise and cream cheese; mix until smooth. Stir in pepperoncini, cilantro and crumbled bacon.

3. Spread about 2 tablespoons mayonnaise mixture onto each warm tortilla. Top each with 1 rounded tablespoon tomato, ⅙ of turkey and 1 lettuce leaf. Roll up each tortilla tightly. Cut each roll into 8 pieces; secure each piece with cocktail toothpick.

4. Serve immediately, or cover tightly and refrigerate until serving time.

make-ahead tip
Roll-ups can be refrigerated up to 2 hours.

NUTRITION INFORMATION PER SERVING: SERVING SIZE: 1 Appetizer • Calories 45 • Calories from Fat 25 • % Daily Value: Total Fat 3 g 5% • Saturated Fat 1 g 5% • Cholesterol 10 mg 3% • Sodium 75 mg 3% • Total Carbohydrate 3 g 1% • Dietary Fiber 0 g 0% • Sugars 0 g • Protein 2 g • Vitamin A 0% • Vitamin C 0% • Calcium 0% • Iron 0% • **Dietary Exchanges:** 1 Fat

Sushi-Style Beef Roll-Ups

Inspired by the classic Japanese seafood rolls, this version uses tortillas for the wrap, and beef and a spiced-up cream cheese for the filling. Rice vinegar gives the rice a tangy-sweet flavor.

PREP TIME: 25 MINUTES
(READY IN 5 HOURS 15 MINUTES)
MAKES 24 APPETIZERS

²/₃ cup uncooked medium-grain white rice

1 ¹/₃ cups water

2 tablespoons seasoned rice vinegar

1 (3-oz.) pkg. cream cheese, softened

1 teaspoon whipped horseradish

3 (7- or 8-inch) flour tortillas

1 (2.5-oz.) pkg. thinly sliced corned beef

1 (7- to 8-inch) cucumber

¹/₄ cup roasted red bell pepper pieces
    (from 7.25-oz. jar)

1. Cook rice in water as directed on package. In medium bowl, combine warm cooked rice and vinegar; mix well. Cover; refrigerate 30 minutes or until cool.

2. In small bowl, combine cream cheese and horseradish; mix well. Place each tortilla on 12-inch square of plastic wrap. Spread about 2 tablespoons cream cheese mixture over each tortilla, spreading to edges. Arrange corned beef slices over cream cheese, overlapping slices and leaving 1 inch of top and bottom edges of each tortilla uncovered. (See photo.)

3. Spoon about ¹/₃ cup cold rice mixture across center of each tortilla; press firmly into strip about 2 inches wide and ¹/₂ inch thick.

4. Quarter cucumber lengthwise. Reserve 3 sections for another use. Remove seeds from cucumber quarter; cut into 3 thin lengthwise strips. Press 1 strip into center of each rice strip. Cut roasted peppers into thin strips. Place next to cucumber to form long red stripe.

5. On each tortilla, mound another ¹/₃ cup rice mixture over cucumber and roasted pepper. With wet hands, form rice into firm rolls, completely covering cucumber and roasted pepper.

6. Beginning at bottom edge, roll each tortilla firmly around rice. Wrap each roll securely in plastic wrap. Refrigerate at least 4 hours or until well chilled.

7. To serve, trim uneven ends of each roll. Cut each roll into 8 slices.

make-ahead
tip

Roll-ups can be refrigerated up to 24 hours. Just before serving, cut into slices.

NUTRITION INFORMATION PER SERVING: SERVING SIZE: 1 Appetizer • Calories 50 • Calories from Fat 20 • % Daily Value: Total Fat 2 g 3% • Saturated Fat 1 g 5% • Cholesterol 5 mg 2% • Sodium 55 mg 2% • Total Carbohydrate 7 g 2% • Dietary Fiber 0 g 0% • Sugars 0 g • Protein 2 g • Vitamin A 2% • Vitamin C 4% • Calcium 0% • Iron 2% • **Dietary Exchanges:** ¹/₂ Starch **OR** ¹/₂ Carbohydrate

Spinach and Jalapeño Roll-Ups

Jalapeños punch up this green and red spiral sandwich. If you prefer less zip, you can substitute canned mild green chiles.

PREP TIME: 25 MINUTES
(READY IN 1 HOUR 25 MINUTES)
MAKES 32 APPETIZERS

1 (9-oz.) pkg. frozen spinach in a pouch

1 (8-oz.) pkg. cream cheese, softened

2 jalapeño chiles, minced

4 (8-inch) flour tortillas

Roasted red bell pepper (from 7.25-oz. jar), cut into 4 (8-inch) strips

1. Cook spinach as directed on package. Place in colander or strainer; rinse with cold water to cool. Squeeze spinach to remove as much moisture as possible.

2. In food processor bowl with metal blade, combine cream cheese and chiles; process until smooth. Add spinach; process just until blended.

3. Place 1 tortilla on work surface. Spread ¼ of spinach mixture over tortilla, leaving ½-inch border on one side. Place strips of roasted pepper, piecing together if necessary, across middle of tortilla.

4. Roll tortilla toward border, making sure beginning is tightly rolled, but easing pressure as rolling continues to avoid forcing out filling. Wrap in plastic wrap; repeat with remaining tortillas, spinach mixture and roasted peppers. Refrigerate at least 1 hour before serving.

5. To serve, trim uneven ends of each roll. Cut each roll diagonally into 8 slices.

make-ahead
tip

Roll-ups can be refrigerated up to 8 hours. Just before serving, cut into slices.

NUTRITION INFORMATION PER SERVING: SERVING SIZE: 1 Appetizer • Calories 45 • Calories from Fat 25 • % Daily Value: Total Fat 3 g 5% • Saturated Fat 2 g 10% • Cholesterol 10 mg 3% • Sodium 60 mg 3% • Total Carbohydrate 3 g 1% • Dietary Fiber 0 g 0% • Sugars 0 g • Protein 1 g • Vitamin A 10% • Vitamin C 10% • Calcium 2% • Iron 0% • **Dietary Exchanges:** ½ Vegetable, ½ Fat

Crab Roll-Ups

Surimi, an inexpensive crabmeat alternative made of flavored white fish, works well in this blended filling.

PREP TIME: 15 MINUTES
(READY IN 30 MINUTES)
MAKES 36 APPETIZERS

4 oz. cream cheese, softened

2 tablespoons mayonnaise or salad dressing

2 teaspoons prepared horseradish

½ avocado, pitted, peeled and chopped

6 (8-inch) flour tortillas

1 (8-oz.) pkg. flaked imitation crabmeat (surimi)

¾ cup chopped red bell pepper

⅓ cup sliced green onions

1 (2¼-oz.) can sliced ripe olives, drained

1. In food processor bowl with metal blade or blender container, combine cream cheese, mayonnaise, horseradish and avocado; process on high speed until well mixed.

2. Spread cream cheese mixture evenly over tortillas. Top each tortilla with crabmeat, bell pepper, green onions and olives. Roll up each tortilla; wrap securely in plastic wrap. Refrigerate at least 15 minutes or overnight.

3. To serve, slice rolls diagonally into ¾-inch-thick slices.

NUTRITION INFORMATION PER SERVING: SERVING SIZE: 1 Appetizer • Calories 60 • Calories from Fat 25 • % Daily Value: Total Fat 3 g 5% • Saturated Fat 1 g 5% • Cholesterol 5 mg 2% • Sodium 110 mg 5% • Total Carbohydrate 5 g 2% • Dietary Fiber 0 g 0% • Sugars 1 g • Protein 2 g • Vitamin A 4% • Vitamin C 8% • Calcium 0% • Iron 2% • **Dietary Exchanges:** ½ Starch, ½ Fat **OR** ½ Carbohydrate, ½ Fat

Spinach Dip Crescent Wreath

Perfect for holiday time, this ring-shaped dish looks like an evergreen wreath dotted with holly leaves and berries. You may also make your own spinach dip (see page 30) to really put your stamp on this cheerful hors d'oeuvre.

PREP TIME: 30 MINUTES
(READY IN 1 HOUR 10 MINUTES)
MAKES 20 SERVINGS

2 (8-oz.) cans refrigerated crescent dinner rolls

1½ cups purchased spinach dip

¼ cup chopped red bell pepper

2 tablespoons chopped green onions

1 tablespoon chopped fresh parsley

Green bell pepper, cut into holly leaves

Small cherry tomatoes

1. Heat oven to 375°F. Invert 10-oz. custard cup on center of ungreased large cookie sheet.

2. Remove dough from 1 can, keeping dough in 1 piece; do not unroll. (Keep remaining can of dough in refrigerator.) With hands, roll dough in one direction to form 12-inch log. Cut log into 20 slices. Arrange 16 slices, slightly overlapping and in clockwise direction, around custard cup on cookie sheet.

3. Repeat with second can of dough, cutting log into 20 slices. Arrange slices from second can and remaining 4 slices from first can (total of 24 slices), slightly overlapping each other and in counterclockwise direction, next to but not overlapping first ring. Remove custard cup from center of wreath shape.

4. Bake at 375°F. for 14 to 18 minutes or until light golden brown. Gently loosen wreath from cookie sheet; carefully slide onto wire rack. Cool 30 minutes or until completely cooled.

5. Place cooled wreath on serving tray or platter. Spread spinach dip over wreath. Sprinkle with red bell pepper, 2 tablespoons green onions and parsley. Decorate with bell pepper "holly leaves" and cherry tomato "berries." Serve immediately, or cover and refrigerate up to 2 hours before serving.

NUTRITION INFORMATION PER SERVING: SERVING SIZE: 1/20 of Recipe • Calories 170 • Calories from Fat 120 • % Daily Value: Total Fat 13 g 20% • Saturated Fat 3 g 15% • Cholesterol 15 mg 5% • Sodium 310 mg 13% • Total Carbohydrate 10 g 3% • Dietary Fiber 0 g 0% • Sugars 3 g • Protein 2 g • Vitamin A 4% • Vitamin C 6% • Calcium 0% • Iron 2% • **Dietary Exchanges:** ½ Starch, 2½ Fat **OR** ½ Carbohydrate, 2½ Fat

Guacamole Appetizer Squares

Guacamole, a spicy mashed avocado blend, often serves as a dip for tortilla chips—but it's equally suitable as a spread on these easy-to-serve squares. Store-bought guacamole is fine, but if you have extra time try the recipe on page 52.

page 52

PREP TIME: 20 MINUTES
(READY IN 2 HOURS 10 MINUTES)
MAKES 60 APPETIZERS

2 (8-oz.) cans refrigerated crescent dinner rolls

1/2 teaspoon cumin

1/2 teaspoon chili powder

1 (8-oz.) container soft cream cheese with pineapple

1 (8-oz.) container guacamole

1/2 cup diced seeded Italian plum tomatoes

1/4 cup real bacon pieces

1/4 cup sliced ripe olives

1/4 cup chopped fresh cilantro

1. Heat oven to 375°F. Separate dough into 4 long rectangles. Place rectangles in ungreased 15x10x1-inch baking pan. Press over bottom of pan; firmly press perforations to seal. Sprinkle with cumin and chili powder.

2. Bake at 375°F. for 13 to 17 minutes or until golden brown. Cool 30 minutes or until completely cooled.

3. In medium bowl, combine cream cheese and guacamole; blend well. Spread evenly over cooled crust. Cover with plastic wrap; refrigerate 1 to 2 hours.

4. Just before serving, top with tomatoes, bacon, olives and cilantro. Cut into squares.

NUTRITION INFORMATION PER SERVING: SERVING SIZE: 1 Appetizer • Calories 45 • Calories from Fat 25 • % Daily Value: Total Fat 3 g 5% • Saturated Fat 1 g 5% • Cholesterol 4 mg 1% • Sodium 120 mg 5% • Total Carbohydrate 4 g 1% • Dietary Fiber 0 g 0% • Sugars 1 g • Protein 1 g • Vitamin A 0% • Vitamin C 0% • Calcium 0% • Iron 0% • **Dietary Exchanges:** 1 Fat

Party Pesto Squares

Pesto—a traditional paste of basil, garlic, pine nuts, Parmesan cheese and olive oil—is the signature flavor in these quick, zesty pizza squares.

PREP TIME: 25 MINUTES
(READY IN 55 MINUTES)
MAKES 35 APPETIZERS

2 (8-oz.) cans refrigerated crescent dinner rolls

1/2 cup purchased pesto

1/4 cup sour cream

2 Italian plum tomatoes, cut in half lengthwise, thinly sliced

1/2 cup sliced ripe olives

1/2 cup chopped yellow bell pepper

1. Heat oven to 375°F. Separate dough into 4 long rectangles. Place rectangles crosswise in ungreased 15x10x1-inch baking pan. Press over bottom and 1 inch up sides to form crust.

2. Bake at 375°F. for 14 to 19 minutes or until golden brown. Cool 30 minutes or until completely cooled.

3. In small bowl, combine pesto and sour cream; blend well. Spread over cooled crust. Top with tomato slices, olives and bell pepper.

4. Serve immediately, or cover loosely and refrigerate until serving time. To serve, cut into small squares.

NUTRITION INFORMATION PER SERVING: SERVING SIZE: 1 Appetizer • Calories 60 • Calories from Fat 35 • % Daily Value: Total Fat 4 g 6% • Saturated Fat 1 g 5% • Cholesterol 0 mg 0% • Sodium 130 mg 5% • Total Carbohydrate 6 g 2% • Dietary Fiber 0 g 0% • Sugars 1 g • Protein 1 g • Vitamin A 0% • Vitamin C 4% • Calcium 0% • Iron 2% • **Dietary Exchanges:** 1/2 Starch, 1/2 Fat **OR** 1/2 Carbohydrate, 1/2 Fat

Taco Crescent Wreath

Avocado, like many other fruits, turns brown when the flesh is exposed to air. Dipping the avocado cubes in lime or lemon juice keeps them a creamy, vibrant green.

PREP TIME: 40 MINUTES
(READY IN 1 HOUR)
MAKES 20 SERVINGS

2 (8-oz.) cans refrigerated crescent dinner rolls

2 dried chipotle chiles

1/3 cup sour cream

1/4 cup chopped fresh cilantro

1/4 cup mayonnaise

1 teaspoon sugar

1/4 teaspoon salt

1/4 teaspoon cumin

1 (2 1/4-oz.) can sliced ripe olives, drained

1 avocado, pitted, peeled, diced and dipped in lime juice

1/2 cup chopped fresh tomato

2 oz. (1/2 cup) finely shredded Cheddar cheese

Additional fresh cilantro leaves

1/2 cup chunky-style salsa

1. Heat oven to 375°F. Invert 10-oz. custard cup on center of ungreased large cookie sheet.

2. Remove dough from 1 can, keeping dough in 1 piece; do not unroll. (Keep remaining can of dough in refrigerator.) With hands, roll dough in one direction to form 12-inch log. Cut log into 20 slices. Arrange 16 slices, slightly overlapping and in clockwise direction, around custard cup on cookie sheet.

3. Repeat with second can of dough, cutting log into 20 slices. Arrange slices from second can and remaining 4 slices from first can (total of 24 slices), slightly overlapping each other and in counterclockwise direction, next to but not overlapping first ring. Remove custard cup from center of wreath shape.

4. Bake at 375°F. for 14 to 18 minutes or until light golden brown. Gently loosen wreath from cookie sheet; carefully slide onto wire rack. Cool 30 minutes or until completely cooled.

5. Meanwhile, cover chipotle chiles with water; let stand 10 to 15 minutes. Drain; finely chop. In medium bowl, combine chiles, sour cream, chopped cilantro, mayonnaise, sugar, salt and cumin; mix well.

6. Place cooled wreath on serving tray or platter. Spread sour cream mixture over wreath. Decorate with olives, avocado, tomato, cheese and cilantro leaves. Place salsa in small bowl; place in center of wreath. Serve immediately, or cover and refrigerate up to 2 hours before serving.

NUTRITION INFORMATION PER SERVING: SERVING SIZE: 1/20 of Recipe • Calories 150 • Calories from Fat 90 • % Daily Value: Total Fat 10 g 15% • Saturated Fat 3 g 15% • Cholesterol 5 mg 2% • Sodium 310 mg 13% • Total Carbohydrate 11 g 4% • Dietary Fiber 1 g 4% • Sugars 3 g • Protein 3 g • Vitamin A 15% • Vitamin C 2% • Calcium 4% • Iron 4% • **Dietary Exchanges:** 1/2 Starch, 2 Fat **OR** 1/2 Carbohydrate, 2 Fat

Mini Seafood Tostadas

You can prepare the creamy topping in advance, but spread it on the chips just before serving, to keep them crisp.

PREP TIME: 25 MINUTES
MAKES 24 APPETIZERS

4 oz. 1/3-less-fat cream cheese (Neufchâtel), softened

1 tablespoon chopped fresh cilantro

2 teaspoons fresh lime juice

1/2 to 1 serrano chile, seeded, chopped

24 bite-sized round tortilla chips

1/2 cup shredded leaf lettuce

24 shelled deveined cooked small shrimp, or 1/2 cup chopped crabmeat or imitation crabmeat (surimi)

1/4 cup finely chopped red bell pepper

1. In small bowl, combine cream cheese, cilantro, lime juice and chile; blend well.

2. Spread about 1/2 teaspoon cream cheese mixture onto each tortilla chip. Top each with lettuce, shrimp and bell pepper.

NUTRITION INFORMATION PER SERVING: SERVING SIZE: 1 Appetizer • Calories 35 • Calories from Fat 20 • % Daily Value: Total Fat 2 g 3% • Saturated Fat 1 g 5% • Cholesterol 10 mg 3% • Sodium 45 mg 2% • Total Carbohydrate 2 g 1% • Dietary Fiber 0 g 0% • Sugars 0 g • Protein 2 g • Vitamin A 4% • Vitamin C 10% • Calcium 0% • Iron 0% • **Dietary Exchanges:** 1/2 Very Lean Meat, 1/2 Fat

Caesar Seafood Tacos

This take-off on the Caesar salad uses mild surimi instead of the traditional anchovies, with the salad tucked into crunchy mini taco shells. It could also be spooned into mini pita bread rounds.

PREP TIME: 20 MINUTES
MAKES 24 MINI TACOS

2 (8-oz.) pkg. flaked imitation crabmeat (surimi)

1/2 cup purchased Caesar salad dressing

3 cups shredded romaine lettuce

1 (3.8-oz.) pkg. (24 shells) fun-size mini taco shells

2 oz. (1/2 cup) shredded fresh Parmesan cheese

1. In medium bowl, combine imitation crabmeat and 1/4 cup of the salad dressing; toss to coat. In another medium bowl, combine lettuce and remaining 1/4 cup salad dressing; toss to coat.

2. Layer imitation crabmeat mixture and lettuce mixture in each taco shell. Top each with cheese.

NUTRITION INFORMATION PER SERVING: SERVING SIZE: 1 Mini Taco • Calories 70 • Calories from Fat 35 • % Daily Value: Total Fat 4 g 6% • Saturated Fat 1 g 5% • Cholesterol 5 mg 2% • Sodium 280 mg 12% • Total Carbohydrate 5 g 2% • Dietary Fiber 0 g 0% • Sugars 2 g • Protein 4 g • Vitamin A 2% • Vitamin C 2% • Calcium 4% • Iron 0% • **Dietary Exchanges:** 1/2 Starch, 1/2 Very Lean Meat, 1/2 Fat **OR** 1/2 Carbohydrate, 1/2 Very Lean Meat, 1/2 Fat

Cucumber-Dill Stuffed Cherry Tomatoes

Choose large cherry tomatoes for easiest stuffing. A baby feeding spoon or miniature melon baller works well for scooping the seeds out of the tomatoes.

PREP TIME: 30 MINUTES
(READY IN 2 HOURS 30 MINUTES)
MAKES 24 APPETIZERS

TOMATOES

24 cherry tomatoes

FILLING

1 (3-oz.) pkg. cream cheese, softened

2 tablespoons mayonnaise or salad dressing

1/4 cup finely chopped, seeded cucumber

1 tablespoon finely chopped green onions

2 teaspoons chopped fresh dill or 1/4 teaspoon dried dill weed

1. Remove stems from tomatoes. Cut thin slice from bottom of each tomato. With small spoon or melon baller, carefully hollow out each tomato, leaving 1/8-inch shell. Invert tomato shells onto paper towels to drain. (See photo.)

2. In small bowl, combine cream cheese and mayonnaise; blend well. Stir in cucumber, green onions and dill; mix well.

3. Fill tomato shells with cream cheese mixture. Cover loosely; refrigerate at least 2 hours before serving to blend flavors.

tip

For easy filling, place cream cheese mixture in plastic squeeze bottle. Cut off 3/4 of bottle tip with scissors. Squeeze cream cheese mixture into tomato shells.

make-ahead tip

Stuffed tomatoes can be refrigerated up to 24 hours.

NUTRITION INFORMATION PER SERVING: SERVING SIZE: 1 Appetizer • Calories 20 • Calories from Fat 20 • % Daily Value: Total Fat 2 g 3% • Saturated Fat 1 g 5% • Cholesterol 5 mg 2% • Sodium 15 mg 1% • Total Carbohydrate 0 g 0% • Dietary Fiber 0 g 0% • Sugars 0 g • Protein 0 g • Vitamin A 0% • Vitamin C 0% • Calcium 0% • Iron 0% • **Dietary Exchanges:** 1/2 Fat

CUCUMBER-DILL STUFFED CHERRY TOMATOES

Salmon-Stuffed Cherry Tomatoes

Salmon, capers and dill make a colorful and delicious filling for cherry tomatoes.

PREP TIME: 20 MINUTES
MAKES 18 APPETIZERS

18 cherry tomatoes

1 (6⅛-oz.) can pink salmon, drained, flaked

2 tablespoons mayonnaise

1 tablespoon drained capers, if desired

½ teaspoon dried dill weed

4 sprigs fresh parsley

1. Line cookie sheet with 2 layers of paper towels. Cut thin slice from bottom of each tomato. With small spoon or melon baller, carefully hollow out each tomato, leaving ⅛-inch shell. Invert tomato shells onto paper towels to drain.

2. In small bowl, combine salmon, mayonnaise, capers and dill; mix well. Spoon about 2 teaspoons filling into each tomato. Garnish with small parsley leaves.

make-ahead tip

Stuffed tomatoes can be refrigerated up to 8 hours.

NUTRITION INFORMATION PER SERVING: SERVING SIZE: 1 Appetizer • Calories 30 • Calories from Fat 20 • % Daily Value: Total Fat 2 g 3% • Saturated Fat 0 g 0% • Cholesterol 4 mg 1% • Sodium 50 mg 2% • Total Carbohydrate 1 g 1% • Dietary Fiber 0 g 0% • Sugars 0 g • Protein 2 g • Vitamin A 2% • Vitamin C 4% • Calcium 2% • Iron 0% • **Dietary Exchanges:** ½ Fat

Cheesy Stuffed Cherry Peppers

Sweet, smooth and sharp flavors make these stuffed peppers an intriguing hors d'oeuvre.

PREP TIME: 15 MINUTES
MAKES 16 APPETIZERS

8 pickled sweet red cherry peppers

⅓ cup soft cream cheese with pineapple (from 8-oz. tub)

3 tablespoons finely chopped dried beef

3 tablespoons sliced green onions

1 tablespoon mayonnaise or salad dressing

5 to 6 drops hot pepper sauce

1. Cut peppers in half vertically; remove seeds. Drain on paper towel.

2. In small bowl, combine all remaining ingredients; mix well. Spoon filling into pepper halves.

NUTRITION INFORMATION PER SERVING: SERVING SIZE: 1 Appetizer • Calories 25 • Calories from Fat 20 • % Daily Value: Total Fat 2 g 3% • Saturated Fat 1 g 5% • Cholesterol 5 mg 2% • Sodium 115 mg 5% • Total Carbohydrate 1 g 1% • Dietary Fiber 0 g 0% • Sugars 0 g • Protein 1 g • Vitamin A 4% • Vitamin C 4% • Calcium 0% • Iron 0% • **Dietary Exchanges:** ½ Fat

Shrimp-Stuffed Cherry Tomatoes

Display the stuffed tomatoes on a platter lined with frilly savoy cabbage leaves or sprigs of curly parsley.

PREP TIME: 20 MINUTES
(READY IN 1 HOUR 20 MINUTES)
MAKES 20 APPETIZERS

20 medium cherry tomatoes, stems removed

1/3 cup soft cream cheese with garden vegetables (from 8-oz. tub)

20 shelled deveined cooked medium shrimp

20 small sprigs fresh parsley

1. Cut thin slice from bottom of each tomato. With small spoon or melon baller, carefully hollow out each tomato, leaving 1/8-inch shell. Place on serving platter or tray.

2. In small bowl, beat cream cheese until smooth. Spoon scant teaspoon cream cheese into each tomato shell. Top each with 1 shrimp and 1 parsley sprig. Cover; refrigerate at least 1 hour or until serving time.

make-ahead tip

Stuffed tomatoes can be refrigerated up to 8 hours.

NUTRITION INFORMATION PER SERVING: SERVING SIZE: 1 Appetizer • Calories 15 • Calories from Fat 10 • % Daily Value: Total Fat 1 g 2% • Saturated Fat 1 g 5% • Cholesterol 15 mg 5% • Sodium 25 mg 1% • Total Carbohydrate 1 g 1% • Dietary Fiber 0 g 0% • Sugars 0 g • Protein 1 g • Vitamin A 4% • Vitamin C 6% • Calcium 0% • Iron 0% • **Dietary Exchanges:** Free

Salmon-Stuffed Pea Pods

For a stunning presentation, arrange the stuffed pea pods spoke-fashion on a large round platter, interspersed with stuffed cherry tomatoes (found from page 123 to the recipe at left).

PREP TIME: 25 MINUTES
(READY IN 1 HOUR 25 MINUTES)
MAKES 36 APPETIZERS

36 fresh snow pea pods

1 (3-oz.) pkg. cream cheese, softened

2 tablespoons drained capers

1 (4.5-oz.) pkg. smoked salmon, flaked

Chopped fresh parsley

1. Rinse pea pods. If not crisp, soak in ice water for 30 minutes. Drain; remove stem end. With thin knife, open pea pods along straight side.

2. In medium bowl, combine cream cheese and capers; mix well. Add salmon; mix gently. Spoon about 1 teaspoon mixture into each pea pod. Garnish with parsley. Cover; refrigerate at least 1 hour or until serving time.

make-ahead tip

Stuffed pea pods can be refrigerated up to 8 hours.

NUTRITION INFORMATION PER SERVING: SERVING SIZE: 1 Appetizer • Calories 10 • Calories from Fat 10 • % Daily Value: Total Fat 1 g 2% • Saturated Fat 1 g 5% • Cholesterol 3 mg 1% • Sodium 40 mg 2% • Total Carbohydrate 0 g 0% • Dietary Fiber 0 g 0% • Sugars 0 g • Protein 1 g • Vitamin A 0% • Vitamin C 4% • Calcium 0% • Iron 0% • **Dietary Exchanges:** Free

Smoked Salmon on Endive

Endive's slight, pleasant bitterness goes well with a blend of smoked salmon and oniony cream cheese.

PREP TIME: 25 MINUTES
MAKES 24 APPETIZERS

1 (8-oz.) container soft cream cheese with chives and onions

1 (4.5-oz.) pkg. smoked salmon, skin removed, finely chopped

2 tablespoons mayonnaise

1/8 teaspoon hot pepper sauce

24 Belgian endive leaves (2 to 3 heads)

Chopped fresh chives, if desired

1. In medium bowl, combine all ingredients except endive and chives; mix well. Spoon or pipe scant tablespoon mixture into each endive leaf.

2. Serve immediately, or cover and refrigerate until serving time. Just before serving, sprinkle with chives.

NUTRITION INFORMATION PER SERVING: SERVING SIZE: 1 Appetizer • Calories 45 • Calories from Fat 35 • % Daily Value: Total Fat 4 g 6% • Saturated Fat 2 g 10% • Cholesterol 10 mg 3% • Sodium 70 mg 3% • Total Carbohydrate 0 g 0% • Dietary Fiber 0 g 0% • Sugars 0 g • Protein 2 g • Vitamin A 4% • Vitamin C 0% • Calcium 0% • Iron 0% • **Dietary Exchanges:** 1/2 Lean Meat, 1/2 Fat

Caviar and Cream Cheese-Filled Endive

This appetizer uses ingredients often served with caviar—hard-cooked eggs and onion—but serves them on crisp endive rather than the traditional toast points.

PREP TIME: 45 MINUTES
MAKES 16 APPETIZERS

3 eggs

1/2 cup soft cream cheese with onions and garlic or with herbs and garlic (from 8-oz. tub)

16 leaves Belgian endive

2 tablespoons finely chopped red onion

2 tablespoons caviar

1. Place eggs in single layer in medium saucepan. Add enough water to cover eggs by 1 inch. Bring to a boil. Immediately remove from heat; cover and let stand 15 minutes. Drain; rinse with cold water. Place eggs in bowl of ice water; let stand 10 minutes.

2. Peel eggs; coarsely chop. Pipe or spoon cream cheese onto endive leaves. Top with onion, chopped egg and caviar.

3. Serve immediately, or cover loosely and refrigerate until serving time.

make-ahead tip

Eggs can be cooked in advance. Wrap tightly; refrigerate up to 24 hours. Chop eggs just before assembling appetizers.

NUTRITION INFORMATION PER SERVING: SERVING SIZE: 1 Appetizer • Calories 60 • Calories from Fat 45 • % Daily Value: Total Fat 5 g 8% • Saturated Fat 3 g 15% • Cholesterol 60 mg 20% • Sodium 95 mg 4% • Total Carbohydrate 1 g 1% • Dietary Fiber 0 g 0% • Sugars 0 g • Protein 2 g • Vitamin A 6% • Vitamin C 0% • Calcium 0% • Iron 2% • **Dietary Exchanges:** 1/2 High-Fat Meat

Fig-Filled Endive Leaves

The natural sweetness and chewiness of dried figs is a wonderful and sophisticated touch in this orange-scented appetizer.

PREP TIME: 25 MINUTES
MAKES 16 APPETIZERS

1/2 cup soft cream cheese with pineapple (from 8-oz. tub)

1 tablespoon powdered sugar

2 teaspoons orange-flavored liqueur

1/4 teaspoon grated orange peel

1/4 cup coarsely chopped dried Calimyrna figs

16 small Belgian endive leaves

16 small pieces fresh orange

1. In small bowl, combine cream cheese, powdered sugar, liqueur and orange peel; mix well. Add figs; stir gently to mix.

2. Spoon mixture into each endive leaf. Top each with piece of orange. Serve immediately, or cover loosely and refrigerate until serving time.

NUTRITION INFORMATION PER SERVING: SERVING SIZE: 1 Appetizer • Calories 45 • Calories from Fat 25 • % Daily Value: Total Fat 3 g 5% • Saturated Fat 2 g 10% • Cholesterol 10 mg 3% • Sodium 20 mg 1% • Total Carbohydrate 3 g 1% • Dietary Fiber 1 g 4% • Sugars 3 g • Protein 1 g • Vitamin A 4% • Vitamin C 4% • Calcium 0% • Iron 0% • **Dietary Exchanges:** 1/2 Fat

Elegant Cheese and Fruit Platter

The variety of flavors and textures makes this easily assembled platter very appealing. For best flavor, set out the cheese about a half hour before serving.

PREP TIME: 15 MINUTES
(READY IN 45 MINUTES)
MAKES 24 SERVINGS

1 (8-oz.) wedge Stilton or Gorgonzola cheese

1 (8-oz.) block white Cheddar cheese

1 (8-oz.) round Camembert or Brie cheese

1 large crisp red apple, sliced

1 medium pear, sliced

1 pint (2 cups) strawberries, halved

3/4 lb. seedless green grapes, cut into small clusters

3/4 lb. seedless red grapes, cut into small clusters

1 (7-oz.) pkg. dried apricots

1/4 cup dried cherries

Lemon leaves or fresh rosemary sprigs

1. Arrange cheeses in center of large serving platter. Cover; let stand at room temperature about 30 minutes.

2. Arrange fresh fruit in groups around cheese. Sprinkle dried apricots and cherries over cheese and fruit. Tuck lemon leaves among fruit.

3. To serve, provide cheese spreaders for soft cheeses and cheese planes for harder cheeses. If desired, serve cheese and fruit with crackers.

NUTRITION INFORMATION PER SERVING: SERVING SIZE: 1/24 of Recipe • Calories 160 • Calories from Fat 70 • % Daily Value: Total Fat 8 g 12% • Saturated Fat 5 g 25% • Cholesterol 25 mg 8% • Sodium 270 mg 11% • Total Carbohydrate 15 g 5% • Dietary Fiber 2 g 8% • Sugars 12 g • Protein 7 g • Vitamin A 20% • Vitamin C 20% • Calcium 15% • Iron 4% • **Dietary Exchanges:** 1 Fruit, 1 High-Fat Meat **OR** 1 Carbohydrate, 1 High-Fat Meat

Savory Herb Shortbread

This rich, crumbly "cookie" comes as a savory surprise on the appetizer table and makes a good hostess gift, too.

PREP TIME: 45 MINUTES
MAKES 24 APPETIZERS

¼ cup chopped walnuts

2 oz. (½ cup) shredded fresh Parmesan cheese

2 oz. (½ cup) shredded sharp Cheddar cheese

¼ cup butter, cut into chunks

⅔ cup all-purpose flour

½ teaspoon dried sage leaves

¼ teaspoon dry mustard

¼ teaspoon coarse-ground black pepper

1. Heat oven to 350°F. Spread walnuts on small cookie sheet. Bake at 350°F. for 5 to 7 minutes or until golden brown, stirring occasionally. Cool 5 minutes or until completely cooled. Increase oven temperature to 425°F.

2. In food processor bowl with metal blade, combine cheeses and butter; process with on/off pulses until mixture is crumbly. Add cooled toasted walnuts and all remaining ingredients; process until dough forms.

3. Divide dough into 4 equal parts. On lightly floured surface, pat or press each part into disk. Roll each to form 5-inch round. Cut each round into 6 wedges. Place on ungreased cookie sheet.

4. Bake at 425°F. for 6 to 8 minutes or until light golden brown around edges. Remove from cookie sheet; place on wire rack. Cool 15 minutes or until completely cooled before serving.

Prepare shortbread as directed in recipe. Store for up to 24 hours in tightly covered container.

NUTRITION INFORMATION PER SERVING: SERVING SIZE: 1 Appetizer • Calories 60 • Calories from Fat 35 • % Daily Value: Total Fat 4 g 6% • Saturated Fat 2 g 10% • Cholesterol 10 mg 3% • Sodium 70 mg 3% • Total Carbohydrate 3 g 1% • Dietary Fiber 0 g 0% • Sugars 0 g • Protein 2 g • Vitamin A 2% • Vitamin C 0% • Calcium 4% • Iron 0% • **Dietary Exchanges:** ½ High-Fat Meat

Twenty-Minute Party for 6 to 8 People

Don't let a tight schedule deprive you of the fun of getting together with friends. A quick trip through the grocery store will yield everything you need.

PREP TIME: 20 MINUTES
MAKES 6 TO 8 SERVINGS

1 lb. shelled deveined cooked medium shrimp (from fresh meat counter)

1 (2-oz.) container caviar (from canned meat section) or 1 (8-oz.) jar pickled herring (from deli or refrigerated section)

1 lb. sliced cheese (from deli) or cheese ball and spreads (from refrigerated section)

½ lb. sliced sausage or meat (from deli) or 8 oz. pâté (from deli or canned meat section)

1 lb. Italian vegetable or tortellini salad (from deli)

1 lb. cut-up fresh fruit (from deli or produce section)

1 bottle seafood cocktail sauce

1 box crackers

1 (8-oz.) loaf cocktail rye or pumpernickel bread, sliced

Cans and/or bottles of sparkling water, soda pop, wine coolers and/or beer

Arrange all items except beverages on 2 or 3 large serving platters. Serve with cocktail toothpicks and/or small forks.

NUTRITION INFORMATION PER SERVING: Not possible to calculate because of recipe variables.

Sun-Dried Tomato Cream Puffs

These showy puffs are not hard to make but are so impressive to serve to guests.

PREP TIME: 25 MINUTES
(READY IN 1 HOUR)
MAKES 40 APPETIZERS

1/2 cup water

1/4 cup margarine or butter, cut into small pieces

1/2 cup all-purpose flour

2 tablespoons finely chopped sun-dried tomatoes
   (not oil-packed)

1/4 teaspoon dried basil leaves

1/4 teaspoon salt

1/8 teaspoon ground red pepper (cayenne)

2 eggs

4 oz. cream cheese or flavored cream cheese, softened

1. Heat oven to 425°F. In medium saucepan, combine water and margarine; heat over medium heat until mixture comes to a boil and margarine is melted.

2. Stir in all remaining ingredients except eggs and cream cheese. Cook over medium heat for about 1 minute, stirring vigorously until mixture leaves sides of saucepan in smooth compact ball. Remove from heat.

3. Add eggs 1 at a time, beating with hand mixer for 1 minute after each addition until mixture is smooth and glossy. Drop mixture by tablespoonfuls or pipe from decorating bag onto ungreased cookie sheet to form 20 puffs.

4. Bake at 425°F. for 15 to 20 minutes or until puffed and golden brown. Remove from oven; cut small slit in side of each puff to allow steam to escape. Cool 15 minutes or until completely cooled.

5. To serve, cut puffs in half. Spoon or pipe about 1 teaspoon cream cheese into each half. Serve immediately.

HIGH ALTITUDE (ABOVE 3500 FEET): No change.

NUTRITION INFORMATION PER SERVING: SERVING SIZE: 1 Appetizer • Calories 60 • Calories from Fat 45 • % Daily Value: Total Fat 5 g 8% • Saturated Fat 2 g 10% • Cholesterol 25 mg 8% • Sodium 85 mg 4% • Total Carbohydrate 3 g 1% • Dietary Fiber 0 g 0% • Sugars 0 g • Protein 1 g • Vitamin A 4% • Vitamin C 0% • Calcium 0% • Iron 0% • Dietary Exchanges: 1 Vegetable, 1 Fat

hot appetizers

Orange-Pineapple Appetizer Meatballs

If you shape meatballs by hand, slip on plastic deli gloves or sandwich bags to keep your hands clean. Or use a meatball tool, which resembles tongs fitted with half spheres. Dip the tool in water between squeezes to prevent sticking.

PREP TIME: 30 MINUTES
MAKES 12 SERVINGS

MEATBALLS

1 lb. extra-lean ground beef

1/4 cup quick-cooking rolled oats

1/4 cup finely chopped green onions

1/2 teaspoon salt, if desired

1/4 teaspoon allspice

1/4 teaspoon pepper

1/4 cup refrigerated or frozen fat-free egg product, thawed

SAUCE

1 (8-oz.) can pineapple tidbits in unsweetened juice, drained

1/2 cup reduced-sugar orange marmalade

1 tablespoon finely chopped green onions

1/8 teaspoon allspice

1. In medium bowl, combine all meatball ingredients; mix well. Shape into about 36 (1-inch) balls.

2. Spray large nonstick skillet with nonstick cooking spray. Heat over medium-high heat until hot. Add meatballs; cook 8 to 10 minutes or until meatballs are browned, thoroughly cooked and no longer pink in center, turning frequently.

3. Stir in all sauce ingredients. Cook over medium heat for 3 to 4 minutes or until thoroughly heated, stirring once.

make-ahead tip

Prepare meatballs in sauce as directed in recipe. Place in covered container; refrigerate up to 24 hours. To reheat, place in microwave-safe bowl. Microwave on HIGH until thoroughly heated, stirring occasionally.

NUTRITION INFORMATION PER SERVING: SERVING SIZE: 1/12 of Recipe • Calories 110 • Calories from Fat 45 • % Daily Value: Total Fat 5 g 8% • Saturated Fat 2 g 10% • Cholesterol 25 mg 8% • Sodium 115 mg 5% • Total Carbohydrate 7 g 2% • Dietary Fiber 0 g 0% • Sugars 5 g • Protein 8 g • Vitamin A 0% • Vitamin C 2% • Calcium 0% • Iron 6% • **Dietary Exchanges:** 1/2 Fruit, 1 1/2 Lean Meat **OR** 1/2 Carbohydrate, 1 1/2 Lean Meat

Saté Meatballs

Indonesian saté often consists of skewered strips of chicken or beef in a spicy peanutty sauce. Here, the peanut-coconut-lime sauce goes with little meatballs.

PREP TIME: 35 MINUTES
MAKES 32 MEATBALLS; 16 SERVINGS

MEATBALLS

1 lb. extra-lean ground beef

1/2 cup soft white bread crumbs

1/4 cup chopped onion

1 garlic clove, minced

1 tablespoon soy sauce

1 egg, beaten

SAUCE

1 tablespoon oil

1/4 cup chopped onion

1 cup coconut milk

1/3 cup peanut butter

1 tablespoon brown sugar

1 tablespoon lime juice

1 tablespoon fish sauce or soy sauce

1/4 teaspoon ground red pepper (cayenne)

1. Heat oven to 350°F. In medium bowl, combine all meatball ingredients; mix well. Shape into 32 meatballs; place in ungreased 15x10x1-inch baking pan.

2. Bake at 350°F. for 15 to 20 minutes or until meatballs are thoroughly cooked and no longer pink in center.

3. Meanwhile, heat oil in large nonstick skillet over medium heat until hot. Add 1/4 cup onion; cook about 5 minutes or until tender, stirring frequently. Add coconut milk and peanut butter; stir until well combined. Stir in all remaining sauce ingredients until well blended. Reduce heat to low; simmer until thickened.

4. Add meatballs to sauce; stir gently to coat. Serve in chafing dish or slow cooker on low setting.

make-ahead tip

Prepare meatballs in sauce as directed in recipe. Place in covered container; refrigerate up to 24 hours. To reheat, place in large saucepan. Cook over medium heat until thoroughly heated, stirring occasionally.

NUTRITION INFORMATION PER SERVING: SERVING SIZE: 1/16 of Recipe • Calories 150 • Calories from Fat 100 • % Daily Value: Total Fat 11 g 17% • Saturated Fat 5 g 25% • Cholesterol 30 mg 10% • Sodium 190 mg 8% • Total Carbohydrate 4 g 1% • Dietary Fiber 0 g 0% • Sugars 2 g • Protein 8 g • Vitamin A 0% • Vitamin C 0% • Calcium 0% • Iron 6% • **Dietary Exchanges:** 1/2 Starch, 1 Medium-Fat Meat, 1 Fat **OR** 1/2 Carbohydrate, 1 Medium-Fat Meat, 1 Fat

Bourbon Cocktail Meatballs

Meat loaf mixture, sold at the meat counter, usually combines ground beef and pork, and sometimes veal. You may of course substitute your own favorite combination of ground meats.

PREP TIME: 45 MINUTES
MAKES 48 MEATBALLS; 24 SERVINGS

MEATBALLS

1 1/2 lb. meat loaf mixture or lean ground beef

1/2 cup unseasoned dry bread crumbs

1/4 cup finely chopped onion

1 teaspoon salt

1 teaspoon dry mustard

2 tablespoons chili sauce

1 egg

SAUCE

1 (12-oz.) jar pineapple preserves

1/3 cup chili sauce

1/4 cup bourbon

1/4 teaspoon hot pepper sauce

1. Heat oven to 400°F. In large bowl, combine all meatball ingredients; mix well. Shape into 48 (1¼-inch) meatballs; place in ungreased 15x10x1-inch baking pan.

2. Bake at 400°F. for 15 to 20 minutes or until meatballs are thoroughly cooked and no longer pink in center.

3. Meanwhile, in large saucepan, combine all sauce ingredients; mix well. Cook over low heat until mixture is bubbly, stirring frequently.

4. Add meatballs to sauce; stir gently to coat. Cook until thoroughly heated, stirring occasionally.

Prepare meatballs in sauce as directed in recipe. Place in covered container; refrigerate up to 24 hours. To reheat, place in large saucepan. Cook over medium heat until thoroughly heated, stirring occasionally.

NUTRITION INFORMATION PER SERVING: SERVING SIZE: 1/24 of Recipe • Calories 100 • Calories from Fat 25 • % Daily Value: Total Fat 3 g 5% • Saturated Fat 1 g 5% • Cholesterol 20 mg 7% • Sodium 190 mg 8% • Total Carbohydrate 13 g 4% • Dietary Fiber 0 g 0% • Sugars 8 g • Protein 4 g • Vitamin A 0% • Vitamin C 2% • Calcium 0% • Iron 2% • **Dietary Exchanges:** 1 Fruit, 1/2 Medium-Fat Meat **OR** 1 Carbohydrate, 1/2 Medium-Fat Meat

Chutney-Glazed Meatballs

Chutney, a sweet-sour condiment important in Indian cuisine, blends with tomato and grated fresh ginger for a piquant glaze. Serve the meatballs with toothpicks.

PREP TIME: 30 MINUTES
(READY IN 1 HOUR)
MAKES 48 MEATBALLS; 24 SERVINGS

MEATBALLS

1 1/2 lb. lean ground beef

1/2 cup unseasoned dry bread crumbs

1 tablespoon instant minced onion

1/2 teaspoon salt

1/8 teaspoon pepper

1/4 cup milk

1 egg, slightly beaten

SAUCE

1/2 cup chutney

1/2 cup ketchup

1 (8-oz.) can tomato sauce

1 teaspoon grated gingerroot

1. Heat oven to 375°F. In large bowl, combine all meatball ingredients; mix well. Shape into 48 (1-inch) meatballs; place in ungreased 15x10x1-inch baking pan.

2. Bake at 375°F. for 25 to 30 minutes or until meatballs are thoroughly cooked and no longer pink in center.

3. Meanwhile, in large saucepan, combine all sauce ingredients; mix well. Cook over medium heat for 4 to 5 minutes or until bubbly.

4. Add meatballs to sauce; stir to coat. Cook over medium heat for 4 to 5 minutes or until thoroughly heated, stirring occasionally.

Prepare meatballs in sauce as directed in recipe. Place in covered container, refrigerate up to 24 hours. To reheat, place in large saucepan. Cook over medium heat until thoroughly heated, stirring occasionally.

NUTRITION INFORMATION PER SERVING: SERVING SIZE: 1/24 of Recipe • Calories 100 • Calories from Fat 35 • % Daily Value: Total Fat 4 g 6% • Saturated Fat 2 g 10% • Cholesterol 25 mg 8% • Sodium 250 mg 10% • Total Carbohydrate 9 g 3% • Dietary Fiber 0 g 0% • Sugars 4 g • Protein 6 g • Vitamin A 4% • Vitamin C 2% • Calcium 0% • Iron 4% • **Dietary Exchanges:** 1/2 Fruit, 1/2 Medium-Fat Meat **OR** 1/2 Carbohydrate, 1/2 Medium-Fat Meat

Sweet and Zesty Meatballs with Peppers

Grape jelly is the surprise ingredient in the sauce for these golden turkey meatballs. We challenge your guests to identify it, for while the jelly provides sweetness and subtle undertones in the chili-pepper sauce, its distinctive flavor is subdued.

PREP TIME: 40 MINUTES
MAKES 60 MEATBALLS; 30 SERVINGS

MEATBALLS

1 1/2 lb. lean ground turkey

1/2 cup finely chopped onion

1/3 cup unseasoned dry bread crumbs

1/4 teaspoon garlic powder

1/4 teaspoon salt

1/8 teaspoon pepper

1 egg, slightly beaten

SAUCE

1/2 cup grape jelly

3/4 cup chili sauce

1 medium green bell pepper, cut into 1-inch pieces

1 medium red bell pepper, cut into 1-inch pieces

1 medium yellow bell pepper, cut into 1-inch pieces

1. Heat oven to 375°F. In large bowl, combine all meatball ingredients; blend well. Shape into 60 (1-inch) meatballs; place in ungreased 15x10x1-inch baking pan.

2. Bake at 375°F. for 25 to 30 minutes or until meatballs are thoroughly cooked and no longer pink in center.

3. Meanwhile, in large saucepan, combine grape jelly and chili sauce; mix well. Bring to a boil over medium heat.

4. Add meatballs and bell peppers to sauce. Reduce heat to low; simmer 5 minutes, stirring occasionally.

make-ahead tip

Prepare meatballs in sauce as directed in recipe. Do not add bell peppers. Place meatball mixture in covered container; refrigerate up to 24 hours. To reheat, place in large saucepan; add bell peppers. Cook over medium heat until thoroughly heated, stirring occasionally.

NUTRITION INFORMATION PER SERVING: SERVING SIZE: 1/30 of Recipe • Calories 70 • Calories from Fat 20 • % Daily Value: Total Fat 2 g 3% • Saturated Fat 1 g 5% • Cholesterol 25 mg 8% • Sodium 140 mg 6% • Total Carbohydrate 7 g 2% • Dietary Fiber 0 g 0% • Sugars 4 g • Protein 5 g • Vitamin A 6% • Vitamin C 15% • Calcium 0% • Iron 2% • **Dietary Exchanges:** 1/2 Starch, 1/2 Very Lean Meat **OR** 1/2 Carbohydrate, 1/2 Very Lean Meat

Maple-Glazed BBQ Meatballs

Ground turkey is a lighter, leaner alternative to pork or beef meatballs. Since ground poultry is highly perishable, plan to use it or freeze it within a day of purchase.

PREP TIME: 30 MINUTES
MAKES 32 MEATBALLS; 8 SERVINGS

1 lb. lean ground turkey

1/2 cup finely chopped unpeeled apple

1/4 cup corn flake crumbs

1/4 teaspoon onion powder

1/4 teaspoon dried thyme leaves

1 tablespoon real maple syrup or maple-flavored syrup

1 egg

1 cup barbecue sauce

1/3 cup real maple syrup or maple-flavored syrup

1. Heat oven to 400°F. Line 15x10x1-inch baking pan with foil. Spray foil with nonstick cooking spray.

2. In medium bowl, combine ground turkey, apple, corn flake crumbs, onion powder, thyme, 1 tablespoon syrup and egg; mix well. To quickly form turkey mixture into meatballs, firmly press mixture into 8x4-inch rectangle. Cut into 32 (1-inch) squares; if desired, roll each into ball. Place in foil-lined pan.

3. Bake at 400°F. for 15 to 20 minutes or until meatballs are thoroughly cooked and no longer pink in center.

4. In medium saucepan, combine barbecue sauce and 1/3 cup syrup. Bring to a boil. Add baked meatballs; stir until coated.

Prepare meatballs as directed in recipe but do not glaze. Place meatballs in covered container; refrigerate up to 24 hours. Prepare barbecue sauce mixture as directed. Add meatballs; cook and stir over medium heat until coated and thoroughly heated.

NUTRITION INFORMATION PER SERVING: SERVING SIZE: 1/8 of Recipe • Calories 170 • Calories from Fat 45 • % Daily Value: Total Fat 5 g 8% • Saturated Fat 1 g 5% • Cholesterol 65 mg 22% • Sodium 340 mg 14% • Total Carbohydrate 18 g 6% • Dietary Fiber 1 g 4% • Sugars 11 g • Protein 13 g • Vitamin A 8% • Vitamin C 4% • Calcium 4% • Iron 8% • **Dietary Exchanges:** 1 Fruit, 2 Lean Meat **OR** 1 Carbohydrate, 2 Lean Meat

Turkey Meatballs in Cranberry Sauce

For a holiday appetizer buffet, turkey-cranberry meatballs capture the season's signature flavors without the fuss or long cooking time of an entire roasted bird. Garnish the serving dish with thin half-circles of fresh navel orange.

PREP TIME: 35 MINUTES
MAKES 15 SERVINGS

1 lb. lean ground turkey

1/2 cup finely chopped onion

1/4 cup uncooked instant white or brown rice

1/4 cup unseasoned dry bread crumbs

1/4 cup refrigerated or frozen fat-free egg product, thawed

1 teaspoon salt, if desired

1/2 teaspoon poultry seasoning

1 (16-oz.) can jellied cranberry sauce

1/2 cup water

1. In medium bowl, combine all ingredients except cranberry sauce and water; mix well. Shape into about 45 (1-inch) balls.

2. Spray large nonstick skillet with nonstick cooking spray. Heat over medium heat until hot. Add meatballs; cover and cook 8 to 10 minutes or until meatballs are browned, thoroughly cooked and no longer pink in center, turning occasionally.

3. Add cranberry sauce and water; cook over medium-low heat for 3 to 4 minutes or until cranberry sauce is melted and smooth, stirring frequently.

make-ahead tip

Prepare meatballs in sauce as directed in recipe. Place in covered container; refrigerate up to 24 hours. To reheat, place in microwave-safe bowl. Microwave on HIGH until thoroughly heated, stirring occasionally.

NUTRITION INFORMATION PER SERVING: SERVING SIZE: 1/15 of Recipe • Calories 120 • Calories from Fat 25 • % Daily Value: Total Fat 3 g 5% • Saturated Fat 1 g 5% • Cholesterol 20 mg 7% • Sodium 190 mg 8% • Total Carbohydrate 15 g 5% • Dietary Fiber 0 g 0% • Sugars 11 g • Protein 7 g • Vitamin A 0% • Vitamin C 0% • Calcium 0% • Iron 4% • **Dietary Exchanges:** 1 Fruit, 1 Lean Meat **OR** 1 Carbohydrate, 1 Lean Meat

Spinach Balls
with Mustard Dip

For contrast with these emerald colored meatballs, decorate a holiday serving tray with cherry or grape tomatoes.

PREP TIME: 30 MINUTES
MAKES 15 SERVINGS

1 lb. lean ground turkey

1 (9-oz.) pkg. frozen spinach in a pouch, thawed, well drained

¼ cup unseasoned dry bread crumbs

¼ cup finely chopped onion

½ teaspoon garlic powder

½ teaspoon salt, if desired

¼ cup refrigerated or frozen fat-free egg product, thawed

1 (12-oz.) bottle creamy mustard-mayonnaise sauce

1. In medium bowl, combine turkey, spinach, bread crumbs, onion, garlic powder, salt, egg product and 2 tablespoons of the mustard-mayonnaise sauce; mix well. Shape into about 45 (1-inch) balls.

2. Spray large nonstick skillet with nonstick cooking spray. Heat over medium-high heat until hot. Add spinach balls; cover and cook 8 to 10 minutes or until spinach balls are firm and centers are no longer pink, turning occasionally. Keep warm.

3. Pour remaining mustard-mayonnaise sauce into small microwave-safe serving bowl. Microwave on HIGH for 1½ to 2 minutes or until thoroughly heated. Stir sauce. Serve hot spinach balls with sauce.

tip

To quickly thaw spinach, cut small slit in center of pouch; microwave on HIGH for 2 to 3 minutes or until thawed. Remove spinach from pouch; squeeze dry with paper towels.

make-ahead tip

Prepare and cook spinach balls as directed above. Place in covered container; refrigerate up to 24 hours. To reheat, place spinach balls in foil-lined 15x10x1-inch baking pan. Heat at 400°F. for 8 to 12 minutes or until thoroughly heated. Heat sauce as directed in recipe.

NUTRITION INFORMATION PER SERVING: SERVING SIZE: ⅟₁₅ of Recipe • Calories 130 • Calories from Fat 70 • % Daily Value: Total Fat 8 g 12% • Saturated Fat 3 g 15% • Cholesterol 20 mg 7% • Sodium 430 mg 18% • Total Carbohydrate 7 g 2% • Dietary Fiber 0 g 0% • Sugars 0 g • Protein 7 g • Vitamin A 10% • Vitamin C 4% • Calcium 2% • Iron 4% • **Dietary Exchanges:** 1 Vegetable, 1 Lean Meat, 1 Fat

Veggie Balls in Barbecue Sauce

Unlike many other dried beans, lentils cook quickly, making an earthy-flavored base for vegetarian "meat" balls.

PREP TIME: 55 MINUTES
MAKES 18 SERVINGS

2¾ cups water

½ cup dried lentils, sorted, rinsed

1 cup uncooked instant rice

¼ cup finely chopped onion

1 teaspoon dried Italian seasoning

¼ teaspoon salt

¼ cup unseasoned dry bread crumbs

⅓ cup refrigerated or frozen fat-free egg product, thawed

1⅓ cups barbecue sauce

1. In medium saucepan, combine water and lentils. Bring to a boil. Reduce heat to medium-low; cover and cook 8 minutes, stirring occasionally.

2. Add rice, onion, Italian seasoning and salt; mix well. Return to a boil. Reduce heat to medium-low; cover and cook 8 to 10 minutes or until liquid is absorbed and lentils and rice are tender, stirring occasionally.

3. Remove saucepan from heat; uncover and let stand 10 minutes.

4. Add bread crumbs, egg product and 2 tablespoons of the barbecue sauce to lentil mixture; stir, mashing mixture slightly while mixing. With wet hands, shape into 36 (1-inch) balls.

5. Spray large nonstick skillet with nonstick cooking spray. Heat over medium-high heat until hot. Add veggie balls; cook 6 to 8 minutes or until browned on all sides, turning frequently with 2 spoons.

6. Reduce heat to medium. Pour remaining barbecue sauce over veggie balls; cook 5 minutes or until thoroughly heated, stirring frequently.

make-ahead tip

Prepare veggie balls in sauce as directed in recipe. Place in covered container; refrigerate up to 24 hours. To reheat, place in microwave-safe bowl. Microwave on HIGH until thoroughly heated, stirring occasionally.

NUTRITION INFORMATION PER SERVING: SERVING SIZE: ⅟₁₈ of Recipe • Calories 60 • Calories from Fat 0 • % Daily Value: Total Fat 0 g 0% • Saturated Fat 0 g 0% • Cholesterol 0 mg 0% • Sodium 200 mg 8% • Total Carbohydrate 11 g 4% • Dietary Fiber 2 g 8% • Sugars 1 g • Protein 3 g • Vitamin A 4% • Vitamin C 2% • Calcium 0% • Iron 6% • **Dietary Exchanges:** 1 Starch **OR** 1 Carbohydrate

Easy Sausage and Provolone Cheese Balls

Most meatball recipes use a finely ground dry ingredient, such as bread crumbs, to bind the mixture with egg or cheese so it won't crumble during cooking. In these Italian-inspired meatballs, pancake mix does the trick.

PREP TIME: 55 MINUTES
MAKES 48 APPETIZERS

1 lb. bulk Italian pork sausage

1 cup buttermilk complete pancake and waffle mix

½ teaspoon dried basil leaves

8 oz. (2 cups) shredded provolone cheese

¼ cup chopped green onions

1. Heat oven to 375°F. Line 15x10x1-inch baking pan with foil. Spray foil with nonstick cooking spray.

2. In food processor bowl with metal blade, combine sausage, pancake mix and basil; process just until combined. Add cheese and green onions; process with on/off pulses to blend. Shape mixture into 1-inch balls; place in sprayed foil-lined pan.

3. Bake at 375°F. for 10 to 15 minutes or until meatballs are no longer pink in center. Serve warm with cocktail toothpicks.

make-ahead tip

Prepare sausage balls as directed in recipe but do not bake. Cover; refrigerate up to 24 hours. Uncover; bake as directed in recipe.

NUTRITION INFORMATION PER SERVING: SERVING SIZE: 1 Appetizer • Calories 45 • Calories from Fat 25 • % Daily Value: Total Fat 3 g 5% • Saturated Fat 1 g 5% • Cholesterol 10 mg 3% • Sodium 140 mg 6% • Total Carbohydrate 2 g 1% • Dietary Fiber 0 g 0% • Sugars 1 g • Protein 3 g • Vitamin A 0% • Vitamin C 0% • Calcium 4% • Iron 0% • **Dietary Exchanges:** ½ High-Fat Meat

Sweet Orange-Glazed Chicken Wings

The little morsel of meat on the wing tip is not worth including in an appetizer like this, but you can freeze the tips, along with necks, gizzards and other chicken trimmings (except liver), to use in chicken stock.

PREP TIME: 10 MINUTES
(READY IN 5 HOURS 10 MINUTES)
MAKES 24 APPETIZERS

12 chicken wings (about 2 lb.), tips removed, wings cut in half and skin removed if desired

⅓ cup chili sauce

¼ cup orange marmalade

1 tablespoon red wine vinegar

1½ teaspoons Worcestershire sauce

½ teaspoon prepared mustard

¼ teaspoon garlic powder

1. Place chicken wings in resealable food storage plastic bag. Add all remaining ingredients; seal bag. Turn bag to coat wings. Refrigerate 4 to 24 hours to marinate, turning bag occasionally.

2. Heat oven to 375°F. Drain chicken wings; reserve marinade. Place chicken on broiler pan.

3. Bake at 375°F. for 45 to 60 minutes or until chicken is no longer pink next to bone, brushing occasionally with reserved marinade. Discard any remaining marinade.

make-ahead tip

Prepare and bake wings as directed in recipe. Place in covered container; refrigerate up to 24 hours. To reheat, place in foil-lined 15x10x1-inch baking pan. Heat at 350°F. for 20 minutes or until thoroughly heated.

NUTRITION INFORMATION PER SERVING: SERVING SIZE: 1 Appetizer • Calories 50 • Calories from Fat 25 • % Daily Value: Total Fat 3 g 5% • Saturated Fat 1 g 5% • Cholesterol 15 mg 5% • Sodium 25 mg 1% • Total Carbohydrate 1 g 1% • Dietary Fiber 0 g 0% • Sugars 1 g • Protein 5 g • Vitamin A 0% • Vitamin C 0% • Calcium 0% • Iron 0% • **Dietary Exchanges:** 1 Lean Meat

SWEET ORANGE-GLAZED CHICKEN WINGS; CRAB AND ASIAGO BUNDLES, PAGE 225

Chinese Glazed Chicken Wings

(Pictured on page 132.)

Think of duck sauce as thin, tangy marmalade or jam. It's made with fruit—usually apricots, peaches or plums—plus sugar, vinegar and sometimes chile pepper.

PREP TIME: 20 MINUTES
(READY IN 1 HOUR 20 MINUTES)
MAKES 24 APPETIZERS

12 chicken wings (about 2 lb.), tips removed, wings cut in half

1/2 cup hoisin sauce

2 tablespoons duck sauce (containing apricots and peaches)

2 tablespoons soy sauce

2 teaspoons chili paste or 1/4 teaspoon crushed red pepper flakes

1 garlic clove, minced

1. Heat oven to 375°F. Line 15x10x1-inch baking pan with foil. Arrange chicken wings in foil-lined pan. In small bowl, combine all remaining ingredients; mix well. Brush or spoon about half of sauce onto chicken wings. Bake at 375°F. for 30 minutes.

2. Remove pan from oven. Turn wings over; brush with remaining sauce.

3. Return to oven; bake an additional 30 minutes or until chicken is no longer pink next to bone.

make-ahead tip

Prepare and bake wings as directed in recipe. Place in covered container; refrigerate up to 24 hours. To reheat, place in foil-lined 15x10x1-inch baking pan. Heat at 350°F. for 20 minutes or until thoroughly heated.

NUTRITION INFORMATION PER SERVING: SERVING SIZE: 1 Appetizer • Calories 70 • Calories from Fat 35 • % Daily Value: Total Fat 4 g 6% • Saturated Fat 1 g 5% • Cholesterol 15 mg 5% • Sodium 240 mg 10% • Total Carbohydrate 4 g 1% • Dietary Fiber 0 g 0% • Sugars 3 g • Protein 5 g • Vitamin A 0% • Vitamin C 0% • Calcium 0% • Iron 2% • **Dietary Exchanges:** 1/2 Fruit, 1/2 High-Fat Meat **OR** 1/2 Carbohydrate, 1/2 High-Fat Meat

Maple-Apple Party Riblets

The maple glaze makes these sweet riblets hard to resist. Just remember to set out plenty of napkins.

PREP TIME: 25 MINUTES
(READY IN 1 HOUR 25 MINUTES)
MAKES 16 SERVINGS

1 (2-lb.) rack pork back ribs, cut in half lengthwise across bones

1/2 cup real maple syrup

1/4 cup apple jelly

1 tablespoon soy sauce

1/4 cup chopped fresh chives

1/2 teaspoon dry mustard

1. Heat oven to 450°F. Line 15x10x1-inch baking pan with foil. Cut ribs into individual riblets. Place riblets, meaty side down, in foil-lined pan; cover with foil. Bake at 450°F. for 30 minutes.

2. Meanwhile, in small saucepan, combine syrup, jelly, soy sauce, chives and dry mustard; mix well. Cook over low heat for 8 to 10 minutes or until hot and well blended, stirring occasionally. Remove from heat.

3. Reduce oven temperature to 350°F. Remove riblets from oven. Uncover; drain off liquid in pan. Turn riblets meaty side up; brush with syrup mixture.

4. Return to oven; bake, uncovered, at 350°F. for 30 minutes.

5. Brush riblets with syrup mixture. Bake an additional 10 to 15 minutes or until riblets are tender and no longer pink next to bone.

make-ahead tip

Prepare and bake riblets as directed in recipe. Place in covered container; refrigerate up to 24 hours. To reheat, place in foil-lined 15x10x1-inch baking pan. Heat at 350°F. for 20 minutes or until thoroughly heated.

NUTRITION INFORMATION PER SERVING: SERVING SIZE: 1/16 of Recipe • Calories 140 • Calories from Fat 70 • % Daily Value: Total Fat 8 g 12% • Saturated Fat 3 g 15% • Cholesterol 30 mg 10% • Sodium 90 mg 4% • Total Carbohydrate 10 g 3% • Dietary Fiber 0 g 0% • Sugars 8 g • Protein 7 g • Vitamin A 0% • Vitamin C 0% • Calcium 2% • Iron 4% • **Dietary Exchanges:** 1/2 Fruit, 1 High-Fat Meat **OR** 1/2 Carbohydrate, 1 High-Fat Meat

Chinese Spare Riblets

What curry is to Indian cooking, five-spice powder is to China's cuisine. It's a fragrant blend of sweet and sharp flavors—usually anise, star anise, cloves, Szechuan peppercorns and cinnamon.

PREP TIME: 30 MINUTES
(READY IN 3 HOURS 30 MINUTES)
MAKES 16 SERVINGS

⅓ cup soy sauce

⅓ cup plum jelly

2 tablespoons water

2 tablespoons dry sherry

2 garlic cloves, minced

1 teaspoon Chinese five-spice powder

1 (2-lb.) rack pork spareribs, cut in half lengthwise across bones

1. In small saucepan, combine all ingredients except riblets. Cook over low heat, stirring until jelly is melted. Cool.

2. Cut ribs into individual riblets. Place riblets in resealable food storage plastic bag. Pour marinade into bag. Squeeze out air; seal. Refrigerate 2 to 3 hours to marinate, turning bag several times.

3. Heat oven to 450°F. Line shallow baking pan with foil. Remove riblets from plastic bag; reserve marinade. Place riblets, meaty side down, in foil-lined pan; cover with foil. Bake at 450°F. for 30 minutes.

4. Reduce oven temperature to 350°F. Remove riblets from oven. Uncover; drain off liquid in pan. Turn riblets meaty side up; brush with reserved marinade.

5. Return to oven; bake, uncovered, at 350°F. for 30 minutes.

6. Drain liquid if necessary. Brush riblets again with marinade. Bake an additional 10 to 15 minutes or until riblets are tender and no longer pink next to bone. Discard any remaining marinade.

Prepare and bake riblets as directed in recipe. Place in covered container; refrigerate up to 24 hours. To reheat, place in foil-lined 15x10x1-inch baking pan. Heat at 350°F. for 20 minutes or until thoroughly heated.

NUTRITION INFORMATION PER SERVING: SERVING SIZE: ⅟₁₆ of Recipe • Calories 110 • Calories from Fat 60 • % Daily Value: Total Fat 7 g 11% • Saturated Fat 2 g 10% • Cholesterol 25 mg 8% • Sodium 350 mg 15% • Total Carbohydrate 5 g 2% • Dietary Fiber 0 g 0% • Sugars 3 g • Protein 7 g • Vitamin A 0% • Vitamin C 0% • Calcium 0% • Iron 4% • **Dietary Exchanges:** ½ Fruit, 1 High-Fat Meat **OR** ½ Carbohydrate, 1 High-Fat Meat

Cranberry-Barbecue Riblets

Cranberry and orange have become so inseparable that we can forget it took an ingenious matchmaker to introduce them in the first place. Cranberries grow in northern bogs, while oranges thrive in southern groves.

PREP TIME: 15 MINUTES
(READY IN 1 HOUR 25 MINUTES)
MAKES 16 SERVINGS

- 1 (2-lb.) rack pork back ribs, cut in half lengthwise across bones
- 1 cup barbecue sauce
- ½ cup frozen cranberry-orange relish, thawed
- ¼ cup chopped fresh chives
- ¼ teaspoon dry mustard
- ¼ teaspoon dried marjoram leaves

1. Heat oven to 375°F. Line 15x10x1-inch baking pan with foil. Spray foil with nonstick cooking spray. Cut ribs into individual riblets. Place riblets, meaty side down, in sprayed foil-lined pan; cover with foil. Bake at 375°F. for 30 minutes.

2. Meanwhile, in small bowl, combine all remaining ingredients; mix well.

3. Remove riblets from oven. Uncover; drain off liquid in pan. Turn riblets meaty side up; spoon sauce mixture over riblets.

4. Return to oven; bake, uncovered, an additional 30 to 45 minutes or until riblets are tender and no longer pink next to bone, turning and brushing with sauce once or twice. Serve warm riblets with sauce from pan.

make-ahead tip

Prepare and bake riblets as directed in recipe. Place in covered container; refrigerate up to 24 hours. To reheat, place in foil-lined 15x10x1-inch baking pan. Heat at 350°F. for 20 minutes or until thoroughly heated.

NUTRITION INFORMATION PER SERVING: SERVING SIZE: 1/16 of Recipe • Calories 120 • Calories from Fat 70 • % Daily Value: Total Fat 8 g 12% • Saturated Fat 3 g 15% • Cholesterol 30 mg 10% • Sodium 160 mg 7% • Total Carbohydrate 6 g 2% • Dietary Fiber 0 g 0% • Sugars 4 g • Protein 7 g • Vitamin A 4% • Vitamin C 4% • Calcium 0% • Iron 4% • **Dietary Exchanges:** ½ Starch, 1 High-Fat Meat **OR** ½ Carbohydrate, 1 High-Fat Meat

Honey-Mustard Drummies

Honey not only sweetens the glaze but also caramelizes in the oven to form a nicely browned exterior. Since the recipe calls for brushing the remaining sauce on the finished chicken, be sure to drizzle the glaze over the raw chicken, to avoid contaminating it with a brush or spoon that has touched the raw chicken.

PREP TIME: 5 MINUTES
(READY IN 1 HOUR 5 MINUTES)
MAKES 20 APPETIZERS

20 chicken wing drummettes

1/3 cup honey

2 tablespoons Dijon mustard

3 tablespoons soy sauce

1. In ungreased 12x8-inch (2-quart) glass baking dish, arrange chicken drummettes in single layer.

2. In 1-cup microwave-safe measuring cup, combine honey, mustard and soy sauce; mix well. Microwave on HIGH for 30 seconds. Stir until well blended. Drizzle honey mixture over chicken, brushing as necessary to coat chicken. If desired, cover and refrigerate up to 2 hours.

3. Heat oven to 375°F. Uncover dish; turn chicken drummettes. Bake 50 to 60 minutes or until chicken is tender, glazed and no longer pink next to bone, turning chicken once halfway through baking time.

4. Just before serving, brush with honey mixture from dish.

make-ahead tip

Prepare and bake drummettes as directed in recipe. Place in covered container; refrigerate up to 24 hours. To reheat, place in foil-lined 15x10x1-inch baking pan. Heat at 350°F. for 20 minutes or until thoroughly heated.

NUTRITION INFORMATION PER SERVING: SERVING SIZE: 1 Appetizer • Calories 70 • Calories from Fat 25 • % Daily Value: Total Fat 3 g 5% • Saturated Fat 1 g 5% • Cholesterol 15 mg 5% • Sodium 210 mg 9% • Total Carbohydrate 5 g 2% • Dietary Fiber 0 g 0% • Sugars 5 g • Protein 5 g • Vitamin A 0% • Vitamin C 0% • Calcium 0% • Iron 0% • **Dietary Exchanges:** 1/2 Fruit, 1/2 High-Fat Meat **OR** 1/2 Carbohydrate, 1/2 High-Fat Meat

Sesame Chicken Drummies

To toast sesame seeds and bring out their nutty flavor, spread the seeds in a single layer in a dry frying pan and cook over medium heat, stirring occasionally, until the seeds deepen in color and become fragrant. They can also be toasted on a toaster-oven tray or on a cookie sheet in the oven. Watch carefully to prevent burning.

PREP TIME: 20 MINUTES
(READY IN 55 MINUTES)
MAKES 20 APPETIZERS

Nonstick cooking spray

2 tablespoons all-purpose flour

1/2 cup unseasoned dry bread crumbs

3 tablespoons sesame seed, toasted

1/2 teaspoon garlic salt

1/4 teaspoon ground red pepper (cayenne)

2 egg whites

2 lb. chicken wing drummettes

Purchased sweet-and-sour sauce, if desired

1. Heat oven to 425°F. Line 15x10x1-inch baking pan with foil. Spray foil with nonstick cooking spray.

2. In small bowl, combine flour, bread crumbs, sesame seed, garlic salt and ground red pepper; mix well. In another small bowl, beat egg whites. Dip chicken drummettes in egg whites; coat with flour mixture. Place in sprayed foil-lined pan. Spray chicken with nonstick cooking spray.

3. Bake at 425°F. for 25 to 35 minutes or until chicken is no longer pink next to bone. Serve with sweet-and-sour sauce.

NUTRITION INFORMATION PER SERVING: SERVING SIZE: 1 Appetizer • Calories 80 • Calories from Fat 45 • % Daily Value: Total Fat 5 g 8% • Saturated Fat 1 g 5% • Cholesterol 15 mg 5% • Sodium 120 mg 5% • Total Carbohydrate 4 g 1% • Dietary Fiber 0 g 0% • Sugars 1 g • Protein 6 g • Vitamin A 0% • Vitamin C 0% • Calcium 0% • Iron 2% • **Dietary Exchanges:** 1 Lean Meat, 1/2 Fat

Spicy Honey Chicken Drummettes

(Pictured on page 228.)

As a kindness to guests with delicate palates, label dishes that might be too spicy for some with a little flame drawn on an index card or the word *spicy* in red letters. For fire-lovers, set out extra hot-pepper sauce.

PREP TIME: 10 MINUTES
(READY IN 2 HOURS 10 MINUTES)
MAKES 12 APPETIZERS

1/4 cup honey

1/4 cup soy sauce

1/4 cup chili sauce

1/2 teaspoon hot pepper sauce

1/4 teaspoon ginger

1/4 teaspoon dry mustard

12 chicken wing drummettes

1. In 12x8-inch (2-quart) glass baking dish, combine all ingredients except chicken; mix well. Add chicken drummettes; turn to coat. Cover; refrigerate 1 hour to marinate.

2. Heat oven to 375°F. Uncover dish; bake chicken in marinade at 375°F. for 45 to 60 minutes or until chicken is tender and no longer pink next to bone, brushing with marinade occasionally.

Prepare and bake drummettes as directed in recipe. Place in covered container; refrigerate up to 24 hours. To reheat, place in foil-lined 15x10x1-inch baking pan. Heat at 350°F. for 20 minutes or until thoroughly heated.

NUTRITION INFORMATION PER SERVING: SERVING SIZE: 1 Appetizer • Calories 50 • Calories from Fat 25 • % Daily Value: Total Fat 3 g 5% • Saturated Fat 1 g 5% • Cholesterol 15 mg 5% • Sodium 120 mg 5% • Total Carbohydrate 2 g 1% • Dietary Fiber 0 g 0% • Sugars 2 g • Protein 4 g • Vitamin A 0% • Vitamin C 0% • Calcium 0% • Iron 0% • **Dietary Exchanges:** 1 Lean Meat

Boneless Buffalo Chicken Appetizers

Cool blue cheese soothes the palate for those who find this tantalizing chicken a bit on the hot side. Celery sticks are another traditional accompaniment.

PREP TIME: 20 MINUTES
(READY IN 50 MINUTES)
MAKES 12 SERVINGS

CHICKEN

1/3 cup honey

1/3 cup chili sauce

4 teaspoons soy sauce

2 teaspoons hot pepper sauce

1 teaspoon cider vinegar

1/8 teaspoon ginger

1/8 teaspoon cumin

4 boneless skinless chicken breast halves, cut crosswise into 1/2-inch-wide strips

DIPPING SAUCE

1/2 cup purchased light blue cheese salad dressing

1/4 cup light sour cream

2 tablespoons chopped fresh parsley

2 tablespoons crumbled blue cheese, if desired

1. In medium bowl, combine all chicken ingredients except chicken; mix well. Add chicken; toss to coat well. Cover; refrigerate at least 30 minutes to marinate.

2. Meanwhile, in small bowl, combine salad dressing and sour cream; mix well. Refrigerate until serving time.

3. Heat large nonstick skillet over medium-high heat until hot. With slotted spoon, remove chicken from marinade; reserve marinade. Add chicken to skillet; cook and stir 4 minutes. Add reserved marinade; cook over medium-high heat for 6 to 7 minutes or until sauce thickens and chicken is no longer pink in center, stirring occasionally.

4. Spoon dipping sauce into small serving bowl; sprinkle with parsley and blue cheese. Place bowl on serving platter; arrange warm chicken around bowl. Serve with cocktail toothpicks.

NUTRITION INFORMATION PER SERVING: SERVING SIZE: 1/12 of Recipe • Calories 120 • Calories from Fat 35 • % Daily Value: Total Fat 4 g 6% • Saturated Fat 1 g 5% • Cholesterol 30 mg 10% • Sodium 330 mg 14% • Total Carbohydrate 11 g 4% • Dietary Fiber 0 g 0% • Sugars 10 g • Protein 10 g • Vitamin A 4% • Vitamin C 2% • Calcium 8% • Iron 2% • **Dietary Exchanges:** 1/2 Fruit, 1 1/2 Very Lean Meat, 1/2 Fat **OR** 1/2 Carbohydrate, 1 1/2 Very Lean Meat, 1/2 Fat

Coconut Shrimp with Gingered Cocktail Sauce

This tropical shrimp cocktail features shrimp in a crisp, golden-brown coconut coating, dipped in sauce spiked with grated fresh ginger.

PREP TIME: 30 MINUTES
MAKES 16 SERVINGS

SHRIMP

1 cup coconut

½ cup unseasoned dry bread crumbs

¼ teaspoon salt

Dash ground red pepper (cayenne)

1½ lb. shelled deveined uncooked medium shrimp

¼ cup honey

SAUCE

1 (12-oz.) jar seafood cocktail sauce

1 tablespoon grated gingerroot

1. Heat oven to 425°F. Line large cookie sheet with foil; lightly grease foil. In food processor bowl with metal blade, combine coconut, bread crumbs, salt and ground red pepper; process 10 seconds to combine slightly. Place in pie pan or shallow dish.

2. Pat shrimp dry with paper towels; place in medium bowl. Heat honey in small saucepan over low heat just until melted. Pour over shrimp; toss to coat. Roll shrimp in coconut mixture to coat; place in single layer on greased foil-lined cookie sheet.

3. Bake at 425°F. for 9 to 12 minutes or until shrimp turn pink and coconut begins to brown.

4. In small serving bowl, combine cocktail sauce and gingerroot; mix well. Arrange shrimp on serving platter. Serve shrimp with sauce.

NUTRITION INFORMATION PER SERVING: SERVING SIZE: 1⁄16 of Recipe • Calories 110 • Calories from Fat 20 • % Daily Value: Total Fat 2 g 3% • Saturated Fat 2 g 10% • Cholesterol 60 mg 20% • Sodium 400 mg 17% • Total Carbohydrate 14 g 5% • Dietary Fiber 1 g 4% • Sugars 10 g • Protein 8 g • Vitamin A 4% • Vitamin C 4% • Calcium 0% • Iron 8% • **Dietary Exchanges:** ½ Starch, ½ Fruit, 1 Very Lean Meat **OR** 1 Carbohydrate, 1 Very Lean Meat

Jerk Chicken Wings with Creamy Dipping Sauce

"Jerk" is a spicy Jamaican way of cooking chicken or meat slowly over low heat. These wings are similarly flavored with sweet-sharp-earthy-hot seasonings, but need less than an hour in the oven.

PREP TIME: 10 MINUTES
(READY IN 1 HOUR 55 MINUTES)
MAKES 12 SERVINGS

CHICKEN WINGS

2 tablespoons dried thyme leaves

1 tablespoon brown sugar

1 tablespoon minced garlic (3 to 4 medium cloves)

3 teaspoons allspice

1 teaspoon salt

2 tablespoons cider vinegar

2 tablespoons hot pepper sauce

1 (3-lb.) pkg. frozen chicken wing drummettes, thawed

DIPPING SAUCE

1/2 cup chopped green onions

1/2 cup sour cream

1/2 cup mayonnaise

1. In large nonmetal bowl, combine thyme, brown sugar, garlic, allspice, salt, vinegar and hot pepper sauce; mix well. Add chicken drummettes; toss to coat evenly. Cover; refrigerate 1 hour to marinate.

2. Heat oven to 425°F. Line two 15x10x1-inch baking pans with foil. Spray foil with nonstick cooking spray. Place chicken drummettes in sprayed foil-lined pans. Discard any remaining marinade.

3. Bake at 425°F. for 45 minutes or until chicken is no longer pink next to bone.

4. Meanwhile, in small bowl, combine all dipping sauce ingredients; blend well. Serve chicken drummettes with sauce.

make-ahead tip

Prepare and bake drummettes as directed in recipe. Place in covered container; refrigerate up to 24 hours. To reheat, place in foil-lined 15x10x1-inch baking pan. Heat at 350°F. for 20 minutes or until thoroughly heated.

NUTRITION INFORMATION PER SERVING: SERVING SIZE: 1/12 of Recipe • Calories 170 • Calories from Fat 120 • % Daily Value: Total Fat 13 g 20% • Saturated Fat 3 g 15% • Cholesterol 50 mg 17% • Sodium 140 mg 6% • Total Carbohydrate 1 g 1% • Dietary Fiber 0 g 0% • Sugars 1 g • Protein 13 g • Vitamin A 2% • Vitamin C 0% • Calcium 2% • Iron 4% • **Dietary Exchanges:** 2 Medium-Fat Meat, 1/2 Fat

Chicken Peanut Saté

African and Asian recipes often use the rich nuttiness of peanut butter for enriching, smoothing and thickening savory sauces, soups and stews.

PREP TIME: 30 MINUTES
MAKES 20 APPETIZERS

SATÉ

20 (6-inch) bamboo or wooden skewers

10 slices bacon

4 boneless skinless chicken breast halves

PEANUT SAUCE

2 tablespoons peanut butter

2 tablespoons soy sauce

2 tablespoons apple juice or water

1/8 to 1/4 teaspoon crushed red pepper flakes

1. Soak skewers in water for 15 minutes. Meanwhile, cook bacon in large nonstick skillet over medium heat for about 5 minutes or until partially cooked but not crisp. Remove bacon from skillet; drain on paper towels. Cut each slice in half crosswise.

2. Cut each chicken breast half lengthwise into 5 strips, each about 1/2 inch thick. Place 1 piece of bacon on each chicken strip. Thread each bacon-topped chicken strip loosely onto 1 skewer; place on broiler pan.

3. In small bowl, combine all peanut sauce ingredients; mix well.

4. Broil skewered chicken 4 to 6 inches from heat for 3 to 4 minutes. Brush with peanut sauce; turn. Broil an additional 3 to 4 minutes or until chicken is no longer pink in center. Brush with remaining sauce.

NUTRITION INFORMATION PER SERVING: SERVING SIZE: 1 Appetizer • Calories 40 • Calories from Fat 20 • % Daily Value: Total Fat 2 g 3% • Saturated Fat 1 g 5% • Cholesterol 15 mg 5% • Sodium 90 mg 4% • Total Carbohydrate 0 g 0% • Dietary Fiber 0 g 0% • Sugars 0 g • Protein 6 g • Vitamin A 0% • Vitamin C 0% • Calcium 0% • Iron 0% • **Dietary Exchanges:** 1 Very Lean Meat, 1/2 Fat

Shrimp and Pineapple Kabobs

(Pictured on page 228.)

The intestinal vein of a shrimp appears as a dark line running along the back, just under the flesh. It's edible, but many people prefer to remove it. If you have to devein the shrimp yourself, use a small, sharp knife to slit the shrimp along the inside curve. Pick out the dark vein with the tip of the knife and run the shrimp under water to remove any remaining fragments.

PREP TIME: 40 MINUTES
MAKES 12 KABOBS

12 (4- to 6-inch) wooden or bamboo skewers

1/2 cup purchased sweet-and-sour sauce

1/2 teaspoon dry mustard

2 teaspoons chopped fresh chives or 1 teaspoon freeze-dried chopped chives

2 medium green bell peppers, cut into 24 (1-inch) pieces

24 (1- to 1 1/2-inch) chunks fresh pineapple

12 uncooked medium shrimp, shelled, deveined

1. Soak skewers in water for 15 minutes. Meanwhile, in small bowl, combine sweet-and-sour sauce, mustard and chives; mix well.

2. On each skewer, thread 1 pepper piece, 1 pineapple chunk, 1 shrimp, 1 pineapple chunk and 1 pepper piece. Place kabobs on broiler pan. Brush kabobs with sweet-and-sour mixture.

3. Broil 4 to 6 inches from heat for 3 minutes. Turn kabobs; brush with remaining mixture. Broil an additional 2 to 4 minutes or until shrimp turn pink.

NUTRITION INFORMATION PER SERVING: SERVING SIZE: 1 Kabob • Calories 40 • Calories from Fat 0 • % Daily Value: Total Fat 0 g 0% • Saturated Fat 0 g 0% • Cholesterol 10 mg 3% • Sodium 75 mg 3% • Total Carbohydrate 9 g 3% • Dietary Fiber 1 g 4% • Sugars 6 g • Protein 1 g • Vitamin A 2% • Vitamin C 20% • Calcium 0% • Iron 2% • **Dietary Exchanges:** 1/2 Fruit **OR** 1/2 Carbohydrate

Shrimp Kabobs with Bacon-Wrapped Water Chestnuts

Each skewer combines the varying flavors and textures of crisp water chestnuts, salty bacon, briny shrimp, zesty salsa and sweet pepper or pineapple.

PREP TIME: 20 MINUTES
MAKES 24 APPETIZERS

24 shelled deveined uncooked medium shrimp (about 6 to 7 oz.)

3 tablespoons barbecue sauce

3 tablespoons chunky-style salsa

24 wooden toothpicks

4 slices reduced-sodium bacon, each cut into 6 pieces

24 canned whole water chestnuts, well drained

½ medium red bell pepper, cut into 12 pieces

12 canned pineapple chunks in unsweetened juice, well drained

1. Rinse shrimp; pat dry with paper towels. In medium bowl, combine barbecue sauce and salsa; mix well. Reserve 2 tablespoons mixture in small bowl. Add shrimp to remaining mixture; toss gently to coat evenly.

2. Spray broiler pan with nonstick cooking spray. Insert toothpick through both ends of each shrimp, so shrimp forms a "C" on pick. Wrap 1 bacon piece around half of each water chestnut; carefully insert onto toothpicks. Add EITHER bell pepper piece OR pineapple chunk to end of toothpick. (Leave room around bacon to allow it to cook thoroughly.) Arrange kabobs on sprayed pan.

3. Broil 6 to 8 inches from heat for 5 minutes. With tongs and fork, or spoon and fork, carefully turn kabobs. Broil an additional 4 to 5 minutes or until edges of bacon begin to brown and shrimp is no longer pink.

4. With brush or teaspoon, top each shrimp with reserved sauce mixture. Arrange kabobs on serving platter.

NUTRITION INFORMATION PER SERVING: SERVING SIZE: 1 Appetizer • Calories 30 • Calories from Fat 10 • % Daily Value: Total Fat 1 g 2% • Saturated Fat 0 g 0% • Cholesterol 15 mg 5% • Sodium 65 mg 3% • Total Carbohydrate 3 g 1% • Dietary Fiber 0 g 0% • Sugars 1 g • Protein 2 g • Vitamin A 2% • Vitamin C 4% • Calcium 0% • Iron 0% • **Dietary Exchanges:** ½ Lean Meat

Cilantro-Lime Shrimp with Chile Aïoli

Ail is French for garlic, and aïoli is a garlic mayonnaise, which traditional French chefs prepare from scratch. This shortcut version spices up purchased mayonnaise with chiles as well as garlic.

PREP TIME: 30 MINUTES
MAKES 24 SERVINGS

SHRIMP

24 fresh uncooked large shrimp (about 1 lb.), shelled with tails left on

1 tablespoon chopped fresh cilantro

2 tablespoons lime juice

1 tablespoon olive oil

1 garlic clove, minced

SAUCE

1 cup mayonnaise

3 tablespoons milk

2 canned chipotle chiles in adobo sauce, chopped (about 4 teaspoons)

2 garlic cloves, chopped

2 teaspoons chopped fresh cilantro

1. Heat oven to 350°F. Cut shrimp along outside curve almost to other side; spread open. Remove any visible vein. Place cut side down on ungreased cookie sheet so that tails stand up and curve over shrimp.

2. In small bowl, combine all remaining shrimp ingredients; mix well. Brush mixture over shrimp.

3. Bake at 350°F. for 5 to 7 minutes or until shrimp turn pink.

4. Meanwhile, in blender container, combine all sauce ingredients except cilantro; blend until smooth.

5. To serve, drizzle small amount of sauce onto serving platter. Sprinkle with 2 teaspoons chopped cilantro. Place cooked shrimp over sauce. Serve with remaining sauce.

NUTRITION INFORMATION PER SERVING: SERVING SIZE: ½4 of Recipe • Calories 80 • Calories from Fat 70 • % Daily Value: Total Fat 8 g 12% • Saturated Fat 1 g 5% • Cholesterol 20 mg 7% • Sodium 80 mg 3% • Total Carbohydrate 1 g 1% • Dietary Fiber 0 g 0% • Sugars 0 g • Protein 2 g • Vitamin A 2% • Vitamin C 0% • Calcium 0% • Iron 0% • **Dietary Exchanges:** ½ Very Lean Meat, 1½ Fat

Orange-Ginger Shrimp Snacks

Soaking the wooden skewers (sold in grocery stores and kitchen shops) prevents them from scorching under the broiler.

PREP TIME: 25 MINUTES
MAKES 15 SERVINGS

½ cup oil

¼ cup vinegar

¼ cup frozen orange juice concentrate, thawed

1 tablespoon chopped red onion

2 teaspoons grated gingerroot

¾ teaspoon crushed red pepper flakes

1 lb. shelled deveined uncooked medium shrimp

5 (12-inch) bamboo or wooden skewers

1. In blender container, combine all ingredients except shrimp and skewers; process until blended.

2. Place shrimp in resealable food storage plastic bag. Pour oil mixture over shrimp; seal bag. Let stand at room temperature for 15 minutes to marinate. Soak skewers in water while shrimp are marinating.

3. Drain shrimp; discard marinade. Thread shrimp onto skewers; place on ungreased cookie sheet.

4. Broil 6 inches from heat for 3 to 5 minutes or until shrimp turn pink, turning once. Before serving, cut each skewer into 3 pieces with kitchen scissors.

NUTRITION INFORMATION PER SERVING: SERVING SIZE: ⅕ of Recipe • Calories 40 • Calories from Fat 20 • % Daily Value: Total Fat 2 g 3% • Saturated Fat 0 g 0% • Cholesterol 45 mg 15% • Sodium 50 mg 2% • Total Carbohydrate 1 g 1% • Dietary Fiber 0 g 0% • Sugars 0 g • Protein 5 g • Vitamin A 0% • Vitamin C 2% • Calcium 0% • Iron 4% • **Dietary Exchanges:** 1 Very Lean Meat

Lemon-Garlic Skewered Shrimp

Shrimp turn pale pink when cooked. To double-check for doneness, cut into the flesh to make sure it has lost its grayish translucence and instead looks opaque white all the way through.

PREP TIME: 20 MINUTES
(READY IN 1 HOUR 20 MINUTES)
MAKES 10 SERVINGS

¼ cup olive oil

¼ cup lemon juice

3 garlic cloves, minced

2 teaspoons salt

2 teaspoons dried basil leaves

¼ teaspoon crushed red pepper flakes

30 shelled deveined fresh uncooked large shrimp (about 1½ lb.)

10 (8-inch) wooden or bamboo skewers

Fresh basil sprigs

Lemon slices or wedges

1. In small bowl, combine oil, lemon juice, garlic, salt, basil and red pepper flakes; mix well. Place shrimp in resealable food storage plastic bag or large glass bowl. Pour marinade over shrimp; seal bag or cover bowl. Refrigerate 1 to 2 hours to marinate. Soak skewers in water for at least 30 minutes.

2. When ready to grill, heat grill. Carefully oil grill rack. Remove shrimp from marinade; reserve marinade. Thread 3 shrimp on each skewer, leaving some space between shrimp.

3. Place skewers on gas grill over medium heat or on charcoal grill 4 to 6 inches from medium coals. Cook 8 to 10 minutes or until shrimp turn pink, turning twice and brushing with reserved marinade. Discard any remaining marinade.

4. To serve, arrange skewers on medium platter. Garnish with fresh basil and lemon.

tip

To broil shrimp, place on oiled broiler pan; broil 4 to 6 inches from heat using times above as a guide, turning twice and brushing with reserved marinade.

NUTRITION INFORMATION PER SERVING: SERVING SIZE: $\frac{1}{10}$ of Recipe • Calories 100 • Calories from Fat 50 • % Daily Value: Total Fat 6 g 9% • Saturated Fat 1 g 5% • Cholesterol 95 mg 32% • Sodium 540 mg 23% • Total Carbohydrate 1 g 1% • Dietary Fiber 0 g 0% • Sugars 0 g • Protein 11 g • Vitamin A 4% • Vitamin C 6% • Calcium 2% • Iron 10% • **Dietary Exchanges:** 1½ Lean Meat, 1 Fat

Crab Cakes Italiano

Pesto, fragrant with basil, blends with mayonnaise for a superb sauce to crown these golden crab cakes.

PREP TIME: 35 MINUTES
MAKES 8 SERVINGS

SAUCE

1/2 cup mayonnaise or reduced-fat mayonnaise

2 tablespoons purchased pesto

CRAB CAKES

1 lb. fresh lump crabmeat, cleaned and rinsed, or imitation crabmeat (surimi), shredded

1/2 cup Italian-style dry bread crumbs

1/3 cup mayonnaise or light mayonnaise

2 tablespoons purchased pesto

1 egg, beaten

2 tablespoons olive oil

GARNISH, IF DESIRED

Italian plum tomato slices

Fresh basil sprigs

Julienne-cut sun-dried tomatoes

1. In small bowl, combine sauce ingredients; mix well. Cover; refrigerate until serving time.

2. In large bowl, combine all crab cake ingredients except olive oil; mix well. Using 1/3 cup mixture for each, shape into eight 3-inch patties.

3. Heat oil in large nonstick skillet over medium heat until hot. Add patties; cook 4 to 5 minutes on each side or until golden brown and thoroughly cooked. Drain on paper towels. Serve crab cakes topped with sauce. Garnish as desired.

tip

Canned crabmeat, drained, or frozen crabmeat, thawed and drained, can be substituted for the fresh crabmeat.

NUTRITION INFORMATION PER SERVING: SERVING SIZE: 1/8 of Recipe • Calories 340 • Calories from Fat 240 • % Daily Value: Total Fat 27 g 42% • Saturated Fat 4 g 20% • Cholesterol 70 mg 23% • Sodium 970 mg 40% • Total Carbohydrate 9 g 3% • Dietary Fiber 1 g 4% • Sugars 2 g • Protein 14 g • Vitamin A 6% • Vitamin C 10% • Calcium 8% • Iron 8% • **Dietary Exchanges:** 1/2 Starch, 2 Very Lean Meat, 5 Fat **OR** 1/2 Carbohydrate, 2 Very Lean Meat, 5 Fat

Easy Egg Rolls

Cooked shrimp can substitute for the chicken in this home-cooked version of a favorite take-out appetizer. Thaw the frozen wrappers at room temperature; the microwave does not work well for this. Serve with Mustard Dipping Sauce (page 178) and Sweet Chili-Plum Sauce (page 178).

PREP TIME: 45 MINUTES
MAKES 8 EGG ROLLS

1 teaspoon cornstarch

4 teaspoons soy sauce

½ teaspoon sesame oil

1 tablespoon oil

4 cups purchased coleslaw blend

1 cup fresh bean sprouts

2 tablespoons sliced green onions

½ teaspoon grated gingerroot

½ cup shredded cooked chicken

Oil for deep frying

8 egg roll skins (from 1-lb. pkg.)

1. In small bowl, combine cornstarch, soy sauce and sesame oil; blend well. Set aside.

2. Heat 1 tablespoon oil in large skillet or wok over medium-high heat until hot. Add coleslaw blend, bean sprouts, green onions and gingerroot; cook and stir 3 to 4 minutes or until tender. Add chicken and cornstarch mixture; cook and stir 1 to 2 minutes or until mixture is thoroughly coated. Remove from skillet; cool to room temperature.

3. In deep fryer, heavy saucepan or wok, heat 3 to 4 inches of oil to 375°F.

4. Meanwhile, place 1 egg roll skin on work surface with 1 corner facing you. (Cover remaining skins with damp paper towel to prevent drying out.) Place ¼ cup coleslaw mixture slightly below center of egg roll skin. Fold corner of egg roll skin closest to filling over filling, tucking point under. Fold in and overlap right and left corners. Wet remaining corner with water; gently roll egg roll toward remaining corner and press to seal. (Cover filled egg roll with damp paper towel to prevent drying out.) Repeat with remaining egg roll skins and coleslaw mixture.

5. Fry egg rolls, a few at a time, in hot oil (375°F.) for 4 to 6 minutes or until golden brown, turning once. Drain on paper towels. Serve warm egg rolls with dipping sauces.

tip

To prepare in oven, heat oven to 400°F. Spray cookie sheet with nonstick cooking spray. Place uncooked egg rolls, seam side down, on sprayed cookie sheet. Lightly spray top and sides of egg rolls with cooking spray. Bake at 400°F. for 15 to 20 minutes or until golden brown.

NUTRITION INFORMATION PER SERVING: SERVING SIZE: 1 Egg Roll • Calories 240 • Calories from Fat 130 • % Daily Value: Total Fat 14 g 22% • Saturated Fat 2 g 10% • Cholesterol 10 mg 3% • Sodium 370 mg 15% • Total Carbohydrate 22 g 7% • Dietary Fiber 1 g 4% • Sugars 3 g • Protein 7 g • Vitamin A 20% • Vitamin C 15% • Calcium 4% • Iron 8% • **Dietary Exchanges:** 1 Starch, 1 Vegetable, 3 Fat **OR** 1 Carbohydrate, 1 Vegetable, 3 Fat

Prosciutto-Wrapped Scallops

(Pictured on page 189.)

Thin strips of prosciutto and fresh basil leaves infuse the sea scallops with wonderful Mediterranean flavors.

PREP TIME: 25 MINUTES
MAKES 20 APPETIZERS

1 lb. uncooked sea scallops, halved if large

1 tablespoon olive oil

20 fresh basil leaves

¼ lb. prosciutto, cut into 3x1½-inch strips

1. Heat oven to 425°F. In small bowl, combine scallops and oil; toss to coat.

2. Place basil leaf on center of each prosciutto strip; top each with scallop. Roll up; place, seam side down, in ungreased 15x10x1-inch baking pan.

3. Bake at 425°F. for 8 to 10 minutes or until scallops turn opaque. Insert decorative toothpick into each.

NUTRITION INFORMATION PER SERVING: SERVING SIZE: 1 Appetizer • Calories 30 • Calories from Fat 10 • % Daily Value: Total Fat 1 g 2% • Saturated Fat 0 g 0% • Cholesterol 10 mg 3% • Sodium 115 mg 5% • Total Carbohydrate 1 g 1% • Dietary Fiber 0 g 0% • Sugars 0 g • Protein 5 g • Vitamin A 0% • Vitamin C 0% • Calcium 0% • Iron 0% • **Dietary Exchanges:** ½ Very Lean Meat

Cream Cheese Puffs

(Pictured on page 176.)

Wonton "skins," as they're called, are readily available in supermarkets. Cream cheese may not be a traditional wonton filling, but it is absolutely delicious, and many Chinese-American take-out shops offer a version of this addictive starter.

PREP TIME: 40 MINUTES
MAKES 14 APPETIZERS

Oil for deep frying

14 wonton skins

½ cup soft cream cheese with chives and onions (from 8-oz. tub) or plain soft cream cheese

1. In deep fryer, heavy saucepan or wok, heat 2 to 3 inches of oil to 375°F.

2. Meanwhile, place 1 wonton skin on work surface with 1 corner facing you. Cover remaining skins with damp paper towel to prevent drying out. Lightly brush edges of wonton skin with water. Place 2 teaspoons cream cheese just below center of wonton skin. Fold corner farthest from you down over filling to form a triangle; press edges to seal well. Bring 2 outer points of triangle together; press to seal well, using small amount of water if necessary. Repeat with remaining wonton skins and cream cheese. Cover cream cheese puffs with plastic wrap to prevent drying out.

3. Fry cream cheese puffs, a few at a time, in hot oil (375°F.) for 1 to 3 minutes or until golden brown, turning once. Drain on paper towels. Serve warm cream cheese puffs with a variety of dipping sauces, pages 177 to 179.

NUTRITION INFORMATION PER SERVING: SERVING SIZE: 1 Appetizer • Calories 90 • Calories from Fat 60 • % Daily Value: Total Fat 7 g 11% • Saturated Fat 2 g 10% • Cholesterol 10 mg 3% • Sodium 70 mg 3% • Total Carbohydrate 5 g 2% • Dietary Fiber 0 g 0% • Sugars 0 g • Protein 1 g • Vitamin A 2% • Vitamin C 0% • Calcium 0% • Iron 2% • **Dietary Exchanges:** ½ Starch, 1 Fat **OR** ½ Carbohydrate, 1 Fat

Bacon-Wrapped Rumaki

Rumaki is an appetizer that combines bacon and water chestnuts. Most "authentic" versions also include chicken liver, which is found in one of the variations below.

PREP TIME: 20 MINUTES
(READY IN 50 MINUTES)
MAKES 24 APPETIZERS

1 (8-oz.) can whole water chestnuts, drained, cut into 24 equal pieces if necessary

¼ cup soy sauce

1 tablespoon sugar

8 slices bacon, cut into thirds

1. In small bowl, combine water chestnut pieces, soy sauce and sugar; mix well. Let stand at room temperature for 30 minutes to marinate.

2. Drain water chestnuts; discard marinade. Wrap 1 piece of bacon around each water chestnut; secure with toothpick. Place on broiler pan or on rack in shallow baking pan.

3. Broil 4 to 6 inches from heat for 4 to 7 minutes on each side or until bacon is crisp.

make-ahead tip

Prepare rumaki as directed in recipe; do not broil. Place in covered container; refrigerate up to 24 hours. Broil as directed in recipe.

NUTRITION INFORMATION PER SERVING: SERVING SIZE: 1 Appetizer • Calories 20 • Calories from Fat 10 • % Daily Value: Total Fat 1 g 2% • Saturated Fat 0 g 0% • Cholesterol 0 mg 0% • Sodium 75 mg 3% • Total Carbohydrate 2 g 1% • Dietary Fiber 0 g 0% • Sugars 0 g • Protein 1 g • Vitamin A 0% • Vitamin C 0% • Calcium 0% • Iron 0% • **Dietary Exchanges:** ½ Fat

VARIATIONS
CHICKEN LIVER RUMAKI

Cut ½ lb. chicken livers into 24 equal pieces. In small bowl, combine chicken livers, ½ cup purchased French salad dressing and ¼ teaspoon garlic salt. Let stand at room temperature for 15 minutes to marinate. Drain chicken livers; discard marinade. Wrap with bacon; broil as directed in recipe.

OLIVE RUMAKI

Use 24 pimiento-stuffed green olives for the water chestnuts. Prepare, marinate and broil as directed in recipe.

PINEAPPLE RUMAKI

In small bowl, combine 24 fresh, canned or frozen pineapple chunks, well drained, and ⅓ cup purchased French salad dressing. Let stand at room temperature for 15 minutes to marinate. Drain pineapple; discard marinade. Wrap with bacon; broil as directed in recipe.

SCALLOP RUMAKI

Use ½ lb. fresh or frozen scallops, thawed, cut into 24 equal pieces for the water chestnuts. Prepare, marinate and broil as directed in recipe.

SMOKED OYSTER RUMAKI

Use two 3.75-oz. cans (about 24) smoked oysters, drained, for the water chestnuts. Prepare, marinate and broil as directed in recipe.

Sweet-and-Sour Crescent Drummettes

These boneless "drummettes" are made from a mix of chopped cashews and cooked chicken, encased in golden-brown crescent rolls shaped like a chicken drumstick.

PREP TIME: 20 MINUTES
(READY IN 40 MINUTES)
MAKES 8 APPETIZERS

½ cup chopped cooked chicken

½ cup Parmesan dry bread crumbs

2 tablespoons coarsely chopped cashews

3 tablespoons purchased sweet-and-sour sauce

1 (8-oz.) can refrigerated crescent dinner rolls

1 egg

Sweet-and-sour sauce

Green onion fans, if desired

1. Heat oven to 375°F. Lightly grease cookie sheet. In small bowl, combine chicken, 1 tablespoon of the bread crumbs, cashews and 3 tablespoons sweet-and-sour sauce; mix well.

2. Separate dough into 8 triangles. Press shortest side of each triangle to widen slightly. Place about 1 tablespoon chicken mixture on widened end of each triangle. Fold 2 corners over filling; press dough around filling to form ball. Fold up long pointed end of dough 1 inch toward filling; firmly twist to form drumstick shape.

3. Place remaining bread crumbs in shallow bowl. In another shallow bowl, beat egg. Dip each drumstick in egg; coat with crumbs. Place seam side down on greased cookie sheet.

4. Bake at 375°F. for 14 to 17 minutes or until deep golden brown. Cool 5 minutes.

5. To serve, arrange appetizers on serving platter. Serve warm with additional sweet-and-sour sauce. Garnish with green onion fans.

NUTRITION INFORMATION PER SERVING: SERVING SIZE: 1 Appetizer • Calories 180 • Calories from Fat 60 • % Daily Value: Total Fat 7 g 11% • Saturated Fat 2 g 10% • Cholesterol 35 mg 12% • Sodium 580 mg 24% • Total Carbohydrate 22 g 7% • Dietary Fiber 1 g 4% • Sugars 7 g • Protein 6 g • Vitamin A 0% • Vitamin C 0% • Calcium 2% • Iron 6% • **Dietary Exchanges:** 1 Starch, ½ Fruit, ½ Lean Meat, 1 Fat **OR** 1½ Carbohydrate, ½ Lean Meat, 1 Fat

Pork and Shrimp Pot Stickers

Pot stickers are little dumplings that are cooked in oil on top of the stove until the outside is exquisitely golden brown, then steamed to finish the cooking. Serve them with Hoisin Dipping Sauce (page 179) or Soy-Ginger Sauce (page 177).

PREP TIME: 1 HOUR
MAKES 48 APPETIZERS

¹⁄₂ lb. bulk pork sausage

¹⁄₂ cup finely chopped water chestnuts

¹⁄₄ cup chopped fresh parsley

1 (5-oz.) pkg. frozen cooked tiny shrimp, thawed, chopped

1 (4-oz.) can mushroom pieces and stems, drained, finely chopped

3 tablespoons cornstarch

1 tablespoon sugar

1 teaspoon soy sauce

1 teaspoon sherry

¹⁄₂ teaspoon sesame oil, if desired

¹⁄₄ teaspoon ginger

48 (about 15 oz.) pot sticker (gyoza) wrappers

2 tablespoons oil

²⁄₃ cup water

1. In large bowl, combine all ingredients except pot sticker wrappers, oil and water; mix well.

2. Working with 6 to 8 wrappers at a time, spoon 1 heaping teaspoon meat mixture onto each wrapper. (Cover remaining wrappers with damp paper towel to prevent drying out.) Gather up sides, letting wrapper pleat naturally. (See photo at left.) Give middle a light squeeze; tap bottom lightly on flat surface. (Some filling will show.) Set upright in baking pan or on cookie sheet; cover with plastic wrap or damp cloth towel. Repeat with remaining wrappers.

3. In 12-inch electric skillet or 10-inch skillet over medium heat, heat 1 tablespoon of the oil. Set half of pot stickers (24) in skillet. Cook, uncovered, 5 to 7 minutes or until bottoms are deep golden brown.

4. Pour in ¹⁄₃ cup of the water. Reduce heat to low; cover and simmer an additional 10 minutes. Drain skillet and repeat with remaining pot stickers. Serve warm pot stickers with a variety of dipping sauces, pages 177 to 179.

NUTRITION INFORMATION PER SERVING: SERVING SIZE: 1 Appetizer • Calories 35 • Calories from Fat 10 • % Daily Value: Total Fat 1 g 2% • Saturated Fat 0 g 0% • Cholesterol 10 mg 3% • Sodium 85 mg 4% • Total Carbohydrate 5 g 2% • Dietary Fiber 0 g 0% • Sugars 0 g • Protein 2 g • Vitamin A 0% • Vitamin C 0% • Calcium 0% • Iron 0% • **Dietary Exchanges:** ¹⁄₂ Starch

Sweet and Spicy Shrimp Bundles

For this Chinese version of stuffed cabbage, a peppery blend of rice and shrimp becomes the filling for crisp lettuce leaves.

PREP TIME: 15 MINUTES
(READY IN 35 MINUTES)
MAKES 12 APPETIZERS

1/3 cup uncooked regular long-grain white rice

2/3 cup water

1 (5-oz.) pkg. frozen cooked small shrimp, thawed

2 green onions, thinly sliced

1/8 teaspoon crushed red pepper flakes

1 tablespoon hoisin sauce

12 small Bibb or iceberg lettuce leaves, washed, dried

1. In small saucepan, bring rice and water to a boil over medium-high heat. Reduce heat; cover and simmer 15 to 18 minutes or until rice is tender and water is absorbed.

2. Add all remaining ingredients except lettuce leaves to rice; remove from heat. Keep warm until serving time.

3. To serve, spoon filling onto center of serving platter; place lettuce leaves around edge. Have guests spoon about 2 tablespoons filling onto 1 lettuce leaf; fold or roll leaf around filling. If desired, serve bundles with dipping sauces such as hoisin sauce or sweet-and-sour sauce.

tip

If lettuce leaves are large, cut into pieces about 6 inches square, removing thick center rib.

make-ahead tip

Prepare filling and fill lettuce leaves as directed in recipe. Place, seam side down, in shallow pan; cover with plastic wrap. Refrigerate up to 24 hours. Serve cold.

NUTRITION INFORMATION PER SERVING: SERVING SIZE: 1 Appetizer • Calories 30 • Calories from Fat 0 • % Daily Value: Total Fat 0 g 0% • Saturated Fat 0 g 0% • Cholesterol 25 mg 8% • Sodium 40 mg 2% • Total Carbohydrate 5 g 2% • Dietary Fiber 0 g 0% • Sugars 0 g • Protein 3 g • Vitamin A 2% • Vitamin C 0% • Calcium 0% • Iron 4% • **Dietary Exchanges:** 1/2 Starch **OR** 1/2 Carbohydrate

Light Shrimp Toast

To grate fresh ginger, pare the brown skin away with a vegetable peeler or small, sharp knife. Grate the ginger over a bowl with a fine-hole grater. In a hurry, you can substitute minced pickled ginger from a jar, but the flavor will be slightly different.

PREP TIME: 30 MINUTES
MAKES 15 APPETIZERS

1 (4¼-oz.) can broken shrimp, drained

¼ cup finely chopped celery

3 tablespoons finely chopped carrot

1 tablespoon chopped green onions

2 tablespoons duck sauce (containing apricots and peaches)

½ teaspoon grated gingerroot

15 (¼-inch-thick) slices baguette-style French bread

1. In small bowl, combine all ingredients except bread slices; mix well. Spread 1 tablespoon shrimp mixture on each slice of bread. Place on ungreased cookie sheet.

2. Broil 4 to 6 inches from heat for 1 to 2 minutes or until appetizers are hot and edges of bread are toasted.

NUTRITION INFORMATION PER SERVING: SERVING SIZE: 1 Appetizer • Calories 15 • Calories from Fat 0 • % Daily Value: Total Fat 0 g 0% • Saturated Fat 0 g 0% • Cholesterol 15 mg 5% • Sodium 55 mg 2% • Total Carbohydrate 2 g 1% • Dietary Fiber 0 g 0% • Sugars 1 g • Protein 2 g • Vitamin A 10% • Vitamin C 0% • Calcium 0% • Iron 0% • **Dietary Exchanges:** Free

Smoked Salmon Toast

Homemade Melba toast is basically bread that has been toasted until very dry. The purchased variety provides a crisp, neutral base for a variety of toppings, including this contemporary spread made with smoked salmon and shredded mozzarella.

PREP TIME: 20 MINUTES
MAKES 32 APPETIZERS

4 oz. smoked salmon, minced

2 oz. (½ cup) shredded reduced-fat mozzarella cheese

½ cup fat-free mayonnaise or salad dressing

¼ cup finely chopped red onion

2 tablespoons drained capers, rinsed

32 Melba toast rounds

Chopped fresh parsley, if desired

1. Heat oven to 350°F. In medium bowl, combine salmon, cheese, mayonnaise, onion and capers; mix well. Spread 1 heaping teaspoon salmon mixture on each toast round to cover; place on ungreased cookie sheet.

2. Bake at 350°F. for 8 to 10 minutes or until thoroughly heated. Sprinkle with parsley.

NUTRITION INFORMATION PER SERVING: SERVING SIZE: 1 Appetizer • Calories 45 • Calories from Fat 10 • % Daily Value: Total Fat 1 g 2% • Saturated Fat 0 g 0% • Cholesterol 3 mg 1% • Sodium 210 mg 9% • Total Carbohydrate 6 g 2% • Dietary Fiber 1 g 4% • Sugars 1 g • Protein 3 g • Vitamin A 0% • Vitamin C 0% • Calcium 2% • Iron 0% • **Dietary Exchanges:** ½ Starch OR ½ Carbohydrate

Shrimp Balls

Water chestnuts are not actually nuts at all, but rather the tuber of an East Asian aquatic plant. They keep their crisp texture even when cooked.

PREP TIME: 1 HOUR
MAKES 24 APPETIZERS

Oil for deep frying

1 lb. shelled deveined uncooked shrimp

1 (8-oz.) can sliced water chestnuts, drained

4 teaspoons cornstarch

2 tablespoons chopped green onions

1 tablespoon dry sherry

¾ teaspoon grated gingerroot

½ teaspoon salt

1 egg, beaten

1. In deep fryer, heavy saucepan or wok, heat 2 to 3 inches of oil to 375°F.

2. Meanwhile, in food processor bowl with metal blade, combine all remaining ingredients except egg; process until finely chopped. Add egg; process until combined.

3. Drop shrimp mixture by teaspoonfuls into hot oil (375°F.). Fry 3 to 4 minutes or until shrimp turn pink and balls are deep golden brown. Drain on paper towels. Serve warm shrimp balls with a variety of dipping sauces, from recipe at right through page 179.

NUTRITION INFORMATION PER SERVING: SERVING SIZE: 1 Appetizer • Calories 45 • Calories from Fat 25 • % Daily Value: Total Fat 3 g 5% • Saturated Fat 0 g 0% • Cholesterol 35 mg 12% • Sodium 85 mg 4% • Total Carbohydrate 2 g 1% • Dietary Fiber 0 g 0% • Sugars 0 g • Protein 3 g • Vitamin A 0% • Vitamin C 0% • Calcium 0% • Iron 2% • **Dietary Exchanges:** ½ Very Lean Meat, ½ Fat

Soy-Ginger Sauce

Keep a bag of Chinese dumplings on hand for an easy appetizer when friends drop by or the work day has been busy. The simple four-ingredient sauce below makes a perfect dip.

PREP TIME: 5 MINUTES
MAKES ⅓ CUP

¼ cup soy sauce

1 tablespoon oil

2 teaspoons grated gingerroot

1 teaspoon sugar

In small bowl, combine all ingredients; mix well. Serve at room temperature.

NUTRITION INFORMATION PER SERVING: SERVING SIZE: 1 Tablespoon • Calories 40 • Calories from Fat 25 • % Daily Value: Total Fat 3 g 5% • Saturated Fat 0 g 0% • Cholesterol 0 mg 0% • Sodium 820 mg 34% • Total Carbohydrate 2 g 1% • Dietary Fiber 0 g 0% • Sugars 1 g • Protein 1 g • Vitamin A 0% • Vitamin C 0% • Calcium 0% • Iron 0% • **Dietary Exchanges:** 1 Fat

Mustard Dipping Sauce

Don't try to rush this recipe by turning up the heat, or the egg mixture may become stringy instead of creamy. Keep the heat low and stir continuously for a smooth result.

PREP TIME: 30 MINUTES
MAKES 1 CUP

1/4 cup dry mustard

2 tablespoons sugar

1/8 teaspoon salt

1/4 cup cider vinegar

1 egg, slightly beaten

1/2 cup mayonnaise or salad dressing

1. In small saucepan, combine mustard, sugar and salt; mix well. Add vinegar and egg; blend well. Cook over low heat for 2 to 3 minutes or until thickened, stirring constantly. Refrigerate 10 to 15 minutes or until cooled.

2. Stir in mayonnaise until well blended. Store in refrigerator up to 2 weeks.

NUTRITION INFORMATION PER SERVING: SERVING SIZE: 1 Tablespoon • Calories 100 • Calories from Fat 80 • % Daily Value: Total Fat 9 g 14% • Saturated Fat 1 g 5% • Cholesterol 25 mg 8% • Sodium 80 mg 3% • Total Carbohydrate 3 g 1% • Dietary Fiber 0 g 0% • Sugars 2 g • Protein 2 g • Vitamin A 0% • Vitamin C 0% • Calcium 0% • Iron 2% • **Dietary Exchanges:** 2 Fat

Sweet Chili-Plum Sauce

Fresh orange juice and orange peel add a tangy burst to the plum sauce. To remove the peel (or "zest") from the orange, scrape the surface gently with a citrus zester tool or use a fine-holed grater to remove the flavorful colored part of the rind only, not the bitter white pith below.

PREP TIME: 20 MINUTES
MAKES 1 CUP

2 teaspoons oil

1/3 cup chopped onion

1 (8.5-oz.) jar (3/4 cup) Chinese plum sauce

2 tablespoons fresh orange juice

2 teaspoons chili paste

1/2 teaspoon grated orange peel

1. Heat oil in medium skillet over medium-high heat until hot. Add onion; cook until tender, stirring constantly.

2. Add all remaining ingredients; cook until thoroughly heated, stirring occasionally. Serve warm.

make-ahead tip

Prepare sauce as directed in recipe. Place in covered container; refrigerate up to 24 hours. To reheat, place in small saucepan; heat over low heat until heated, stirring occasionally.

NUTRITION INFORMATION PER SERVING: SERVING SIZE: 1 Tablespoon • Calories 35 • Calories from Fat 10 • % Daily Value: Total Fat 1 g 2% • Saturated Fat 0 g 0% • Cholesterol 0 mg 0% • Sodium 190 mg 8% • Total Carbohydrate 7 g 2% • Dietary Fiber 0 g 0% • Sugars 6 g • Protein 0 g • Vitamin A 0% • Vitamin C 0% • Calcium 0% • Iron 0% • **Dietary Exchanges:** 1/2 Fruit **OR** 1/2 Carbohydrate

Hoisin Dipping Sauce

Hoisin is a thick, sweetish soy-based sauce that's spread on mu-shu pancakes in Chinese restaurants and also used in marinades and stir-fries. Set out this embellished hoisin as one of the dipping sauces for Shrimp Balls (page 177).

PREP TIME: 10 MINUTES
MAKES ⅓ CUP

¼ cup hoisin sauce

2 tablespoons ketchup

1 tablespoon honey

2 teaspoons soy sauce

In small saucepan, combine all ingredients; mix well. Cook over medium-low heat until thoroughly heated, stirring occasionally. Serve warm.

make-ahead tip

Prepare sauce as directed in recipe. Place in covered container; refrigerate up to 24 hours. To reheat, place in small saucepan; heat over low heat until heated, stirring occasionally.

NUTRITION INFORMATION PER SERVING: SERVING SIZE: 1 Tablespoon • Calories 50 • Calories from Fat 0 • % Daily Value: Total Fat 0 g 0% • Saturated Fat 0 g 0% • Cholesterol 0 mg 0% • Sodium 450 mg 19% • Total Carbohydrate 13 g 4% • Dietary Fiber 0 g 0% • Sugars 10 g • Protein 1 g • Vitamin A 0% • Vitamin C 0% • Calcium 0% • Iron 2% • **Dietary Exchanges:** 1 Fruit **OR** 1 Carbohydrate

Crisp-Coated Mushrooms

The crisp coating and juicy interior might make these mushrooms seem deep-fried, but they're actually oven-baked—not only easier, but much healthier than deep frying.

PREP TIME: 25 MINUTES
MAKES 20 APPETIZERS

¼ cup refrigerated or frozen fat-free egg product, thawed, or 1 egg

½ teaspoon onion salt

8 to 10 drops hot pepper sauce, if desired

¼ cup all-purpose flour

¾ cup crushed Melba round snacks (about 18 snacks)

1 (8-oz.) pkg. fresh whole mushrooms

Olive oil nonstick cooking spray, if desired

1. Heat oven to 450°F. Line 15x10x1-inch baking pan with foil.

2. In small bowl, combine egg product, onion salt and hot pepper sauce; blend well. Place flour in resealable food storage plastic bag or another small bowl. Place snack crumbs on sheet of waxed paper or in another small bowl.

3. Brush mushrooms or wipe clean with damp cloth. Place mushrooms in bag with flour; shake to coat. For each mushroom, shake off excess flour. Dip each in egg product mixture; coat well with snack crumbs. Place in foil-lined pan. For crispier mushrooms, spray all sides of mushrooms with nonstick cooking spray.

4. Bake at 450°F. for 8 to 12 minutes or until hot and crisp.

NUTRITION INFORMATION PER SERVING: SERVING SIZE: 1 Appetizer • Calories 20 • Calories from Fat 0 • % Daily Value: Total Fat 0 g 0% • Saturated Fat 0 g 0% • Cholesterol 0 mg 0% • Sodium 75 mg 3% • Total Carbohydrate 4 g 1% • Dietary Fiber 0 g 0% • Sugars 0 g • Protein 1 g • Vitamin A 0% • Vitamin C 0% • Calcium 0% • Iron 0% • **Dietary Exchanges:** Free

Mushroom Caps with Thyme-Cornbread Stuffing

Made with cornbread instead of plain bread crumbs, these stuffed mushrooms are more special but just as easy to prepare. Save the mushroom stems to stir into spaghetti sauce, soup or stew.

PREP TIME: 20 MINUTES
(READY IN 40 MINUTES)
MAKES 20 APPETIZERS

1 (8-oz.) pkg. fresh whole mushrooms

1/4 cup chopped onion

1 tablespoon margarine or butter

1 tablespoon chopped fresh parsley

1/2 teaspoon dried thyme leaves

1/2 cup dry cornbread stuffing

1/4 cup water

Paprika

1. Heat oven to 350°F. Brush mushrooms or wipe clean with damp cloth. Remove stems from mushrooms; set caps aside. Chop enough stems to make 1/3 cup. Discard remaining stems or reserve for another use.

2. Spray medium nonstick skillet with non-stick cooking spray. Heat over medium-high heat until hot. Add chopped mushroom stems; cook 3 minutes or until golden brown, stirring occasionally.

3. Reduce heat to medium. Add onion; cook 2 to 3 minutes or until onion is tender, stirring frequently. Add margarine, parsley and thyme; cook and stir until margarine is melted. Stir in stuffing and water until well mixed.

4. Remove skillet from heat. Spoon stuffing mixture evenly into mushroom caps; press down gently with spoon to hold stuffing in place. Sprinkle with paprika; place in ungreased shallow baking dish.

5. Bake at 350°F. for 20 minutes or until thoroughly heated. If desired, serve on platter garnished with curly endive.

Stuff mushrooms as directed in recipe; place in baking dish. Do not bake. Cover; refrigerate up to 24 hours. Uncover; bake as directed in recipe.

NUTRITION INFORMATION PER SERVING: SERVING SIZE: 1 Appetizer • Calories 15 • Calories from Fat 10 • % Daily Value: Total Fat 1 g 2% • Saturated Fat 0 g 0% • Cholesterol 0 mg 0% • Sodium 20 mg 1% • Total Carbohydrate 2 g 1% • Dietary Fiber 0 g 0% • Sugars 0 g • Protein 0 g • Vitamin A 0% • Vitamin C 0% • Calcium 0% • Iron 0% • **Dietary Exchanges:** Free

Stuffed Party Mushrooms

Don't soak fresh mushrooms in water to clean them—they'll get soggy. Instead, brush them with a small, clean kitchen brush or gently wipe them with a damp cloth to clean the surface and remove any loose particles.

PREP TIME: 20 MINUTES
(READY IN 45 MINUTES)
MAKES 40 APPETIZERS; 20 SERVINGS

1 lb. medium-sized fresh whole mushrooms (about 40)

1/4 cup grated Parmesan cheese

1/4 cup unseasoned dry bread crumbs

1/4 cup finely chopped onion

1/2 teaspoon dried oregano leaves

1/4 teaspoon salt

1/8 teaspoon pepper

1 garlic clove, minced

1. Heat oven to 350°F. Brush mushrooms or wipe clean with damp cloth. Remove stems from mushrooms; set caps aside. Finely chop mushroom stems.

2. In medium bowl, combine chopped stems and all remaining ingredients; mix well. Press mixture firmly into mushroom caps, mounding on top. Place in ungreased 13x9-inch pan.

3. Bake at 350°F. for 18 to 23 minutes or until thoroughly heated.

make-ahead tip

Stuff mushrooms as directed in recipe; place in pan. Do not bake. Cover; refrigerate up to 24 hours. Uncover; bake as directed in recipe.

NUTRITION INFORMATION PER SERVING: SERVING SIZE: 1/20 of Recipe • Calories 20 • Calories from Fat 10 • % Daily Value: Total Fat 1 g 2% • Saturated Fat 0 g 0% • Cholesterol 0 mg 0% • Sodium 60 mg 3% • Total Carbohydrate 2 g 1% • Dietary Fiber 0 g 0% • Sugars 0 g • Protein 1 g • Vitamin A 0% • Vitamin C 0% • Calcium 2% • Iron 0% • **Dietary Exchanges:** Free

Walnut-Blue Cheese Stuffed Mushrooms

Because nuts are available year-round, we don't always think of them as a seasonal crop—but like most fruits, they are harvested just once a year. To maintain freshness, store nuts in the refrigerator or freezer to prevent the essential oils from turning rancid.

PREP TIME: 25 MINUTES
(READY IN 45 MINUTES)
MAKES 40 APPETIZERS

1 lb. medium-sized fresh whole mushrooms (about 40)

1 (8-oz.) container soft cream cheese with chives and onions

2 tablespoons chopped walnuts

2 tablespoons crumbled blue cheese

1/4 teaspoon dried basil leaves

Chopped fresh parsley

1. Heat oven to 350°F. Brush mushrooms or wipe clean with damp cloth. Remove stems from mushrooms; discard stems or reserve for another use.

2. Place mushroom caps, stem side up, in ungreased 15x10x1-inch baking pan. In medium bowl, combine all remaining ingredients except parsley; mix well. Spoon about 1 teaspoon mixture into each mushroom cap.

3. Bake at 350°F. for 15 to 20 minutes or until thoroughly heated. Sprinkle with parsley.

make-ahead tip

Stuff mushrooms as directed in recipe; place in pan. Do not bake. Cover; refrigerate up to 24 hours. Uncover; bake as directed in recipe.

NUTRITION INFORMATION PER SERVING: SERVING SIZE: 1 Appetizer • Calories 50 • Calories from Fat 45 • % Daily Value: Total Fat 5 g 8% • Saturated Fat 2 g 10% • Cholesterol 5 mg 2% • Sodium 25 mg 1% • Total Carbohydrate 1 g 1% • Dietary Fiber 0 g 0% • Sugars 0 g • Protein 1 g • Vitamin A 0% • Vitamin C 0% • Calcium 0% • Iron 0% • **Dietary Exchanges:** 1 Fat

Stuffed Reuben Mushrooms

Here are the classic flavors of a New York deli Reuben sandwich—corned beef piled high and with sauerkraut and melted cheese—but in a neat, delicate package, layered inside a mushroom cap.

PREP TIME: 25 MINUTES
(READY IN 50 MINUTES)
MAKES 16 APPETIZERS

16 large fresh whole mushrooms

1/4 lb. thinly sliced cooked corned beef

1/3 cup sauerkraut, drained

3 tablespoons purchased Thousand Island salad dressing

2 oz. (1/2 cup) finely shredded Swiss cheese

1 teaspoon chopped fresh or freeze-dried chives

1. Heat oven to 350°F. Brush mushrooms or wipe clean with damp cloth. Remove stems from mushrooms; discard or reserve stems for another use.

2. Fold and fit 1 slice of corned beef inside mushroom cap. Top with 1 teaspoon sauerkraut, 1/2 teaspoon salad dressing and about 1 teaspoon cheese. Place in ungreased 15x10x1-inch baking pan. Repeat with remaining mushrooms. Sprinkle with chives.

3. Bake at 350°F. for 20 to 25 minutes or until thoroughly heated.

make-ahead tip

Stuff mushrooms as directed in recipe; place in pan. Do not bake. Cover; refrigerate up to 24 hours. Uncover; bake as directed in recipe.

NUTRITION INFORMATION PER SERVING: SERVING SIZE: 1 Appetizer • Calories 45 • Calories from Fat 25 • % Daily Value: Total Fat 3 g 5% • Saturated Fat 1 g 5% • Cholesterol 10 mg 3% • Sodium 120 mg 5% • Total Carbohydrate 1 g 1% • Dietary Fiber 0 g 0% • Sugars 1 g • Protein 3 g • Vitamin A 0% • Vitamin C 0% • Calcium 4% • Iron 2% • **Dietary Exchanges:** 1/2 High-Fat Meat

Broccoli-Stuffed Mushrooms

Flavorful, brown cremini mushrooms are also known as common brown, or Roman, mushrooms. White buttom mushrooms can be used instead, and if you prefer, use Swiss or Cheddar cheese in place of the chèvre (goat) cheese.

PREP TIME: 45 MINUTES
MAKES 18 APPETIZERS

2 (6-oz.) pkg. cremini mushrooms (16 to 18 mushrooms)

Nonstick cooking spray

2 tablespoons butter

1 cup frozen chopped broccoli

1/4 cup Italian-style bread crumbs

1 oz. (1/4 cup) crumbled chèvre (goat) cheese

2 tablespoons chopped fresh chives

1. Heat oven to 350°F. Brush mushrooms or wipe clean with damp cloth. Remove stems from mushrooms. Chop stems to make about 3/4 cup; set aside.

2. Place mushroom caps, stem side down, in ungreased 15x10x1-inch baking pan. Spray mushrooms lightly with nonstick cooking spray. Bake at 350°F. for 10 minutes.

3. Meanwhile, melt butter in medium saucepan over medium heat. Add chopped mushroom stems and broccoli; cook and stir 3 minutes or until tender. Stir in bread crumbs.

4. Remove mushrooms from oven. Turn mushrooms stem side up. Spoon broccoli mixture into each mushroom. Sprinkle each with cheese and chives.

5. Return to oven; bake an additional 10 minutes or until thoroughly heated. Serve warm.

NUTRITION INFORMATION PER SERVING: SERVING SIZE: 1 Appetizer • Calories 30 • Calories from Fat 20 • % Daily Value: Total Fat 2 g 3% • Saturated Fat 1 g 5% • Cholesterol 5 mg 2% • Sodium 45 mg 2% • Total Carbohydrate 2 g 1% • Dietary Fiber 0 g 0% • Sugars 0 g • Protein 1 g • Vitamin A 2% • Vitamin C 4% • Calcium 2% • Iron 2% • **Dietary Exchanges:** 1/2 Fat

Chili Potato Dippers with Cheddar Jalapeño Dip

All chili powders start with ground dried chile peppers, but flavor and heat vary with the other spices added to the seasoning mix.

PREP TIME: 15 MINUTES
(READY IN 40 MINUTES)
MAKES 8 SERVINGS

DIPPERS

4 medium russet potatoes

2 tablespoons olive or vegetable oil

1 teaspoon chili powder

1/2 teaspoon garlic powder

CHEDDAR JALAPEÑO DIP

1/3 cup sour cream

1/3 cup mayonnaise or salad dressing

1/4 cup finely chopped tomato

1 oz. (1/4 cup) finely shredded extra-sharp Cheddar cheese

1 to 2 jalapeño chiles, seeded, finely chopped

2 tablespoons sliced green onions

1. Heat oven to 450°F. Line 15x10x1-inch baking pan with foil. Spray foil with nonstick cooking spray.

2. Cut potatoes into thin wedges. In large bowl, combine potatoes, oil, chili powder and garlic powder; toss to coat. Place in single layer in sprayed foil-lined pan.

3. Bake at 450°F. for 20 to 30 minutes or until tender and golden brown, turning once.

4. Meanwhile, in medium bowl, combine all dip ingredients except green onions; mix well. Sprinkle with green onions. Serve warm potato dippers with dip.

NUTRITION INFORMATION PER SERVING: SERVING SIZE: 1/8 of Recipe • Calories 210 • Calories from Fat 130 • % Daily Value: Total Fat 14 g 22% • Saturated Fat 4 g 20% • Cholesterol 15 mg 5% • Sodium 90 mg 4% • Total Carbohydrate 17 g 6% • Dietary Fiber 2 g 8% • Sugars 2 g • Protein 3 g • Vitamin A 6% • Vitamin C 20% • Calcium 4% • Iron 6% • **Dietary Exchanges:** 1 Starch, 3 Fat **OR** 1 Carbohydrate, 3 Fat

Nutty Gorgonzola-Roasted Potato Slices

Gorgonzola is a pungent Italian blue cheese that's also good in salad or served with apples or pears.

PREP TIME: 25 MINUTES
MAKES 30 APPETIZERS

10 small red potatoes (about 2 inches in diameter)

1 tablespoon olive oil

1/4 teaspoon salt

1/8 teaspoon pepper

4 oz. (1 cup) crumbled Gorgonzola cheese, room temperature

1/2 cup chopped walnuts

2 tablespoons chopped fresh chives

1. Heat oven to 400°F. Slice off each end of each potato; discard. Cut potatoes into 3/8-inch slices (about 3 per potato).

2. In medium bowl, combine potato slices and oil; toss to coat. Arrange slices on ungreased cookie sheet. Sprinkle with salt and pepper. Bake at 400°F. for 20 minutes or until tender.

3. Meanwhile, in small bowl, combine cheese, walnuts and chives; mix well.

4. Top each roasted potato slice with scant 1 tablespoon cheese mixture.

NUTRITION INFORMATION PER SERVING: SERVING SIZE: 1 Appetizer • Calories 70 • Calories from Fat 25 • % Daily Value: Total Fat 3 g 5% • Saturated Fat 1 g 5% • Cholesterol 3 mg 1% • Sodium 75 mg 3% • Total Carbohydrate 8 g 3% • Dietary Fiber 1 g 4% • Sugars 0 g • Protein 2 g • Vitamin A 0% • Vitamin C 4% • Calcium 2% • Iron 2% • **Dietary Exchanges:** 1/2 Starch, 1/2 Fat **OR** 1/2 Carbohydrate, 1/2 Fat

CHILI POTATO DIPPERS WITH CHEDDAR JALAPEÑO DIP

Ranch-Style Corn Cakes Appetizers

Sour cream adds both tang and tenderness to these golden corn cakes. Regular or nonfat plain yogurt can stand in for the sour cream.

PREP TIME: 30 MINUTES
MAKES 36 CORN CAKES; 12 SERVINGS

¾ cup chunky-style salsa

1 (11-oz.) can white shoepeg corn, drained

1 (8½-oz.) pkg. corn muffin mix

1 cup regular or nonfat sour cream

1 egg, slightly beaten

¼ cup pine nuts or shelled sunflower seeds, lightly toasted

1. In small bowl, combine ½ cup of the salsa and ¼ cup of the corn; mix well. Set aside.

2. In medium bowl, combine corn muffin mix, ½ cup of the sour cream, egg, remaining ¼ cup salsa and remaining corn; mix well.

3. Spray large nonstick skillet or griddle with nonstick cooking spray. Heat over medium heat until hot. Drop batter by scant tablespoonfuls into skillet. Cook 1½ to 2 minutes on each side or until golden brown.

4. Just before serving, place 3 corn cakes on each individual serving plate. Top each corn cake with spoonful of remaining sour cream and salsa–corn mixture. Sprinkle with pine nuts.

tips

To toast pine nuts, spread on cookie sheet; bake at 350°F. for 3 to 6 minutes or until light golden brown, stirring occasionally.

Corn cakes can be kept warm in 200°F. oven until serving time.

NUTRITION INFORMATION PER SERVING: SERVING SIZE: ¹⁄₁₂ of Recipe • Calories 190 • Calories from Fat 80 • % Daily Value: Total Fat 9 g 14% • Saturated Fat 4 g 20% • Cholesterol 25 mg 8% • Sodium 430 mg 18% • Total Carbohydrate 22 g 7% • Dietary Fiber 2 g 8% • Sugars 3 g • Protein 4 g • Vitamin A 6% • Vitamin C 4% • Calcium 4% • Iron 4% • **Dietary Exchanges:** 1½ Starch, 1½ Fat **OR** 1½ Carbohydrate, 1½ Fat

Sour Cream 'n Chive Twice-Baked Potato Bites

Red potatoes have a pleasant "waxy" texture that holds up well to boiling. This recipe is easily doubled for a larger crowd.

PREP TIME: 40 MINUTES
MAKES 12 APPETIZERS

6 small red potatoes

1 teaspoon chopped fresh chives

¼ teaspoon dried thyme leaves or ¾ teaspoon chopped fresh thyme

¼ teaspoon salt

Dash garlic powder

2 tablespoons sour cream

1 tablespoon margarine or butter, melted

1 tablespoon milk

Paprika, if desired

Chopped fresh chives, if desired

1. Place potatoes in medium saucepan; cover with cold water. Bring to a boil. Reduce heat; cook 15 to 20 minutes or until tender. Drain.

2. Cut potatoes in half. If necessary, cut thin slice from bottom of potato halves to level. With small spoon or melon baller, scoop out center of cooked potatoes, leaving ⅛-inch shell. Place scooped out potato (not shells) in small bowl. Add 1 teaspoon chives, thyme, salt, garlic powder, sour cream, margarine and milk; mash until smooth.

3. Pipe or spoon potato mixture into potato shells. Place on ungreased cookie sheet.

4. Broil 4 to 6 inches from heat for 3 to 5 minutes or until hot and lightly browned. Sprinkle with paprika and chives. Arrange filled potatoes on serving plate. If desired, garnish plate with fresh thyme.

make-ahead
tip

Prepare potatoes and top as directed in recipe; place in shallow pan. Do not broil. Cover; refrigerate up to 24 hours. Broil as directed in recipe.

NUTRITION INFORMATION PER SERVING: SERVING SIZE: 1 Appetizer • Calories 60 • Calories from Fat 20 • % Daily Value: Total Fat 2 g 3% • Saturated Fat 1 g 5% • Cholesterol 0 mg 0% • Sodium 60 mg 3% • Total Carbohydrate 10 g 3% • Dietary Fiber 1 g 4% • Sugars 1 g • Protein 1 g • Vitamin A 0% • Vitamin C 6% • Calcium 0% • Iron 4% • **Dietary Exchanges:** ½ Starch, ½ Fat **OR** ½ Carbohydrate, ½ Fat

Microwave Dill Tater Snacks

Besides making a tasty snack, these potatoes are also a good side dish for roasted meat or poultry. If you need to cook the potatoes in batches, cut them just before cooking or keep the cut slices submerged in cold water to prevent discoloration.

PREP TIME: 20 MINUTES
MAKES 20 APPETIZERS

3 slices lean turkey bacon

10 small new red potatoes, unpeeled, halved

½ cup light sour cream

2 tablespoons sliced green onions

½ teaspoon dried dill weed

Dash pepper

¼ cup grated Parmesan cheese

1. Cook bacon in microwave as directed on package. Cool slightly. Crumble; set aside.

2. Place potatoes, cut side down, in 12x8-inch (2-quart) microwave-safe dish. Add 2 tablespoons water. Cover tightly with microwave-safe plastic wrap.

3. Microwave on HIGH for 9 to 12 minutes or until tender, rotating dish ¼ turn halfway through cooking. Let stand 3 minutes. Drain; cool slightly.

4. In small bowl, combine sour cream, green onions and dill; mix well. Turn potatoes over. If necessary, trim thin slice off rounded bottom of each potato half to make potatoes stand upright. Sprinkle each with pepper and Parmesan cheese. Top each with dollop of sour cream mixture; sprinkle with bacon. If desired, garnish with fresh dill weed or parsley.

tip

If 12x8-inch dish will not fit in microwave oven, use microwave-safe pie pan and cook half of potatoes at a time. Microwave on HIGH for 6 to 8 minutes or until tender.

NUTRITION INFORMATION PER SERVING: SERVING SIZE: 1 Appetizer • Calories 70 • Calories from Fat 10 • % Daily Value: Total Fat 1 g 2% • Saturated Fat 1 g 5% • Cholesterol 4 mg 1% • Sodium 60 mg 3% • Total Carbohydrate 13 g 4% • Dietary Fiber 1 g 4% • Sugars 1 g • Protein 2 g • Vitamin A 0% • Vitamin C 8% • Calcium 4% • Iron 4% • **Dietary Exchanges:** 1 Starch **OR** 1 Carbohydrate

Easy Bruschetta Snacks

As a variation, substitute crushed dried rosemary for the sesame seed. Rosemary is much more assertive than the sesame seed, however, so use only about half as much.

PREP TIME: 20 MINUTES
(READY IN 40 MINUTES)
MAKES 15 APPETIZERS

6 teaspoons olive oil

4 1/2 teaspoons sesame seed

1 (8-oz.) can refrigerated crescent dinner rolls

1 (6-oz.) can pitted ripe olives, drained

1 cup finely chopped tomato

3/4 cup grated Parmesan and Romano cheese blend

1. Heat oven to 375°F. Brush large cookie sheet with 1 teaspoon of the oil; sprinkle evenly with 2 teaspoons of the sesame seed. Unroll dough; place over sesame seed, firmly pressing perforations to seal. Press to form 15x12-inch rectangle.

2. Brush dough with 2 teaspoons of the oil; sprinkle evenly with remaining sesame seed. Bake at 375°F. for 10 minutes.

3. Meanwhile, in food processor bowl with metal blade or blender container, combine olives and remaining 3 teaspoons olive oil. Process until olives are finely chopped.

4. Remove partially baked crust from oven. Spread olive mixture over crust. Top with tomato and cheese.

5. Return to oven; bake an additional 5 to 7 minutes or until edges are golden brown. Cut into rectangles.

NUTRITION INFORMATION PER SERVING: SERVING SIZE: 1 Appetizer • Calories 120 • Calories from Fat 70 • % Daily Value: Total Fat 8 g 12% • Saturated Fat 2 g 10% • Cholesterol 5 mg 2% • Sodium 300 mg 13% • Total Carbohydrate 7 g 2% • Dietary Fiber 1 g 4% • Sugars 2 g • Protein 4 g • Vitamin A 2% • Vitamin C 2% • Calcium 8% • Iron 4% • **Dietary Exchanges:** 1/2 Starch, 1/2 Lean Meat, 1 Fat **OR** 1/2 Carbohydrate, 1/2 Lean Meat, 1 Fat

Bruschetta with Pears, Fontina and Pistachios

Fontina is a fairly mild yellow cheese laced with small holes. You may substitute slices of mozzarella or Muenster.

PREP TIME: 25 MINUTES
MAKES 24 APPETIZERS

24 (1/4- to 1/2-inch-thick) slices baguette-style or small French bread

3 tablespoons olive oil

1/2 teaspoon garlic salt

1/4 teaspoon pepper

24 small slices fontina cheese (9 oz.)

1/4 cup chopped shelled pistachios

1 red or green pear, unpeeled, cut into thin slices

1. Heat oven to 375°F. Place slices of bread on ungreased cookie sheet. Brush each with oil. Sprinkle with garlic salt and pepper. Bake at 375°F. for 8 to 10 minutes or until crisp.

2. Remove cookie sheet from oven. Top each bread slice with cheese and pistachios.

3. Return to oven; bake an additional 2 to 3 minutes or until cheese is melted. Top each with pear slice; press in lightly.

Prepare bruschetta as directed in recipe but do not top with pear slices; place in single layer in shallow pan. Cover; refrigerate up to 2 hours. Uncover; bake at 375°F. for 2 to 3 minutes or until cheese is melted. Top each bruschetta with pear slice; press lightly.

NUTRITION INFORMATION PER SERVING: SERVING SIZE: 1 Appetizer • Calories 80 • Calories from Fat 50 • % Daily Value: Total Fat 6 g 9% • Saturated Fat 2 g 10% • Cholesterol 10 mg 3% • Sodium 170 mg 7% • Total Carbohydrate 4 g 1% • Dietary Fiber 0 g 0% • Sugars 1 g • Protein 3 g • Vitamin A 2% • Vitamin C 0% • Calcium 6% • Iron 0% • **Dietary Exchanges:** 1/2 Starch, 1 Fat **OR** 1/2 Carbohydrate, 1 Fat

BRUSCHETTA WITH PEARS, FONTINA AND PISTACHIOS;
PROSCIUTTO-WRAPPED SCALLOPS, PAGE 170

Crostini with Roasted Onion and Garlic Topping

Sweet onions spare you from the tears caused by high sulfur content in other onions. Baking them with honey and oil accentuates their natural sweetness.

PREP TIME: 15 MINUTES
(READY IN 1 HOUR 15 MINUTES)
MAKES 24 APPETIZERS

1 large sweet onion (Vidalia®, Walla Walla or Maui)

3 garlic cloves, peeled

3 tablespoons olive oil

1 tablespoon honey

24 (1/4- to 1/2-inch-thick) slices baguette-style or small French bread

1 1/3 oz. (1/3 cup) shredded fresh Parmesan cheese

Chopped fresh cilantro

1. Heat oven to 350°F. Peel onion; cut into quarters. Place in ungreased 9-inch pie pan. Add garlic. Drizzle with 1 tablespoon of the oil and honey; mix gently.

2. Bake at 350°F. for 40 to 45 minutes or until onion is tender. Cool 15 minutes or until completely cooled.

3. Meanwhile, place bread slices on ungreased cookie sheet. Brush lightly with remaining 2 tablespoons oil.

4. Bake at 350°F. for 8 to 10 minutes or until crisp. Cool 10 minutes.

5. Transfer onion mixture to food processor bowl with metal blade or blender container; process until smooth. Add cheese; mix well.

6. Just before serving, spread about 2 teaspoons onion mixture on each bread slice. Broil 4 to 6 inches from heat for 2 to 3 minutes until topping is hot. Sprinkle with cilantro.

NUTRITION INFORMATION PER SERVING: SERVING SIZE: 1 Appetizer • Calories 40 • Calories from Fat 20 • % Daily Value: Total Fat 2 g 3% • Saturated Fat 0 g 0% • Cholesterol 0 mg 0% • Sodium 55 mg 2% • Total Carbohydrate 4 g 1% • Dietary Fiber 0 g 0% • Sugars 1 g • Protein 1 g • Vitamin A 0% • Vitamin C 0% • Calcium 2% • Iron 0% • **Dietary Exchanges:** 1/2 Starch **OR** 1/2 Carbohydrate

Garlic Cream Cheese Crostini

Assembling the cheese-topped bread slices goes quickly. It's the perfect job for a friend of any age who offers to help in the kitchen.

PREP TIME: 20 MINUTES
MAKES 20 APPETIZERS

20 (1/2-inch-thick) slices French bread

1 tablespoon olive or vegetable oil

1/2 cup soft cream cheese with herbs and garlic (from 8-oz. tub)

1/4 cup chopped green onions

1. Place bread slices on ungreased cookie sheet. Lightly brush each with oil. Broil 4 to 6 inches from heat for about 1 minute or until light golden brown.

2. Meanwhile, in small bowl, combine cream cheese and green onions; blend well.

3. Remove cookie sheet from oven. Spread mixture on toasted bread slices.

4. Return to oven; broil an additional minute or until cream cheese bubbles.

NUTRITION INFORMATION PER SERVING: SERVING SIZE: 1 Appetizer • Calories 50 • Calories from Fat 25 • % Daily Value: Total Fat 3 g 5% • Saturated Fat 1 g 5% • Cholesterol 5 mg 2% • Sodium 95 mg 4% • Total Carbohydrate 5 g 2% • Dietary Fiber 0 g 0% • Sugars 1 g • Protein 1 g • Vitamin A 0% • Vitamin C 0% • Calcium 0% • Iron 0% • **Dietary Exchanges:** 1/2 Starch, 1/2 Fat **OR** 1/2 Carbohydrate, 1/2 Fat

Roasted Red Pepper Crostini

Pine nuts, *pignoli* in Italian, really do come from a Mediterranean pine tree. They're often paired with sweet peppers, as in this recipe, and are also a key ingredient in pesto.

PREP TIME: 15 MINUTES
MAKES 12 APPETIZERS

1 (7.25-oz.) jar roasted red bell peppers, drained

2 tablespoons shredded fresh Parmesan cheese

1/4 teaspoon salt

1 tablespoon balsamic vinegar

1 garlic clove, minced

12 (1/2-inch-thick) slices French bread

2 tablespoons pine nuts, toasted if desired

1. Heat grill. Finely chop roasted peppers; place in small bowl. Add cheese, salt, vinegar and garlic; mix well. Set aside.

2. When ready to grill, place half the bread slices on gas grill over medium heat or on charcoal grill 4 to 6 inches from medium coals. Cook 1 minute or until bread begins to brown on bottom.

3. Turn bread over; top each evenly with half the roasted pepper mixture. Cook an additional 1 to 2 minutes or until breads are browned. Remove from grill; place on serving platter. Sprinkle with half the pine nuts. Repeat with remaining bread slices.

tips

To broil crostini, place bread slices on cookie sheet; broil 4 to 6 inches from heat until bread begins to brown on top. Turn bread over; top each evenly with roasted pepper mixture. Broil an additional 1 to 2 minutes or until breads are browned.

NUTRITION INFORMATION PER SERVING: SERVING SIZE: 1 Appetizer • Calories 45 • Calories from Fat 10 • % Daily Value: Total Fat 1 g 2% • Saturated Fat 0 g 0% • Cholesterol 0 mg 0% • Sodium 130 mg 5% • Total Carbohydrate 7 g 2% • Dietary Fiber 1 g 4% • Sugars 1 g • Protein 2 g • Vitamin A 10% • Vitamin C 25% • Calcium 2% • Iron 2% • **Dietary Exchanges:** 1/2 Starch **OR** 1/2 Carbohydrate

Chicken Pizza Crostini

Purchase preshredded mozzarella for easiest preparation of this French-bread pizza. For the most tender topping, however, buy fresh mozzarella, available at some deli counters and gourmet or specialty Italian markets, and cut it into thin slices.

PREP TIME: 35 MINUTES
MAKES 24 APPETIZERS

24 (1/2-inch-thick) slices baguette-style or small French bread

2 tablespoons olive oil

3/4 cup chunky pizza sauce

1/2 lb. thinly sliced cooked chicken, cut into 24 pieces

2 oz. (1/2 cup) shredded mozzarella cheese

2 to 4 tablespoons chopped fresh parsley

1. Heat oven to 350°F. Brush bread slices with oil; place on ungreased cookie sheet. Bake at 350°F. for 8 to 10 minutes or until crisp.

2. Remove cookie sheet from oven. Top each bread slice with pizza sauce, chicken, cheese and parsley.

3. Return to oven; bake an additional 5 to 8 minutes or until topping is hot and cheese is melted.

NUTRITION INFORMATION PER SERVING: SERVING SIZE: 1 Appetizer • Calories 60 • Calories from Fat 25 • % Daily Value: Total Fat 3 g 5% • Saturated Fat 1 g 5% • Cholesterol 10 mg 3% • Sodium 100 mg 4% • Total Carbohydrate 3 g 1% • Dietary Fiber 0 g 0% • Sugars 1 g • Protein 4 g • Vitamin A 0% • Vitamin C 0% • Calcium 2% • Iron 0% • **Dietary Exchanges:** 1 Lean Meat

Crostini with Brie and Cherry Relish

Laced with brandy and chopped pecans, the cherry relish could also be used as a topping for scones or mini muffins.

PREP TIME: 45 MINUTES
MAKES 24 APPETIZERS

RELISH

¼ cup sugar

2 tablespoons water

2 tablespoons brandy

1 cup dried cherries

¼ cup chopped pecans

1 tablespoon orange marmalade

CROSTINI

24 slices pumpernickel or rye cocktail bread

24 small slices Brie cheese (6 oz.)

2 tablespoons chopped fresh chives

1. In small saucepan, combine sugar, water and brandy. Cook over medium heat until sugar is dissolved, stirring occasionally. Add cherries. Reduce heat to low; simmer 5 minutes, stirring occasionally. Stir in pecans and marmalade. Set aside.

2. Heat oven to 400°F. Place bread slices on ungreased cookie sheet. Bake at 400°F. for 4 to 5 minutes or until toasted.

3. Remove cookie sheet from oven. Top each bread slice with cheese slice and cherry relish. Sprinkle with chives.

4. Return to oven; bake an additional 4 to 6 minutes or until cheese is melted.

Prepare relish as directed in recipe. Cover; refrigerate up to 24 hours. Prepare crostini as directed in recipe.

NUTRITION INFORMATION PER SERVING: SERVING SIZE: 1 Appetizer • Calories 80 • Calories from Fat 25 • % Daily Value: Total Fat 3 g 5% • Saturated Fat 1 g 5% • Cholesterol 5 mg 2% • Sodium 90 mg 4% • Total Carbohydrate 11 g 4% • Dietary Fiber 1 g 4% • Sugars 6 g • Protein 2 g • Vitamin A 6% • Vitamin C 0% • Calcium 2% • Iron 0% • Dietary Exchanges: ½ Starch, ½ Fat OR ½ Carbohydrate, ½ Fat

Goat Cheese Crostini

Chèvre is a soft, tangy, spreadable cheese made from goat's milk. It's often sold in a small log shape and sometimes coated with herbs or black pepper.

PREP TIME: 30 MINUTES
MAKES 16 APPETIZERS

½ baguette-style French bread, cut into 16 thin slices

3 tablespoons olive oil

1 (6-oz.) pkg. chèvre (goat) cheese

2 tablespoons finely chopped sun-dried tomatoes in herbs and oil

1 teaspoon dried basil leaves

5 to 6 drops hot pepper sauce

1. Heat oven to 375°F. Arrange bread slices on ungreased cookie sheet. Brush with oil. Bake at 375°F. for 10 to 15 minutes or until lightly browned.

2. Meanwhile, in small bowl, combine all remaining ingredients; blend well.

3. Remove cookie sheet from oven. Spread each bread slice with cheese mixture.

4. Return to oven; bake an additional 2 to 3 minutes or until thoroughly heated.

NUTRITION INFORMATION PER SERVING: SERVING SIZE: 1 Appetizer • Calories 90 • Calories from Fat 50 • % Daily Value: Total Fat 6 g 9% • Saturated Fat 3 g 15% • Cholesterol 10 mg 3% • Sodium 115 mg 5% • Total Carbohydrate 5 g 2% • Dietary Fiber 0 g 0% • Sugars 1 g • Protein 3 g • Vitamin A 4% • Vitamin C 0% • Calcium 4% • Iron 2% • Dietary Exchanges: ½ Starch, 1 Fat OR ½ Carbohydrate, 1 Fat

Bacon and Pineapple Yam Bites

Bacon freezes well. Package it in bundles of 3 or 4 strips, well wrapped in plastic. Store all the bundles in a resealable freezer bag and defrost in the microwave as needed.

PREP TIME: 40 MINUTES
MAKES 40 APPETIZERS

1 large fresh yam (about 12 oz.), peeled

2 tablespoons margarine or butter, melted

1 teaspoon Caribbean jerk seasoning

8 slices bacon

1 (20-oz.) can chunk pineapple, drained

2 tablespoons brown sugar

1. Heat oven to 400°F. Cut yam crosswise into ½-inch slices. In small bowl, combine margarine and jerk seasoning; blend well. Brush mixture on both sides of each yam slice; place in ungreased 15x10x1-inch baking pan. Cut each slice into bite-sized pieces to make about 40 pieces. Spread pieces about ¼ inch apart.

2. Bake at 400°F. for 8 to 10 minutes or until yam pieces are crisp-tender.

3. Meanwhile, in medium skillet over medium heat, cook bacon until almost crisp. Cut each bacon slice into about 5 pieces.

4. Top each yam piece in baking pan with bacon piece. Dip each pineapple piece in brown sugar; place on top of bacon. Secure each stack with toothpick.

5. Bake at 400°F. for 5 to 7 minutes or until thoroughly heated. With pancake turner, immediately remove from cookie sheet. Place on serving platter or tray. Cool slightly before serving.

make-ahead tip

Assemble yam bites as directed in recipe; place in pan. Do not bake. Cover; refrigerate up to 2 hours. Uncover; bake as directed in recipe.

NUTRITION INFORMATION PER SERVING: SERVING SIZE: 1 Appetizer • Calories 25 • Calories from Fat 10 • % Daily Value: Total Fat 1 g 2% • Saturated Fat 0 g 0% • Cholesterol 0 mg 0% • Sodium 35 mg 1% • Total Carbohydrate 4 g 1% • Dietary Fiber 0 g 0% • Sugars 2 g • Protein 1 g • Vitamin A 0% • Vitamin C 2% • Calcium 0% • Iron 0% • **Dietary Exchanges:** ½ Fruit **OR** ½ Carbohydrate

Marinara and Shrimp Canapés

Shrimp for dipping are usually served with the tail intact for easy pickup. For canapés, however, the tails should be removed.

PREP TIME: 30 MINUTES
MAKES 16 APPETIZERS

1 (10-oz.) can refrigerated pizza crust

1/3 cup refrigerated marinara sauce

1/3 cup chopped purchased precooked bacon

16 cooked medium shrimp, tails removed

2 tablespoons shredded fresh Parmesan cheese

Chopped fresh chives, if desired

1. Heat oven to 425°F. Spray cookie sheet with nonstick cooking spray. Unroll dough onto work surface. Press out dough with fingers to form 12x8-inch rectangle. With floured 2-inch holiday-shaped cookie cutters, cut dough into shapes; place 1 inch apart on sprayed cookie sheet.

2. Bake at 425°F. for 5 to 7 minutes or until light golden brown.

3. Remove partially baked crusts from oven. Spread each crust with marinara sauce. Sprinkle each with bacon. Place 1 shrimp in center of each. Sprinkle each with cheese.

4. Return to oven; bake an additional 3 to 5 minutes or until cheese is melted. Sprinkle with chives.

NUTRITION INFORMATION PER SERVING: SERVING SIZE: 1 Appetizer • Calories 70 • Calories from Fat 20 • % Daily Value: Total Fat 2 g 3% • Saturated Fat 1 g 5% • Cholesterol 15 mg 5% • Sodium 260 mg 11% • Total Carbohydrate 9 g 3% • Dietary Fiber 0 g 0% • Sugars 1 g • Protein 4 g • Vitamin A 0% • Vitamin C 0% • Calcium 0% • Iron 4% • **Dietary Exchanges:** ½ Starch, ½ Lean Meat **OR** ½ Carbohydrate, ½ Lean Meat

Deviled Crab Puffs

Pre-toasting one side of the bread assures a crisp base for these bubbly spiced crab and cheese morsels.

PREP TIME: 20 MINUTES
(READY IN 1 HOUR)
MAKES 48 APPETIZERS

24 (3/4-inch-thick) slices baguette-style French bread

1 (5-oz.) jar sharp pasteurized process cheese spread

1 tablespoon all-purpose flour

1 teaspoon dry mustard

1/8 teaspoon ground red pepper (cayenne)

6 tablespoons margarine or butter, softened

2 tablespoons mayonnaise

1 teaspoon Worcestershire sauce

1 garlic clove, minced

1 (6-oz.) can crabmeat, drained

1. Arrange bread slices on ungreased cookie sheet. Broil 4 to 6 inches from heat for 1 to 2 minutes or until lightly browned on 1 side. Remove from broiler. Turn slices over; cool completely.

2. Meanwhile, in medium bowl, combine all remaining ingredients except crabmeat; mix until well blended and smooth. Stir in crabmeat.

3. Spread mixture on untoasted sides of bread, covering completely. Leaving slices on cookie sheet, freeze at least 30 minutes or until firm.

4. Cut bread slices in half crosswise; separate slightly. Broil frozen appetizers 4 to 6 inches from heat for 3 to 4 minutes or until puffed, bubbly and lightly browned.

NUTRITION INFORMATION PER SERVING: SERVING SIZE: 1 Appetizer • Calories 45 • Calories from Fat 25 • % Daily Value: Total Fat 3 g 5% • Saturated Fat 1 g 5% • Cholesterol 4 mg 1% • Sodium 95 mg 4% • Total Carbohydrate 3 g 1% • Dietary Fiber 0 g 0% • Sugars 0 g • Protein 1 g • Vitamin A 0% • Vitamin C 0% • Calcium 2% • Iron 0% • **Dietary Exchanges:** 1 Fat

Flaky Deli Slices

This savory "strudel" takes almost no work to assemble. Flaky pie pastry surrounds ham, pepperoni and cheese.

PREP TIME: 10 MINUTES
(READY IN 35 MINUTES)
MAKES 32 APPETIZERS

1 (15-oz.) pkg. refrigerated pie crusts, softened as directed on package

¼ cup grated Parmesan cheese

¾ lb. very thinly sliced cooked ham

¼ lb. thinly sliced pepperoni

4 oz. (1 cup) shredded Cheddar cheese

1. Heat oven to 450°F. Remove crusts from pouches; unfold crusts. Press out fold lines. Sprinkle each crust with Parmesan cheese.

2. Top each crust with ham, pepperoni and Cheddar cheese to within 1 inch of edges. Loosely roll up each crust. Place rolls seam side down on ungreased cookie sheet. Fold ends under.

3. Bake at 450°F. for 12 to 17 minutes or until golden brown. Cool 5 minutes. Cut each roll into 16 slices.

NUTRITION INFORMATION PER SERVING: SERVING SIZE: 1 Appetizer • Calories 110 • Calories from Fat 60 • % Daily Value: Total Fat 7 g 11% • Saturated Fat 3 g 15% • Cholesterol 15 mg 5% • Sodium 310 mg 13% • Total Carbohydrate 7 g 2% • Dietary Fiber 0 g 0% • Sugars 1 g • Protein 4 g • Vitamin A 0% • Vitamin C 0% • Calcium 4% • Iron 0% • **Dietary Exchanges:** ½ Starch, ½ High-Fat Meat, ½ Fat **OR** ½ Carbohydrate, ½ High-Fat Meat, ½ Fat

Artichoke and Roasted Pepper Hearts

Preparing and eating fresh artichokes is a labor of love, but marinated artichoke hearts make it easy to enjoy this distinctive vegetable. Here, it's blended with roasted pepper and spooned onto heart-shaped herb toast.

PREP TIME: 20 MINUTES
MAKES 12 APPETIZERS

1 (6-oz.) jar marinated artichoke hearts, drained

¼ cup drained roasted red bell peppers (from 7.25-oz. jar)

2 teaspoons chopped fresh basil

6 slices bread

2 tablespoons olive oil

½ teaspoon dried Italian seasoning

1. Finely chop artichoke hearts and roasted peppers; place in medium bowl. Add basil; mix well.

2. With 2½-inch heart-shaped cookie cutter or sharp knife, cut 2 hearts from each bread slice. Place hearts on ungreased cookie sheet.

3. Broil 4 to 6 inches from heat for 30 to 60 seconds. Turn hearts; brush with oil. Sprinkle with Italian seasoning. Broil an additional 30 to 60 seconds or until tops are lightly toasted.

4. To serve, spoon about 1 tablespoon artichoke mixture onto each heart.

NUTRITION INFORMATION PER SERVING: SERVING SIZE: 1 Appetizer • Calories 50 • Calories from Fat 35 • % Daily Value: Total Fat 4 g 6% • Saturated Fat 0 g 0% • Cholesterol 0 mg 0% • Sodium 40 mg 2% • Total Carbohydrate 4 g 1% • Dietary Fiber 0 g 0% • Sugars 0 g • Protein 1 g • Vitamin A 2% • Vitamin C 6% • Calcium 0% • Iron 0% • **Dietary Exchanges:** ½ Starch, ½ Fat **OR** ½ Carbohydrate, ½ Fat

Maple Mustard Biscuit Bites

These easy homemade biscuits, filled with sweet-glazed ham, are a nice addition to a breakfast or brunch buffet, and also a good way to use up extra ham left over from the holidays.

PREP TIME: 30 MINUTES
MAKES 12 APPETIZERS

1 cup all-purpose flour

2 tablespoons chopped fresh parsley

2 teaspoons sugar

1½ teaspoons baking powder

¼ teaspoon salt

¼ teaspoon dried sage leaves

⅓ to ½ cup skim milk

1 teaspoon margarine or butter, melted

1 tablespoon prepared mustard

1 tablespoon real maple syrup

Dash coarse-ground black pepper

1 (6-oz.) pkg. thinly sliced extra-lean low-fat cooked ham, cut into 2x¼-inch strips

1. Heat oven to 425°F. In medium bowl, combine flour, parsley, sugar, baking powder, salt and sage; mix well. Add ⅓ cup milk and melted margarine; stir with fork just until dry ingredients are moistened, adding additional milk, 1 tablespoon at a time, if necessary to form a soft dough.

2. On floured surface, knead dough gently until smooth ball forms. Pat dough into ⅜-inch-thick square. With knife, cut into 12 pieces; place on ungreased cookie sheet.

3. Bake at 425°F. for 8 to 14 minutes or until light golden brown.

4. Meanwhile, in small nonstick skillet, combine mustard, syrup and pepper. Cook and stir over medium heat until blended. Add ham; mix well to coat with mustard mixture. Cook until thoroughly heated.

5. To serve, split hot biscuits. Fill each with ham mixture.

HIGH ALTITUDE (ABOVE 3500 FEET): No change.

NUTRITION INFORMATION PER SERVING: SERVING SIZE: 1 Appetizer • Calories 70 • Calories from Fat 10 • % Daily Value: Total Fat 1 g 2% • Saturated Fat 0 g 0% • Cholesterol 5 mg 2% • Sodium 330 mg 14% • Total Carbohydrate 11 g 4% • Dietary Fiber 0 g 0% • Sugars 2 g • Protein 4 g • Vitamin A 0% • Vitamin C 6% • Calcium 6% • Iron 4% • **Dietary Exchanges:** 1 Starch **OR** 1 Carbohydrate

Toasted Mini-Sandwiches with Gouda and Tomato

In this party-perfect version of grilled cheese and tomato sandwiches, mustard and dill add an extra kick.

PREP TIME: 25 MINUTES
MAKES 24 MINI-SANDWICHES

24 slices rye or pumpernickel cocktail bread

2 tablespoons butter, melted

1 tablespoon Dijon mustard

1 teaspoon dried dill weed

4 oz. Gouda cheese, thinly sliced, cut into 24 pieces to fit bread

2 to 3 Italian plum tomatoes, cut into 24 thin slices

1. Brush 1 side of each bread slice with butter. Place 12 bread slices, buttered side down, on ungreased cookie sheet.

2. Spread each slice with mustard; sprinkle with dill weed. Top with cheese, tomato and remaining bread slices, buttered side up.

3. Broil 4 to 6 inches from heat for 1 to 3 minutes on each side or until toasted.

4. To serve, cut each sandwich in half diagonally.

make-ahead tip

Prepare sandwiches as directed in recipe; place in shallow pan. Do not broil. Cover; refrigerate up to 2 hours. Uncover; broil as directed in recipe.

NUTRITION INFORMATION PER SERVING: SERVING SIZE: 1 Mini-Sandwich • Calories 50 • Calories from Fat 25 • % Daily Value: Total Fat 3 g 5% • Saturated Fat 1 g 5% • Cholesterol 10 mg 3% • Sodium 110 mg 5% • Total Carbohydrate 4 g 1% • Dietary Fiber 1 g 4% • Sugars 0 g • Protein 2 g • Vitamin A 2% • Vitamin C 0% • Calcium 4% • Iron 0% • **Dietary Exchanges:** ½ Starch, ½ Fat **OR** ½ Carbohydrate, ½ Fat

Cheeseburger Bites

These bites are perfect to serve buffet-style. Pile an assortment of buns—try sesame and poppy seed—in a large basket, and present the beef mixture in the slow cooker. Add a tray of your favorite burger toppings.

PREP TIME: 15 MINUTES
(READY IN 4 HOURS 15 MINUTES)
MAKES 24 APPETIZERS

BITES

1 lb. lean ground beef

2 tablespoons ketchup

2 teaspoons instant minced onion

1 teaspoon prepared mustard

8 oz. pasteurized processed American cheese, cut into 2-inch cubes (2 cups)

24 miniature sandwich buns, split

TOPPINGS

Dill pickle chips

Sliced Italian plum tomatoes

Shredded lettuce

Additional ketchup and mustard

1. Brown ground beef in large skillet over medium-high heat until thoroughly cooked, stirring frequently to break into small pieces. Drain. Stir in 2 tablespoons ketchup, onion and 1 teaspoon mustard.

2. Spray 3½- to 4-quart slow cooker with nonstick cooking spray. Spoon beef mixture into sprayed slow cooker. Top with cheese.

3. Cover; cook in low setting for 3 to 4 hours.

4. To serve, stir beef mixture. Spoon 1 rounded tablespoon mixture into each bun. Serve with desired toppings.

NUTRITION INFORMATION PER SERVING: SERVING SIZE: 1 Appetizer (with toppings) • Calories 170 • Calories from Fat 70 • % Daily Value: Total Fat 8 g 12% • Saturated Fat 3 g 15% • Cholesterol 20 mg 7% • Sodium 470 mg 20% • Total Carbohydrate 17 g 6% • Dietary Fiber 1 g 4% • Sugars 1 g • Protein 8 g • Vitamin A 6% • Vitamin C 4% • Calcium 10% • Iron 8% • **Dietary Exchanges:** 1 Starch, ½ Medium-Fat Meat, 1 Fat **OR** 1 Carbohydrate, ½ Medium-Fat Meat, 1 Fat

Petite Stuffed Pizza Snacks

Cutting the baked pizzas into diamond shapes yields a few odd-shaped pieces at the edges—the perfect reward for kitchen helpers.

PREP TIME: 15 MINUTES
(READY IN 35 MINUTES)
MAKES 16 SERVINGS

1 (10.6-oz.) pkg. refrigerated Parmesan breadsticks

2 tablespoons grated Parmesan cheese

¼ teaspoon dried oregano leaves

1 egg

25 slices pepperoni (about 1½ oz.)

2 oz. (½ cup) shredded Swiss cheese

¾ cup tomato pasta sauce, heated

1. Heat oven to 350°F. Unroll dough; divide into 2 equal sections along center perforation. Press each section to form 8-inch square. Place 1 square on ungreased cookie sheet.

2. In small bowl, combine Parmesan cheese, oregano and egg; beat well. Spoon mixture over square on cookie sheet; carefully spread to within ½ inch of edge. Arrange pepperoni over egg mixture. Sprinkle with Swiss cheese. Top with remaining dough square; press edges to seal. Spread Parmesan spread from container over dough.

3. Bake at 350°F. for 15 to 20 minutes or until golden brown. To serve, cut into 4 strips with serrated knife; cut 7 diagonal strips to form diamond-shaped pieces. (A few outer pieces will not be diamond shaped.) Serve warm pizza snacks with warm pasta sauce.

NUTRITION INFORMATION PER SERVING: SERVING SIZE: ¹⁄₁₆ of Recipe • Calories 100 • Calories from Fat 45 • % Daily Value: Total Fat 5 g 8% • Saturated Fat 2 g 10% • Cholesterol 20 mg 7% • Sodium 300 mg 13% • Total Carbohydrate 9 g 3% • Dietary Fiber 0 g 0% • Sugars 1 g • Protein 4 g • Vitamin A 2% • Vitamin C 0% • Calcium 6% • Iron 4% • **Dietary Exchanges:** ½ Starch, ½ High-Fat Meat **OR** ½ Carbohydrate, ½ High-Fat Meat

Pepperoni Pizza Snacks

Garlicky dough encases pepperoni and mozzarella, with tomato sauce for dipping.

PREP TIME: 20 MINUTES
(READY IN 40 MINUTES)
MAKES 20 APPETIZERS

1 (10.6-oz.) pkg. refrigerated garlic breadsticks

20 slices pepperoni

20 (½-inch) cubes mozzarella cheese (2½ oz.)

1 cup pizza sauce, heated

1. Heat oven to 375°F. Spray 8- or 9-inch square pan with nonstick cooking spray. Remove dough from can. Unroll dough; separate into strips. Cut each strip in half crosswise to make 20 pieces. Press each piece to form 2½-inch square.

2. Top each square with 1 slice of pepperoni and 1 cheese cube. Wrap dough around filling to completely cover; firmly press edges to seal.

3. Place butter mixture from breadstick package in small microwave-safe bowl. Microwave at HIGH for 10 to 20 seconds or until melted. Dip each filled dough bite in melted butter mixture. Place seam side down with sides touching in sprayed pan.

4. Bake at 400°F. for 15 to 20 minutes or until golden brown. Cool 5 minutes. Remove from pan. Serve warm snacks with warm pizza sauce.

NUTRITION INFORMATION PER SERVING: SERVING SIZE: 1 Appetizer • Calories 70 • Calories from Fat 25 • % Daily Value: Total Fat 3 g 5% • Saturated Fat 1 g 5% • Cholesterol 4 mg 1% • Sodium 230 mg 10% • Total Carbohydrate 7 g 2% • Dietary Fiber 0 g 0% • Sugars 1 g • Protein 3 g • Vitamin A 2% • Vitamin C 0% • Calcium 4% • Iron 2% • **Dietary Exchanges:** ½ Starch, ½ Fat **OR** ½ Carbohydrate, ½ Fat

Halftime Sausage Pizzas

Assemble and bake the pizzas when halftime begins—they take only 5 or 10 minutes to heat.

PREP TIME: 25 MINUTES
MAKES 12 APPETIZERS

3 (6-inch) prebaked Italian pizza crusts

1 medium tomato, chopped

¼ cup chopped onion

¾ teaspoon dried pizza seasoning

½ teaspoon dried basil leaves

¼ teaspoon garlic salt

½ cup chopped fully cooked smoked turkey sausage (from 16-oz. pkg.)

3 oz. (¾ cup) shredded reduced-fat mozzarella cheese

1. Heat oven to 425°F. Place pizza crusts on ungreased cookie sheet.

2. In small bowl, combine tomato, onion, pizza seasoning, basil and garlic salt; mix lightly. Spoon tomato mixture onto each pizza crust. Sprinkle with sausage and cheese.

3. Bake at 425°F. for 5 to 10 minutes or until cheese is melted. Cut each into quarters.

NUTRITION INFORMATION PER SERVING: SERVING SIZE: 1 Appetizer • Calories 110 • Calories from Fat 25 • % Daily Value: Total Fat 3 g 5% • Saturated Fat 1 g 5% • Cholesterol 10 mg 3% • Sodium 340 mg 14% • Total Carbohydrate 14 g 5% • Dietary Fiber 0 g 0% • Sugars 1 g • Protein 7 g • Vitamin A 2% • Vitamin C 2% • Calcium 10% • Iron 6% • **Dietary Exchanges:** 1 Starch, ½ Medium-Fat Meat **OR** 1 Carbohydrate, ½ Medium-Fat Meat

Ham and Swiss Appetizer Pizza

A popular brown-bag sandwich crosses the line to party fare with the flourish of green onions and a swift pass in the oven.

PREP TIME: 25 MINUTES
MAKES 64 APPETIZERS

2 tablespoons Dijon mustard

1 (10-oz.) prebaked Italian bread shell

1 cup diced cooked ham

¼ cup finely chopped green onions

6 oz. (1½ cups) shredded Swiss cheese

1. Heat oven to 425°F. Spread mustard on bread shell; place on ungreased cookie sheet. Top with ham, green onions and cheese.

2. Bake at 425°F. for 6 to 8 minutes or until cheese is melted. Cut into small squares.

NUTRITION INFORMATION PER SERVING: SERVING SIZE: 1 Appetizer • Calories 25 • Calories from Fat 10 • % Daily Value: Total Fat 1 g 2% • Saturated Fat 1 g 5% • Cholesterol 4 mg 1% • Sodium 75 mg 3% • Total Carbohydrate 2 g 1% • Dietary Fiber 0 g 0% • Sugars 0 g • Protein 2 g • Vitamin A 0% • Vitamin C 0% • Calcium 4% • Iron 0% • **Dietary Exchanges:** ½ Lean Meat

Pizza Squares Continental

This is an onion lover's pizza, with generous handfuls of thinly sliced rings between melted provolone and creamy Montrachet cheese.

PREP TIME: 30 MINUTES
(READY IN 55 MINUTES)
MAKES 16 APPETIZERS

2 tablespoons olive oil

2 large onions, thinly sliced (4 cups)

1 (10-oz.) can refrigerated pizza crust

6 oz. sliced provolone cheese

1 (7.25-oz.) jar roasted red bell peppers, drained, cut into thin strips

2 oz. Montrachet or other chèvre (goat) cheese, crumbled (⅓ cup)

2 tablespoons pine nuts, if desired

1. Heat oven to 425°F. Grease 12-inch pizza pan or 13x9-inch pan. Heat oil in large skillet over medium heat until hot. Add onions; cook 10 to 12 minutes or until light golden brown, stirring occasionally.

2. Unroll dough; place in greased pan. Starting at center, press out dough with hands to edge of pan. Arrange provolone cheese over dough. Spoon onions over cheese. Top with roasted peppers and Montrachet cheese.

3. Bake at 425°F. for 16 to 21 minutes or until crust is golden brown. Sprinkle with pine nuts. Cut into squares or wedges.

NUTRITION INFORMATION PER SERVING: SERVING SIZE: 1 Appetizer • Calories 120 • Calories from Fat 50 • % Daily Value: Total Fat 6 g 9% • Saturated Fat 3 g 15% • Cholesterol 10 mg 3% • Sodium 210 mg 9% • Total Carbohydrate 11 g 4% • Dietary Fiber 1 g 4% • Sugars 2 g • Protein 5 g • Vitamin A 10% • Vitamin C 25% • Calcium 10% • Iron 4% • **Dietary Exchanges:** 1 Starch, ½ High-Fat Meat **OR** 1 Carbohydrate, ½ High-Fat Meat

Mini Pizzas

Using cookie cutters on the dough adds a festive touch. If you're in a hurry, simple diamonds or squares are equally tasty.

PREP TIME: 30 MINUTES
MAKES 20 PIZZAS

1 (10-oz.) can refrigerated pizza crust

⅓ cup purchased pesto

20 slices Italian plum tomatoes

4 oz. (1 cup) shredded mozzarella cheese

1. Heat oven to 425°F. Lightly grease cookie sheet. Unroll dough onto work surface. Press out dough with fingers to form 12x8-inch rectangle. With 2½-inch holiday-shaped metal cookie cutters, cut dough into shapes; place 1 inch apart on greased cookie sheet.

2. Bake at 425°F. for 5 to 7 minutes or until light golden brown.

3. Remove partially baked crusts from oven. Spread each crust with pesto. Top each with 1 tomato slice. Sprinkle with cheese.

4. Return to oven; bake an additional 3 to 5 minutes or until cheese is melted.

NUTRITION INFORMATION PER SERVING: SERVING SIZE: 1 Pizza • Calories 70 • Calories from Fat 25 • % Daily Value: Total Fat 3 g 5% • Saturated Fat 1 g 5% • Cholesterol 4 mg 1% • Sodium 160 mg 7% • Total Carbohydrate 8 g 3% • Dietary Fiber 0 g 0% • Sugars 1 g • Protein 3 g • Vitamin A 2% • Vitamin C 2% • Calcium 6% • Iron 2% • **Dietary Exchanges:** ½ Starch, ½ Fat **OR** ½ Carbohydrate, ½ Fat

SPEEDWAY PUBLIC LIBRARY SPEEDWAY, INDIANA

Sun-Dried Tomato and Cheese Pizza

Chopped sun-dried tomatoes give rich, concentrated tomato flavor to this homemade pizza.

PREP TIME: 30 MINUTES
MAKES 35 APPETIZERS

1 (10-oz.) can refrigerated pizza crust

1/2 cup oil-packed sun-dried tomatoes, drained, coarsely chopped

1/2 cup sliced pitted kalamata or ripe olives

6 oz. (1 1/2 cups) shredded Cheddar cheese

2 oz. (1/2 cup) shredded fresh Parmesan cheese

1/2 cup sliced green onions

1. Heat oven to 425°F. Grease 15x10x1-inch baking pan. Unroll dough; place in greased pan. Starting at center, press out with hands to edge of pan. Bake at 425°F. for 8 to 10 minutes or until light golden brown.

2. Remove partially baked crust from oven. Sprinkle crust with all remaining ingredients.

3. Return to oven; bake an additional 3 to 5 minutes or until cheese is melted. Cut into small squares.

NUTRITION INFORMATION PER SERVING: SERVING SIZE: 1 Appetizer • Calories 60 • Calories from Fat 25 • % Daily Value: Total Fat 3 g 5% • Saturated Fat 1 g 5% • Cholesterol 5 mg 2% • Sodium 150 mg 6% • Total Carbohydrate 5 g 2% • Dietary Fiber 0 g 0% • Sugars 1 g • Protein 3 g • Vitamin A 0% • Vitamin C 2% • Calcium 6% • Iron 0% • **Dietary Exchanges:** 1/2 Starch, 1/2 Fat **OR** 1/2 Carbohydrate, 1/2 Fat

Sun-Dried Tomato Mini Pizzas

Sun-dried tomatoes come in two forms: dry or packed in olive oil. Using the oil-packed version, and sautéing the onions in the reserved oil, intensifies the tomato flavor in this recipe.

PREP TIME: 20 MINUTES
(READY IN 40 MINUTES)
MAKES 10 APPETIZERS

1/3 cup oil-packed sun-dried tomatoes, chopped, drained, reserving 1 tablespoon oil

1 cup finely chopped onions

1/4 cup chopped fresh basil

Freshly ground black pepper

1 (10.6-oz.) pkg. refrigerated Parmesan breadsticks

1 oz. (1/4 cup) shredded fresh Asiago cheese or finely shredded mozzarella cheese

1. Heat oven to 350°F. Spray cookie sheet with nonstick cooking spray. Heat reserved 1 tablespoon tomato oil in medium skillet over medium heat until hot. Add onions; cook until tender, stirring occasionally. Remove from heat. Add tomatoes, basil, pepper to taste and Parmesan spread from container; mix well.

2. Separate dough into 10 breadsticks. Reroll each breadstick into pinwheel shape. Place 2 inches apart on sprayed cookie sheet. Press out from center of each pinwheel to form 2 1/2-inch round. (Edges will curl up slightly.) Spoon tomato mixture into center of each pinwheel. Sprinkle with cheese.

3. Bake at 350°F. for 15 to 20 minutes or until edges are golden brown.

NUTRITION INFORMATION PER SERVING: SERVING SIZE: 1 Appetizer • Calories 130 • Calories from Fat 50 • % Daily Value: Total Fat 6 g 9% • Saturated Fat 2 g 10% • Cholesterol 3 mg 1% • Sodium 340 mg 14% • Total Carbohydrate 14 g 5% • Dietary Fiber 1 g 4% • Sugars 3 g • Protein 4 g • Vitamin A 4% • Vitamin C 6% • Calcium 6% • Iron 6% • **Dietary Exchanges:** 1 Starch, 1 Fat **OR** 1 Carbohydrate, 1 Fat

Mini Aloha Puff Pizzettes

In colonial America, the pineapple symbolized hospitality, and the shape was often carved into home furnishings. These pineapple-topped morsels will make your guests feel just as welcome.

PREP TIME: 40 MINUTES
MAKES 24 APPETIZERS

1 (8-oz.) can refrigerated crescent dinner rolls

2 tablespoons purchased thick sweet-and-sour sauce

4 oz. (1 cup) finely shredded Swiss cheese

4 oz. thinly sliced baked ham, cut into short thin strips

1 (8-oz.) can crushed pineapple in unsweetened juice, well drained

1. Heat oven to 375°F. Lightly spray cookie sheet with nonstick cooking spray. Unroll dough into 2 long rectangles; press perforations to seal. Cut each rectangle into 12 squares. Place squares on sprayed cookie sheet.

2. Top each square with ¼ teaspoon sweet-and-sour sauce. Layer squares with half of cheese, all of ham, remaining half of cheese and all of pineapple.

3. Bake at 375°F. for 11 to 12 minutes or until edges are golden brown.

NUTRITION INFORMATION PER SERVING: SERVING SIZE: 1 Appetizer • Calories 60 • Calories from Fat 25 • % Daily Value: Total Fat 3 g 5% • Saturated Fat 1 g 5% • Cholesterol 5 mg 2% • Sodium 160 mg 7% • Total Carbohydrate 5 g 2% • Dietary Fiber 0 g 0% • Sugars 2 g • Protein 3 g • Vitamin A 0% • Vitamin C 0% • Calcium 4% • Iron 0% • **Dietary Exchanges:** ½ Starch, ½ Fat OR ½ Carbohydrate, ½ Fat

Artichoke and Brie Pizzettes

Pimientos are thick-fleshed red peppers, similar in flavor but more heart-shaped than bell peppers. In these pizzettes ("little pizzas"), chopped pimientos brighten the artichoke- and Brie-topped biscuits.

PREP TIME: 30 MINUTES
MAKES 20 APPETIZERS

1 (12-oz.) can refrigerated flaky biscuits

2 (6-oz.) jars marinated artichoke hearts, drained, reserving 1 tablespoon liquid

3 oz. Brie cheese

2 tablespoons chopped pimientos

1. Heat oven to 400°F. Separate dough into 10 biscuits. Separate each biscuit into 2 layers; place biscuit halves on large ungreased cookie sheet. Flatten each slightly.

2. Cut artichoke hearts into ½-inch pieces. Brush top of each biscuit half with reserved artichoke liquid. Divide artichoke pieces evenly on top of biscuits.

3. Bake at 400°F. for 9 to 13 minutes or until edges of biscuits are golden brown. Meanwhile, cut cheese into 20 pieces.

4. Remove cookie sheet from oven. Top each biscuit with piece of cheese.

5. Return to oven; bake an additional 2 to 3 minutes or until cheese softens slightly. Garnish each with pimientos.

NUTRITION INFORMATION PER SERVING: SERVING SIZE: 1 Appetizer • Calories 90 • Calories from Fat 45 • % Daily Value: Total Fat 5 g 8% • Saturated Fat 1 g 5% • Cholesterol 4 mg 1% • Sodium 230 mg 10% • Total Carbohydrate 8 g 3% • Dietary Fiber 0 g 0% • Sugars 1 g • Protein 2 g • Vitamin A 0% • Vitamin C 2% • Calcium 0% • Iron 2% • **Dietary Exchanges:** ½ Starch, 1 Fat OR ½ Carbohydrate, 1 Fat

Brie and Cranberry Pizza

For easiest slicing, use a rolling pizza cutter, available with a straight or fluted edge.

PREP TIME: 10 MINUTES
(READY IN 35 MINUTES)
MAKES 16 APPETIZERS

1 (10-oz.) can refrigerated pizza crust

1 (8-oz.) pkg. Brie cheese, rind removed, cut into ½-inch cubes

¾ cup canned whole berry cranberry sauce

½ cup chopped pecans

1. Heat oven to 425°F. Lightly oil 12-inch pizza pan or 13x9-inch pan with olive or vegetable oil. Unroll dough; place in oiled pan. Starting at center, press out dough with hands to edge of pan. Bake at 425°F. for 5 to 8 minutes or until light golden brown.

2. Remove partially baked crust from oven. Sprinkle cheese over crust. Place cranberry sauce in small bowl; stir to break up pieces. Spoon cranberry sauce by teaspoonfuls evenly over cheese. Sprinkle with pecans.

3. Return to oven; bake an additional 6 to 10 minutes or until cheese is melted and crust is golden brown. Cool 5 minutes. Cut into squares or wedges.

NUTRITION INFORMATION PER SERVING: SERVING SIZE: 1 Appetizer • Calories 140 • Calories from Fat 60 • % Daily Value: Total Fat 7 g 11% • Saturated Fat 3 g 15% • Cholesterol 15 mg 5% • Sodium 190 mg 8% • Total Carbohydrate 14 g 5% • Dietary Fiber 1 g 4% • Sugars 5 g • Protein 5 g • Vitamin A 2% • Vitamin C 0% • Calcium 4% • Iron 4% • **Dietary Exchanges:** ½ Starch, ½ Fruit, ½ High-Fat Meat, ½ Fat **OR** 1 Carbohydrate, ½ High-Fat Meat, ½ Fat

Roasted Chicken Nachos

Chicken and black beans make these nachos a substantial snack that's practically a meal in itself.

PREP TIME: 25 MINUTES
MAKES 8 SERVINGS

8 oz. tortilla chips

¾ cup chunky-style salsa

1 (15-oz.) can black beans, drained, rinsed

3 frozen charbroiled mesquite chicken breast patties, thawed, chopped

1 tomato, chopped

8 oz. (2 cups) finely shredded Mexican cheese blend

1. Heat oven to 400°F. Line 15x10x1-inch baking pan with foil. Spread half of tortilla chips evenly in foil-lined pan.

2. In medium bowl, combine salsa and beans; mix well. Spoon half of bean mixture over chips. Top with half each of chicken, tomato and cheese. Repeat layers.

3. Bake at 400°F. for 12 to 14 minutes or until cheese is melted.

NUTRITION INFORMATION PER SERVING: SERVING SIZE: ⅛ of Recipe • Calories 360 • Calories from Fat 170 • % Daily Value: Total Fat 19 g 29% • Saturated Fat 8 g 40% • Cholesterol 40 mg 13% • Sodium 780 mg 33% • Total Carbohydrate 29 g 10% • Dietary Fiber 4 g 16% • Sugars 2 g • Protein 18 g • Vitamin A 10% • Vitamin C 4% • Calcium 25% • Iron 8% • **Dietary Exchanges:** 2 Starch, 1½ Medium-Fat Meat, 2 Fat **OR** 2 Carbohydrate, 1½ Medium-Fat Meat, 2 Fat

Game-Time Nachos

For a fresh touch, these nachos feature chopped tomatoes and cilantro rather than purchased salsa.

PREP TIME: 15 MINUTES
MAKES 8 SERVINGS

6 oz. light pasteurized prepared cheese product, cubed

1 oz. (¼ cup) shredded reduced-fat sharp Cheddar cheese

3 tablespoons skim milk

1½ teaspoons 40% less-sodium taco seasoning mix (from 1.25-oz. pkg.)

3 oz. baked bite-sized tortilla chips (about 64 chips)

1½ cups finely chopped Italian plum tomatoes (about 5 medium)

¼ cup chopped fresh cilantro

1. In small saucepan, combine cheese product, Cheddar cheese, milk and taco seasoning mix; mix well. Cook over medium-low heat until cheeses are melted and smooth, stirring frequently.

2. Meanwhile, arrange chips on large serving platter. Pour warm cheese mixture over chips. Top with tomatoes and cilantro.

NUTRITION INFORMATION PER SERVING: SERVING SIZE: ⅛ of Recipe • Calories 120 • Calories from Fat 35 • % Daily Value: Total Fat 4 g 6% • Saturated Fat 2 g 10% • Cholesterol 10 mg 3% • Sodium 440 mg 18% • Total Carbohydrate 14 g 5% • Dietary Fiber 1 g 4% • Sugars 3 g • Protein 7 g • Vitamin A 10% • Vitamin C 8% • Calcium 15% • Iron 0% • **Dietary Exchanges:** 1 Starch, ½ Medium-Fat Meat **OR** 1 Carbohydrate, ½ Medium-Fat Meat

Smoked Chicken Nachos

If you can't find Mexican cheese blend, substitute shredded Monterey Jack or mild Cheddar.

PREP TIME: 30 MINUTES
MAKES 6 SERVINGS

NACHOS

1 (4-oz.) pkg. refrigerated mesquite-smoked chicken breast

4 cups tortilla chips (any combination of yellow, red and/or blue corn)

8 oz. (2 cups) shredded Mexican cheese blend

1 (2½-oz.) can sliced ripe olives, drained

DIP

¼ cup chunky-style salsa

2 tablespoons sour cream

1 tablespoon mayonnaise

1 small chipotle chile in adobo sauce (from 7- or 11-oz. can), seeded, finely chopped

1. Heat oven to 375°F. Spray 12-inch round pizza pan with nonstick cooking spray. Cook chicken as directed on package. Finely shred or chop cooked chicken.

2. Arrange tortilla chips evenly on sprayed pan, edges of chips overlapping slightly. Top evenly with chicken, cheese and olives.

3. Bake at 375°F. for 8 to 10 minutes or until cheese is melted.

4. Meanwhile, in small bowl, combine all dip ingredients; blend well. Serve warm nachos with dip.

NUTRITION INFORMATION PER SERVING: SERVING SIZE: ⅙ of Recipe • Calories 290 • Calories from Fat 190 • % Daily Value: Total Fat 21 g 32% • Saturated Fat 10 g 50% • Cholesterol 45 mg 15% • Sodium 680 mg 28% • Total Carbohydrate 13 g 4% • Dietary Fiber 1 g 4% • Sugars 2 g • Protein 13 g • Vitamin A 15% • Vitamin C 0% • Calcium 30% • Iron 4% • **Dietary Exchanges:** 1 Starch, 1½ Lean Meat, 3 Fat **OR** 1 Carbohydrate, 1½ Lean Meat, 3 Fat

Mini Picadillo Empanadas

An empanada is a turnover made with a savory filling between two layers of dough. These little ones are stuffed with a mix of ground beef and salsa, spiked with olives and raisins.

PREP TIME: 25 MINUTES
(READY IN 50 MINUTES)
MAKES 16 APPETIZERS

1/2 lb. lean ground beef or turkey

1 cup chunky-style salsa

2 tablespoons raisins

20 pimiento-stuffed green olives, sliced (about 1/3 cup)

1/2 teaspoon cumin

1/8 teaspoon cinnamon

1 (1 lb. 1.3-oz.) can large refrigerated corn biscuits or 1 (1 lb. 0.3-oz.) can large refrigerated buttermilk biscuits

1. Heat oven to 350°F. Brown ground beef in large skillet over medium-high heat for 8 to 10 minutes or until thoroughly cooked, stirring frequently. Drain.

2. Add all remaining ingredients except biscuits. Bring to a boil. Reduce heat to medium; cook 3 to 4 minutes or until most of liquid has evaporated, stirring occasionally. Remove from heat.

3. Separate dough into 8 biscuits. With serrated knife, cut each biscuit in half horizontally to make 16 rounds. Press or roll each to form 4-inch round. Spoon 2 level measuring tablespoons ground beef mixture in center of each round. Fold dough over filling; press edges with fork to seal. Place on ungreased cookie sheets.

4. Bake at 350°F. for 15 to 20 minutes or until golden brown. Cool 5 minutes before serving.

make-ahead tip

Prepare ground beef mixture as directed in recipe. Place in covered container; refrigerate up to 24 hours. Prepare and fill biscuits as directed in recipe. Bake as directed in recipe.

NUTRITION INFORMATION PER SERVING: SERVING SIZE: 1 Appetizer • Calories 140 • Calories from Fat 60 • % Daily Value: Total Fat 7 g 11% • Saturated Fat 2 g 10% • Cholesterol 10 mg 3% • Sodium 520 mg 22% • Total Carbohydrate 15 g 5% • Dietary Fiber 0 g 0% • Sugars 4 g • Protein 4 g • Vitamin A 0% • Vitamin C 0% • Calcium 2% • Iron 6% • **Dietary Exchanges:** 1 Starch, 1 1/2 Fat **OR** 1 Carbohydrate, 1 1/2 Fat

Chile and Cheese Empanaditas

These little hand-held pies encase a filling of melted peppery cheese and salsa.

PREP TIME: 25 MINUTES
(READY IN 45 MINUTES)
MAKES 16 SERVINGS

4 oz. (1 cup) shredded hot pepper Monterey Jack cheese

1/3 cup chopped green chiles (from 4.5-oz. can)

1 (15-oz.) pkg. refrigerated pie crusts, softened as directed on package

1 egg, beaten

1 cup chunky-style salsa

1. Heat oven to 400°F. In small bowl, combine cheese and green chiles; mix well.

2. With 3¼-inch round cutter, cut each pie crust into 8 rounds. Spoon cheese mixture evenly onto half of each dough round. Brush edge of crust rounds with beaten egg. Fold crust rounds in half; press edges with fork to seal. Place on ungreased cookie sheet. Brush tops with egg. Cut small slit in top of each.

3. Bake at 400°F. for 12 to 16 minutes or until golden brown. Serve warm empanaditas with salsa.

NUTRITION INFORMATION PER SERVING: SERVING SIZE: 1/16 of Recipe • Calories 130 • Calories from Fat 70 • % Daily Value: Total Fat 8 g 12% • Saturated Fat 4 g 20% • Cholesterol 25 mg 8% • Sodium 270 mg 11% • Total Carbohydrate 12 g 4% • Dietary Fiber 0 g 0% • Sugars 1 g • Protein 2 g • Vitamin A 4% • Vitamin C 0% • Calcium 6% • Iron 0% • **Dietary Exchanges:** 1/2 Starch, 1/2 Fruit, 1 1/2 Fat **OR** 1 Carbohydrate, 1 1/2 Fat

Italian Sausage Empanadas

Brushed with egg before baking, the empanadas bake to a glossy, golden finish.

PREP TIME: 50 MINUTES
MAKES 20 SERVINGS

1/2 lb. bulk Italian sausage

1 (14.5-oz.) can pizza sauce

1 (12-oz.) can refrigerated flaky biscuits

4 oz. mozzarella cheese, cut into 1/4-inch cubes

1 egg, beaten

1. Brown sausage in large skillet over medium heat. Drain. Stir in 3 tablespoons of the pizza sauce; set remaining pizza sauce aside.

2. Heat oven to 375°F. Separate dough into 10 biscuits; divide each in half horizontally, forming 20 rounds. Press or roll each into 4-inch round.

3. Place 1 tablespoon sausage mixture in center of each round. Top each with cheese; press lightly. Fold dough over filling to form half circle, stretching to fit. Press edges together; seal and prick top with fork. Place on ungreased cookie sheets. Brush with beaten egg.

4. Bake at 375°F. for 9 to 14 minutes or until golden brown.

5. Meanwhile, in small saucepan, heat remaining pizza sauce over low heat until hot. Serve warm empanadas with warm pizza sauce for dipping.

NUTRITION INFORMATION PER SERVING: SERVING SIZE: 1/20 of Recipe • Calories 110 • Calories from Fat 50 • % Daily Value: Total Fat 6 g 9% • Saturated Fat 2 g 10% • Cholesterol 20 mg 7% • Sodium 420 mg 18% • Total Carbohydrate 9 g 3% • Dietary Fiber 0 g 0% • Sugars 2 g • Protein 5 g • Vitamin A 2% • Vitamin C 0% • Calcium 4% • Iron 4% • **Dietary Exchanges:** 1/2 Starch, 1/2 High-Fat Meat, 1/2 Fat **OR** 1/2 Carbohydrate, 1/2 High-Fat Meat, 1/2 Fat

Turkey-Cranberry Quesadillas

Smoked turkey from the deli or leftover roast turkey, finely chopped, works equally well in these quesadillas.

PREP TIME: 25 MINUTES
MAKES 24 SERVINGS

8 (6- to 7-inch) flour tortillas

1 (10- or 12-oz.) container cranberry-orange sauce, thawed if frozen

6 oz. thinly sliced smoked turkey

5 oz. Havarti cheese, thinly sliced

1 tablespoon oil

1. Top each of 4 tortillas with 1 tablespoon of the cranberry-orange sauce; spread to edges. Top each with turkey, cheese and second tortilla.

2. Heat medium skillet over medium heat. Brush 1 side of 1 quesadilla with oil. Place, oiled side down, in medium skillet; press down with pancake turner. Cook 1 to 2 minutes or until browned.

3. Brush top side of quesadilla with oil; turn quesadilla. Cook an additional 1 to 2 minutes or until browned and cheese is melted. Repeat with remaining quesadillas.

4. To serve, cut each quesadilla into 6 wedges. Serve remaining cranberry-orange sauce as a dip with quesadillas.

NUTRITION INFORMATION PER SERVING: SERVING SIZE: $1/24$ of Recipe • Calories 100 • Calories from Fat 25 • % Daily Value: Total Fat 3 g 5% • Saturated Fat 1 g 5% • Cholesterol 10 mg 3% • Sodium 160 mg 7% • Total Carbohydrate 13 g 4% • Dietary Fiber 1 g 4% • Sugars 4 g • Protein 4 g • Vitamin A 0% • Vitamin C 2% • Calcium 6% • Iron 2% • **Dietary Exchanges:** 1 Starch, $1/2$ Fat **OR** 1 Carbohydrate, $1/2$ Fat

Fiesta Quesadillas

A quesadilla is like a grilled cheese sandwich, with cheese melted between tortillas instead of sliced bread. This hearty version features corn, beans and chiles.

PREP TIME: 25 MINUTES
MAKES 32 APPETIZERS

1 (10-oz.) can diced tomatoes with green chiles, drained

1 (7-oz.) can vacuum-packed whole kernel corn, drained

1 tablespoon chopped fresh cilantro

16 (6-inch) flour tortillas

1 cup fat-free refried beans

8 oz. (2 cups) shredded Mexican cheese blend

1. In medium bowl, combine tomatoes, corn and cilantro; mix well.

2. Spread each of 8 tortillas with 2 table-spoons refried beans. Top each of remaining 8 tortillas with ¼ cup cheese and scant 2 tablespoons corn mixture; spread evenly. Cover each with 1 bean-covered tortilla, bean side down.

3. In large nonstick skillet over medium heat, heat 1 quesadilla for 1 to 2 minutes on each side or until cheese is melted and tortilla is toasted. Remove quesadilla from skillet; repeat with remaining quesadillas.

4. To serve, cut each quesadilla into 4 wedges. If desired, serve with nonfat sour cream and salsa.

make-ahead tip

A large griddle heated to 400°F. can be used to heat 3 or 4 quesadillas at a time.

After removing from skillet, quesadillas can be wrapped in foil and placed in a warm oven until serving time.

NUTRITION INFORMATION PER SERVING: SERVING SIZE: 1 Appetizer • Calories 80 • Calories from Fat 25 • % Daily Value: Total Fat 3 g 5% • Saturated Fat 2 g 10% • Cholesterol 5 mg 2% • Sodium 190 mg 8% • Total Carbohydrate 9 g 3% • Dietary Fiber 1 g 4% • Sugars 1 g • Protein 3 g • Vitamin A 2% • Vitamin C 0% • Calcium 6% • Iron 2% • **Dietary Exchanges:** $1/2$ Starch, $1/2$ Fat **OR** $1/2$ Carbohydrate, $1/2$ Fat

Calabacita Quesadillas

These vegetable-spiked quesadillas make fine party fare or a good meatless lunch. *Calabacita* is Spanish for "little squash"—in this case, zucchini.

PREP TIME: 30 MINUTES
MAKES 24 APPETIZERS

1 tablespoon olive oil

1 small zucchini, thinly sliced

1 small onion, chopped

1 ear corn, husk removed, kernels removed,
    or 2/3 cup frozen whole kernel corn, thawed

1/2 teaspoon salt

6 (8-inch) flour tortillas

1 (4.5-oz.) can chopped green chiles, drained

6 oz. (1 1/2 cups) shredded Cheddar cheese

1 1/2 cups chunky-style salsa

1. Heat oil in large nonstick skillet over medium heat until hot. Add zucchini, onion, corn and salt; cook 4 to 5 minutes or just until vegetables are crisp-tender, stirring frequently.

2. Place 3 tortillas on work surface. Divide vegetable mixture evenly onto tortillas, spreading to within 1/2 inch of edges. Top with chiles; sprinkle with cheese. Top with remaining tortillas.

3. In same large nonstick skillet, cook each quesadilla over medium heat for 2 minutes. Carefully turn quesadilla; cook an additional 2 to 3 minutes.

4. To serve, cut each quesadilla into 8 wedges. Serve with salsa.

NUTRITION INFORMATION PER SERVING: SERVING SIZE: 1 Appetizer • Calories 80 • Calories from Fat 35 • % Daily Value: Total Fat 4 g 6% • Saturated Fat 2 g 10% • Cholesterol 5 mg 2% • Sodium 270 mg 11% • Total Carbohydrate 8 g 3% • Dietary Fiber 1 g 4% • Sugars 1 g • Protein 3 g • Vitamin A 6% • Vitamin C 4% • Calcium 8% • Iron 4% • **Dietary Exchanges:** 1/2 Starch, 1 Fat **OR** 1/2 Carbohydrate, 1 Fat

Taquitos

Tangy goat cheese comes as a surprise in these otherwise traditional mini tacos.

PREP TIME: 20 MINUTES
(READY IN 35 MINUTES)
MAKES 24 APPETIZERS

1 (15-oz.) can black beans, drained, rinsed

3/4 cup chunky-style salsa

1/4 cup chopped fresh cilantro

1 (3.8-oz.) pkg. (24 shells) fun-size mini taco shells

3 oz. chèvre (goat) cheese, crumbled (3/4 cup)

1. Heat oven to 350°F. In medium bowl, combine beans, salsa and cilantro; mix well.

2. Arrange taco shells in 13x9-inch pan. Spoon bean mixture into taco shells. Top each with cheese.

3. Bake at 350°F. for 12 to 15 minutes or until thoroughly heated.

NUTRITION INFORMATION PER SERVING: SERVING SIZE: 1 Appetizer • Calories 50 • Calories from Fat 20 • % Daily Value: Total Fat 2 g 3% • Saturated Fat 1 g 5% • Cholesterol 3 mg 1% • Sodium 120 mg 5% • Total Carbohydrate 6 g 2% • Dietary Fiber 1 g 4% • Sugars 1 g • Protein 2 g • Vitamin A 0% • Vitamin C 0% • Calcium 0% • Iron 2% • **Dietary Exchanges:** 1/2 Starch, 1/2 Fat **OR** 1/2 Carbohydrate, 1/2 Fat

Chicken Macadamia Appetizers

Prick the top of each nutty-chicken appetizer with a fork before baking, to let steam escape and keep the crust crisp.

PREP TIME: 40 MINUTES
(READY IN 1 HOUR 10 MINUTES)
MAKES 16 APPETIZERS

1 (4.25-oz.) can white meat chicken spread

¼ cup light cream cheese with roasted garlic
   (from 8-oz. tub)

¼ cup finely chopped green onions

⅓ cup coarsely chopped macadamia nuts or almonds

1 (15-oz.) pkg. refrigerated pie crusts, softened as
   directed on package

Water

½ cup Italian-style dry bread crumbs

Fresh cilantro sprigs, if desired

Green grapes, if desired

1. Heat oven to 400°F. In small bowl, combine chicken spread, cream cheese, green onions and nuts; mix well.

2. Remove crusts from pouches; press out fold lines. Using 2¼-inch round cutter, cut 16 rounds from each crust. (Rounds must be cut close together.)

3. Spoon about 1 tablespoon chicken mixture onto center of each of 16 rounds. Brush edges with water. Press remaining rounds slightly larger; fit each over chicken mixture. With fork, press edges to seal.

4. Brush top and bottom of each appetizer with water; coat generously with bread crumbs. Place on ungreased cookie sheet. Prick top of each appetizer with fork.

5. Bake at 400°F. for 18 to 23 minutes or until golden brown. Cool 5 minutes. Arrange warm appetizers on serving platter. Garnish with cilantro and grapes.

NUTRITION INFORMATION PER SERVING: SERVING SIZE: 1 Appetizer • Calories 180 • Calories from Fat 100 • % Daily Value: Total Fat 11 g 17% • Saturated Fat 4 g 20% • Cholesterol 15 mg 5% • Sodium 260 mg 11% • Total Carbohydrate 16 g 5% • Dietary Fiber 1 g 4% • Sugars 1 g • Protein 3 g • Vitamin A 0% • Vitamin C 0% • Calcium 0% • Iron 4% • **Dietary Exchanges:** 1 Starch, 2 Fat **OR** 1 Carbohydrate, 2 Fat

Green Chile and Cheese Half-Moons

Italian (flat-leaf) parsley and cilantro look similar, but their personalities are strikingly different. Parsley is flavorful but mild and compatible with almost any food or herb, while cilantro is much more assertive and distinctive.

PREP TIME: 20 MINUTES
(READY IN 45 MINUTES)
MAKES 16 APPETIZERS

4 oz. (1 cup) finely shredded Muenster or Monterey Jack cheese

2 tablespoons finely chopped green onion tops

2 tablespoons finely chopped fresh cilantro or parsley

Dash salt

1 (4.5-oz.) can chopped green chiles, drained

1 (1 lb. 1.3-oz.) can large refrigerated corn biscuits or 1 (1 lb. 0.3-oz.) can large refrigerated buttermilk biscuits

1. Heat oven to 375°F. Spray large cookie sheet with nonstick cooking spray. In small bowl, combine cheese, green onions, cilantro, salt and green chiles; mix well.

2. Separate dough into 8 biscuits. With serrated knife, cut each biscuit in half horizontally to make 16 rounds. Press or roll each to form 3½-inch round. Place 1 tablespoon cheese mixture in center of each round. Fold dough over filling; press edges with fork to seal. Form each filled biscuit into crescent shape. Place on sprayed cookie sheet.

3. Bake at 375°F. for 11 to 16 minutes or until golden brown. With toothpick, make face to resemble moon on each crescent. Cool 5 minutes before serving.

NUTRITION INFORMATION PER SERVING: SERVING SIZE: 1 Appetizer • Calories 140 • Calories from Fat 60 • % Daily Value: Total Fat 7 g 11% • Saturated Fat 3 g 15% • Cholesterol 5 mg 2% • Sodium 370 mg 15% • Total Carbohydrate 14 g 5% • Dietary Fiber 0 g 0% • Sugars 3 g • Protein 4 g • Vitamin A 2% • Vitamin C 6% • Calcium 6% • Iron 4% • **Dietary Exchanges:** 1 Starch, 1½ Fat **OR** 1 Carbohydrate, 1½ Fat

Spinach Quiche Bites

These mini quiches are delicious and inexpensive to make. To form individual quiche tartlets, press rounds of pie dough into miniature muffin cups.

PREP TIME: 30 MINUTES
(READY IN 1 HOUR 5 MINUTES)
MAKES 24 APPETIZERS

1 (15-oz.) pkg. refrigerated pie crusts, softened as directed on package

2 slices bacon

1/4 cup chopped green onions

2 eggs

1/2 cup half-and-half

1/3 cup grated Parmesan cheese

1/4 teaspoon salt

1/8 teaspoon nutmeg

1 (9-oz.) pkg. frozen spinach in a pouch, thawed, squeezed to drain

1. Heat oven to 375°F. Remove pie crusts from pouches. Unfold 1 pie crust; press out fold lines. With 2½-inch round cutter, cut 12 rounds. Press each round in bottom and up sides of ungreased miniature muffin cup. Repeat with second crust.

2. Cook bacon in medium skillet until brown and crisp. Drain on paper towels. Add green onions to same skillet with bacon drippings; cook 2 to 3 minutes or until tender, stirring constantly. Drain.

3. Place green onions in medium bowl. Crumble bacon; add to onion. Add eggs to bacon and onion; beat well. Stir in half-and-half, cheese, salt and nutmeg. Add spinach; mix well. Divide mixture evenly into crust-lined cups.

4. Bake at 375°F. for 20 to 25 minutes or until puffed and golden brown. Cool in pan on wire rack for 10 minutes. Loosen and remove quiches from pan with tip of knife. Serve warm or cool. Store in refrigerator.

make-ahead tip

Prepare and bake quiche bites as directed in recipe. Place in shallow pan; cover. Refrigerate up to 24 hours. To reheat, uncover. Heat at 375°F. for 20 to 25 minutes or until thoroughly heated.

NUTRITION INFORMATION PER SERVING: SERVING SIZE: 1 Appetizer • Calories 80 • Calories from Fat 45 • % Daily Value: Total Fat 5 g 8% • Saturated Fat 2 g 10% • Cholesterol 25 mg 8% • Sodium 135 mg 6% • Total Carbohydrate 7 g 2% • Dietary Fiber 0 g 0% • Sugars 1 g • Protein 2 g • Vitamin A 8% • Vitamin C 2% • Calcium 4% • Iron 0% • **Dietary Exchanges:** ½ Starch, 1 Fat **OR** ½ Carbohydrate, 1 Fat

Mini Swiss Quiches

Nutmeg subtly rounds out the flavor in these tiny green onion and cheese quiches.

PREP TIME: 25 MINUTES
(READY IN 1 HOUR 10 MINUTES)
MAKES 24 APPETIZERS

1 (15-oz.) pkg. refrigerated pie crusts, softened as directed on package

6 oz. (1½ cups) shredded Swiss cheese

2 tablespoons sliced green onions

1 tablespoon chopped pimientos

2 eggs

½ cup milk

¼ teaspoon salt

Dash nutmeg

1. Heat oven to 375°F. Spray 24 miniature muffin cups with nonstick cooking spray. Remove pie crusts from pouches. Unfold 1 pie crust; press out fold lines. With floured 2½-inch round cutter, cut 12 rounds. Press each round in bottom and up sides of sprayed muffin cup. Repeat with second crust.

2. Place 1 tablespoon cheese in each cup. Top each with a few green onion slices and pimiento pieces.

3. In 2-cup measuring cup, combine eggs, milk, salt and nutmeg; beat well with fork. Pour mixture into crust-lined cups, filling each to within ¼ inch of top.

4. Bake at 375°F. for 25 to 30 minutes or until golden brown. Cool slightly; lift quiches from cups with tip of knife. Serve warm.

make-ahead tip

Prepare quiche cups and top with cheese, green onions and pimiento as directed in recipe. Combine the egg mixture as directed. Cover each separately; refrigerate up to 6 hours. Just before serving, pour egg mixture into quiche cups as directed in recipe. Bake as directed in recipe.

NUTRITION INFORMATION PER SERVING: SERVING SIZE: 1 Appetizer • Calories 80 • Calories from Fat 45 • % Daily Value: Total Fat 5 g 8% • Saturated Fat 3 g 15% • Cholesterol 25 mg 8% • Sodium 90 mg 4% • Total Carbohydrate 6 g 2% • Dietary Fiber 0 g 0% • Sugars 1 g • Protein 3 g • Vitamin A 2% • Vitamin C 0% • Calcium 8% • Iron 0% • **Dietary Exchanges:** ½ Starch, 1 Fat **OR** ½ Carbohydrate, 1 Fat

Portobello and Brie Cups

Portobello mushrooms are large, meaty mushrooms that can measure several inches across. Chopped fresh portobellos combine beautifully with melted Brie in these warm two-bite appetizers.

PREP TIME: 45 MINUTES
MAKES 24 APPETIZERS

- 1 (6-oz.) pkg. fresh portobello mushrooms
- 2 tablespoons margarine or butter
- 2 garlic cloves, minced
- ¼ cup sliced green onions
- 1 teaspoon Dijon mustard
- 1 (8-oz.) can refrigerated crescent dinner rolls
- 3 oz. Brie cheese

1. Heat oven to 375°F. Spray 24 miniature muffin cups with nonstick cooking spray. Brush mushrooms or wipe clean with damp cloth. Finely chop.

2. In small skillet, combine mushrooms, margarine and garlic; cook over medium heat for 5 to 6 minutes or until margarine is absorbed and mushrooms are tender, stirring occasionally. Stir in green onions and mustard.

3. Separate dough into 4 rectangles. Firmly press perforations to seal. Cut each rectangle in half lengthwise; make 2 crosswise cuts to form 6 squares of dough from each rectangle. Press 1 square of dough into each sprayed muffin cup, letting corners stand above top of cups. Spoon about 1 tablespoon mushroom mixture into each cup.

4. Bake at 375°F. for 10 to 12 minutes or until light golden brown. Meanwhile, cut cheese into 24 pieces.

5. Remove cups from oven. Place 1 piece of cheese over mushroom mixture in each cup.

6. Return to oven; bake an additional 2 to 4 minutes or until cups are golden brown and cheese is softened. Cool 5 minutes; remove from muffin cups. Cool slightly before serving.

NUTRITION INFORMATION PER SERVING: SERVING SIZE: 1 Appetizer • Calories 60 • Calories from Fat 35 • % Daily Value: Total Fat 4 g 6% • Saturated Fat 1 g 5% • Cholesterol 4 mg 1% • Sodium 110 mg 5% • Total Carbohydrate 4 g 1% • Dietary Fiber 0 g 0% • Sugars 1 g • Protein 2 g • Vitamin A 0% • Vitamin C 0% • Calcium 0% • Iron 0% • **Dietary Exchanges:** ½ Starch, ½ Fat **OR** ½ Carbohydrate, ½ Fat

Gouda and Walnut Tartlets

Be sure to soften the refrigerated pie crust as directed on the package. If you try to unfold the dough before it's ready, it is likely to crack.

PREP TIME: 1 HOUR
MAKES 24 TARTLETS

1 (15-oz.) pkg. refrigerated pie crusts, softened as directed on package

2 eggs

¼ cup half-and-half

2 teaspoons all-purpose flour

¼ teaspoon salt

6 oz. (1½ cups) shredded Gouda cheese

⅓ cup chopped walnuts

⅓ cup chopped drained roasted red bell peppers (from 7.25-oz. jar)

¼ cup chopped fresh chives

1. Heat oven to 375°F. Remove pie crusts from pouches. Unfold crusts; press out fold lines. With 2½-inch round cutter, cut 12 rounds from each crust. Press each round in bottom and up sides of ungreased miniature muffin cup. Reserve dough scraps.

2. Beat eggs in medium bowl. Add half-and-half, flour and salt; beat well. Sprinkle cheese and walnuts into each crust-lined cup. Pour egg mixture into each cup. Sprinkle each with roasted peppers and chives.

3. Bake at 375°F. for 19 to 22 minutes or until filling is set and edges are light golden brown. Cool 5 minutes; remove from pans.

4. If desired, cut small star or other shapes from dough scraps that have been rolled together; place on ungreased cookie sheets. Bake at 375°F. for 7 to 9 minutes or until golden brown. Top each tartlet with baked cutout. Store in refrigerator.

make-ahead tip

Prepare tartlet cups and top with cheese and walnuts as directed in recipe. Combine the egg mixture as directed. Cover each separately; refrigerate up to 6 hours. Just before serving, pour egg mixture into tartlet cups and top as directed in recipe. Bake as directed in recipe. Cut-out shapes can be prepared and placed on cookie sheet. Bake as directed.

NUTRITION INFORMATION PER SERVING: SERVING SIZE: 1 Tartlet • Calories 120 • Calories from Fat 70 • % Daily Value: Total Fat 8 g 12% • Saturated Fat 3 g 15% • Cholesterol 30 mg 10% • Sodium 160 mg 7% • Total Carbohydrate 10 g 3% • Dietary Fiber 0 g 0% • Sugars 1 g • Protein 3 g • Vitamin A 4% • Vitamin C 4% • Calcium 6% • Iron 0% • **Dietary Exchanges:** ½ Starch, 1½ Fat **OR** ½ Carbohydrate, 1½ Fat

Mushroom-Garlic Cream Tartlets

Squares of crescent dough hold mounds of creamy mushrooms flecked with fresh parsley.

PREP TIME: 35 MINUTES
MAKES 24 TARTLETS

2 tablespoons butter

1 (8-oz.) pkg. fresh mushrooms, finely chopped

1 tablespoon all-purpose flour

1 tablespoon finely chopped onion

2 garlic cloves, minced

½ cup whipping cream

¼ cup grated Parmesan cheese

1 (8-oz.) can refrigerated crescent dinner rolls

2 tablespoons chopped fresh parsley

1. Heat oven to 350°F. Melt butter in large skillet over medium heat. Add mushrooms, flour, onion and garlic; mix well. Cook 5 minutes or until vegetables are tender, stirring frequently. Add cream and cheese; mix well. Cook 2 to 3 minutes or until most of liquid has evaporated, stirring frequently.

2. Unroll dough into 2 long rectangles; firmly press perforations to seal. Cut each rectangle into 12 squares. Place 1 square in each of 24 ungreased miniature muffin cups. Firmly press in bottom and up sides, leaving corners of dough extended over edges of each cup. Spoon 1 heaping teaspoon mushroom mixture into each cup.

3. Bake at 350°F. for 9 to 12 minutes or until golden brown. Sprinkle with parsley. Cool 5 minutes. Remove tartlets from pan. Serve warm. Store in refrigerator.

NUTRITION INFORMATION PER SERVING: SERVING SIZE: 1 Tartlet • Calories 70 • Calories from Fat 45 • % Daily Value: Total Fat 5 g 8% • Saturated Fat 2 g 10% • Cholesterol 10 mg 3% • Sodium 95 mg 4% • Total Carbohydrate 5 g 2% • Dietary Fiber 0 g 0% • Sugars 1 g • Protein 1 g • Vitamin A 2% • Vitamin C 0% • Calcium 0% • Iron 0% • **Dietary Exchanges:** ½ Starch, 1 Fat **OR** ½ Carbohydrate, 1 Fat

1. Heat oven to 375°F. Unfold pie crust; place on ungreased cookie sheet. Press out fold lines.

2. In medium bowl, combine all filling ingredients; mix well. Spread over crust to within 1 inch of edges. Fold crust edges over filling to form 1-inch border; flute. (See photo below.)

3. Bake at 375°F. for 25 to 35 minutes or until crust is golden brown. Sprinkle with cilantro. Let stand 10 minutes before serving. Cut into wedges. Serve warm.

NUTRITION INFORMATION PER SERVING: SERVING SIZE: 1/16 of Recipe • Calories 150 • Calories from Fat 110 • % Daily Value: Total Fat 12 g 18% • Saturated Fat 4 g 20% • Cholesterol 15 mg 5% • Sodium 180 mg 8% • Total Carbohydrate 8 g 3% • Dietary Fiber 0 g 0% • Sugars 1 g • Protein 3 g • Vitamin A 6% • Vitamin C 10% • Calcium 8% • Iron 0% • **Dietary Exchanges:** ½ Starch, 2½ Fat **OR** ½ Carbohydrate, 2½ Fat

Tex-Mex Appetizer Tart

Fold over the edge of the dough to keep the filling from running out, then crimp the edge. The simplest crimp is just a two-finger pinch that keeps the dough from unfolding in the hot oven.

PREP TIME: 15 MINUTES
(READY IN 1 HOUR)
MAKES 16 SERVINGS

CRUST
1 refrigerated pie crust (from 15-oz. pkg.), softened as directed on package

FILLING
6 oz. (1½ cups) shredded colby-Monterey Jack cheese blend

½ cup roasted red bell peppers (from 7.25-oz. jar), drained, chopped

½ cup mayonnaise

1 (4.5-oz.) can chopped green chiles

TOPPING
¼ cup chopped fresh cilantro or parsley

Gruyère Chicken Triangles

Phyllo dough, available frozen at the grocery store, needs to thaw slowly in the fridge—overnight. Room temperature thawing may cause the sheets to stick together. The *fines herbes,* sold in the spice section, usually includes chervil, chives, parsley, tarragon, and sometimes other herbs as well.

PREP TIME: 1 HOUR 30 MINUTES
(READY IN 1 HOUR 50 MINUTES)
MAKES 60 APPETIZERS

1 cup finely chopped cooked chicken

1 cup chopped cooked broccoli

4 oz. (1 cup) shredded Gruyère cheese

¼ cup chopped roasted red bell peppers
    (from 7.25-oz. jar)

½ teaspoon dried fines herbes

20 (17x12-inch) sheets frozen phyllo (filo) pastry,
    thawed

Nonstick cooking spray

Paprika

1. Heat oven to 375°F. In medium bowl, combine chicken, broccoli, cheese, roasted peppers and fines herbes; mix well.

2. Unroll phyllo sheets; cover with plastic wrap or cloth towel to prevent drying out. Place 1 phyllo sheet on work surface; spray with nonstick cooking spray. Top with second phyllo sheet; spray again. With sharp knife, cut phyllo into six 12-inch-long strips.

3. For each appetizer, place 1 rounded teaspoon chicken mixture at end of 1 strip. (See photo at left.) Fold 1 corner of strip diagonally over filling. Continue folding to end of strip into a triangular bundle, as if folding a flag. Place on ungreased cookie sheets. Repeat with remaining phyllo sheets.

4. Bake at 375°F. for 15 to 20 minutes or until golden brown. Sprinkle bundles with paprika. Serve warm.

NUTRITION INFORMATION PER SERVING: SERVING SIZE: 1 Appetizer • Calories 50 • Calories from Fat 25 • % Daily Value: Total Fat 3 g 5% • Saturated Fat 1 g 5% • Cholesterol 4 mg 1% • Sodium 40 mg 2% • Total Carbohydrate 4 g 1% • Dietary Fiber 0 g 0% • Sugars 0 g • Protein 2 g • Vitamin A 2% • Vitamin C 4% • Calcium 2% • Iron 0% • **Dietary Exchanges:** ½ Starch, ½ Fat **OR** ½ Carbohydrate, ½ Fat

Crab and Asiago Bundles

(Pictured on page 149.)

Asiago is a hard Italian cheese. Parmesan or romano may be substituted.

PREP TIME: 30 MINUTES
(READY IN 55 MINUTES)
MAKES 12 APPETIZERS

2 teaspoons olive or vegetable oil

¼ cup sliced green onions

1 garlic clove, minced

1 (6-oz.) can crabmeat, drained

1 (2-oz.) jar diced pimientos, drained

2 oz. (½ cup) shredded Asiago cheese

¼ cup Italian-style dry bread crumbs

2 tablespoons chopped fresh basil

2 tablespoons mayonnaise

4 (18x14-inch) sheets frozen phyllo (filo) pastry, thawed

3 tablespoons butter, melted

1. Heat oven to 350°F. Heat oil in medium skillet over medium heat until hot. Add green onions and garlic; cook and stir 1 to 2 minutes or until tender. Remove skillet from heat. Add all remaining ingredients except phyllo sheets and butter; mix well.

2. Unroll phyllo sheets; cover with plastic wrap or towel. Place 1 phyllo sheet on work surface. Brush lightly with butter. Layer with 2 more phyllo sheets, brushing each with butter. Top with last phyllo sheet. Cut stack into 12 (4-inch) squares.

3. Spoon about 4 teaspoons filling in center of each square. (See photo.) For each bundle, bring 2 opposite corners to center to overlap, covering filling. Bring 2 remaining corners to center; press lightly. Place on ungreased cookie sheet. Brush top of each with remaining butter.

4. Bake at 350°F. for 20 to 25 minutes or until golden brown. Let stand 10 minutes before serving.

NUTRITION INFORMATION PER SERVING: SERVING SIZE: 1 Appetizer • Calories 110 • Calories from Fat 60 • % Daily Value: Total Fat 7 g 11% • Saturated Fat 3 g 15% • Cholesterol 20 mg 7% • Sodium 220 mg 9% • Total Carbohydrate 6 g 2% • Dietary Fiber 0 g 0% • Sugars 0 g • Protein 5 g • Vitamin A 6% • Vitamin C 8% • Calcium 8% • Iron 4% • **Dietary Exchanges:** ½ Starch, ½ Very Lean Meat, 1 Fat **OR** ½ Carbohydrate, ½ Very Lean Meat, 1 Fat

Wild Mushroom-Stuffed Phyllo Bundles

Phyllo, often used in Greek and Middle Eastern cooking, consists of paper-thin layers of pastry. Traditionally it is made from scratch, then stretched until it's large enough to cover an entire tabletop.

PREP TIME: 35 MINUTES
(READY IN 55 MINUTES)
MAKES 24 APPETIZERS

1 tablespoon butter

½ cup finely chopped red bell pepper

1 garlic clove, minced

1½ cups chopped fresh wild mushrooms (shiitake, portobello or cremini)

¼ cup chopped fresh chives

2 tablespoons shredded fresh Parmesan cheese

¼ teaspoon salt

¼ teaspoon dried marjoram leaves

¼ teaspoon dried sage leaves

⅛ teaspoon pepper

6 (17x12-inch) sheets frozen phyllo (filo) pastry, thawed

Nonstick cooking spray

Fresh chives, if desired

1. Melt butter in medium skillet over medium heat. Add bell pepper and garlic; cook and stir 1 to 2 minutes or until tender. Add mushrooms; cook 2 to 3 minutes or until tender. Remove from heat. Stir in chives, Parmesan cheese, salt, marjoram, sage and pepper; mix well.

2. Heat oven to 350°F. Unroll phyllo sheets; cover with plastic wrap or towel. Place 1 phyllo sheet on work surface; spray with nonstick cooking spray. Layer with 2 more phyllo sheets, spraying each with cooking spray. With sharp knife, cut through all layers of phyllo sheets to make 12 squares.

3. Place about 1 heaping teaspoon mushroom mixture in center of each square. Bring up edges of pastry; twist together with circular motion to seal. Place on ungreased cookie sheets. Repeat with remaining 3 phyllo sheets and mushroom-cheese mixture.

4. Bake at 350°F. for 18 to 20 minutes or until golden brown. If desired, sprinkle with chopped fresh chives.

NUTRITION INFORMATION PER SERVING: SERVING SIZE: 1 Appetizer • Calories 35 • Calories from Fat 20 • % Daily Value: Total Fat 2 g 3% • Saturated Fat 1 g 5% • Cholesterol 0 mg 0% • Sodium 60 mg 3% • Total Carbohydrate 3 g 1% • Dietary Fiber 0 g 0% • Sugars 0 g • Protein 1 g • Vitamin A 4% • Vitamin C 6% • Calcium 0% • Iron 0% • **Dietary Exchanges:** ½ Fat

Shrimp and Crescent Pinwheels

These elegant spirals require only a half-cup of shrimp, making them easy on the budget.

PREP TIME: 30 MINUTES
MAKES 16 APPETIZERS

1 (8-oz.) can refrigerated crescent dinner rolls

1/3 cup gourmet spreadable cheese with garlic and herbs (from 4- to 6.5-oz. container)

1/2 cup coarsely chopped cooked shrimp

2 tablespoons chopped green onions

1. Heat oven to 350°F. Spray cookie sheet with nonstick cooking spray. Unroll dough into 2 long rectangles. Firmly press perforations to seal. Spread each rectangle with cheese. Sprinkle each with shrimp and green onions; press in gently.

2. Starting at short side of each rectangle, roll up tightly; gently press edge to seal. Cut each roll into 8 slices. Arrange slices, cut side down, on sprayed cookie sheet.

3. Bake at 350°F. for 15 to 20 minutes or until edges are deep golden brown.

make-ahead tip

Prepare pinwheels as directed in recipe; place on cookie sheet. Do not bake. Cover with plastic wrap; refrigerate up to 2 hours. Uncover; bake as directed in recipe.

NUTRITION INFORMATION PER SERVING: SERVING SIZE: 1 Appetizer • Calories 70 • Calories from Fat 35 • % Daily Value: Total Fat 4 g 6% • Saturated Fat 2 g 10% • Cholesterol 10 mg 3% • Sodium 150 mg 6% • Total Carbohydrate 6 g 2% • Dietary Fiber 0 g 0% • Sugars 1 g • Protein 2 g • Vitamin A 0% • Vitamin C 0% • Calcium 0% • Iron 2% • **Dietary Exchanges:** 1/2 Starch, 1 Fat **OR** 1/2 Carbohydrate, 1 Fat

Easy Italian Pinwheels

Roll mozzarella and pepperoni in crescent dough, then cut the resulting log crosswise to reveal tasty spirals.

PREP TIME: 40 MINUTES
MAKES 24 APPETIZERS

2 oz. (1/2 cup) shredded mozzarella cheese

1/2 cup sliced pepperoni, finely chopped

1/4 teaspoon dried oregano leaves

1 egg yolk

1 (8-oz.) can refrigerated crescent dinner rolls

1 egg white, beaten

1. Heat oven to 375°F. In small bowl, combine cheese, pepperoni, oregano and egg yolk; mix well.

2. Separate dough into 4 rectangles. Firmly press perforations to seal. Spread each rectangle with about 3 tablespoons pepperoni mixture.

3. Starting at shortest side, roll up each rectangle; pinch edges to seal. Cut each roll into 6 slices. Place, cut side down, 1 inch apart on ungreased cookie sheet. Brush with beaten egg white.

4. Bake at 375°F. for 12 to 15 minutes or until golden brown.

make-ahead tip

Prepare pinwheels as directed in recipe; place on cookie sheet. Do not bake. Cover with plastic wrap; refrigerate up to 2 hours. Uncover; bake as directed in recipe.

NUTRITION INFORMATION PER SERVING: SERVING SIZE: 1 Appetizer • Calories 60 • Calories from Fat 35 • % Daily Value: Total Fat 4 g 6% • Saturated Fat 1 g 5% • Cholesterol 15 mg 5% • Sodium 170 mg 7% • Total Carbohydrate 4 g 1% • Dietary Fiber 0 g 0% • Sugars 1 g • Protein 2 g • Vitamin A 0% • Vitamin C 0% • Calcium 2% • Iron 0% • **Dietary Exchanges:** 1/2 Starch, 1/2 Fat **OR** 1/2 Carbohydrate, 1/2 Fat

Easy Pesto Pinwheels

Basil and pepper are always good partners, and the red-green combination is well suited for a holiday buffet.

PREP TIME: 30 MINUTES
MAKES 16 APPETIZERS

1 (8-oz.) can refrigerated crescent dinner rolls

⅓ cup purchased pesto

¼ cup chopped roasted red bell peppers
   (from 7.25-oz. jar)

1. Heat oven to 350°F. Unroll dough into 2 long rectangles. Firmly press perforations to seal. Spread rectangles with pesto to within ¼ inch of edges. Sprinkle with roasted peppers.

2. Starting at shortest side, roll up each rectangle; pinch edges to seal. Cut each roll into 8 slices. Place, cut side down, on ungreased cookie sheet.

3. Bake at 350°F. for 13 to 17 minutes or until golden brown. Immediately remove from cookie sheet.

make-ahead tip

Prepare pinwheels as directed in recipe; place on cookie sheet. Do not bake. Cover with plastic wrap; refrigerate up to 2 hours. Uncover; bake as directed in recipe.

NUTRITION INFORMATION PER SERVING: SERVING SIZE: 1 Appetizer • Calories 60 • Calories from Fat 35 • % Daily Value: Total Fat 4 g 6% • Saturated Fat 1 g 5% • Cholesterol 0 mg 0% • Sodium 125 mg 5% • Total Carbohydrate 6 g 2% • Dietary Fiber 0 g 0% • Sugars 1 g • Protein 1 g • Vitamin A 0% • Vitamin C 4% • Calcium 0% • Iron 0% • **Dietary Exchanges:** ½ Starch, ½ Fat **OR** ½ Carbohydrate, ½ Fat

Sun-Dried Tomato and Parmesan Pinwheels

An easy snip-and-fold technique turns dough squares into playful pinwheel shapes.

PREP TIME: 35 MINUTES
MAKES 32 APPETIZERS

1 (8-oz.) can refrigerated crescent dinner rolls

½ cup grated Parmesan cheese

⅓ cup chopped drained sun-dried tomatoes packed
   in oil

1. Heat oven to 375°F. Line cookie sheets with parchment paper or spray with nonstick cooking spray. Unroll dough; separate crosswise into 2 sections. Sprinkle 2 tablespoons of the cheese onto 1 section; pat into dough. Turn section over; sprinkle other side with 2 tablespoons cheese. Pat and press dough to form 8-inch square, sealing perforations. Repeat with second section of dough.

2. Cut each section into 16 squares. In each square, make diagonal slash in each corner almost to center of square. Fold tips of alternate slashed corners toward center, forming a pinwheel. Place on paper-lined cookie sheet. In center of each pinwheel, place ¼ to ½ teaspoon sun-dried tomatoes.

3. Bake at 375°F. for 8 to 10 minutes or until golden brown. Immediately remove from cookie sheet.

make-ahead tip

Prepare pinwheels as directed in recipe; place on cookie sheet. Do not bake. Cover with plastic wrap; refrigerate up to 2 hours. Uncover; bake as directed in recipe.

NUTRITION INFORMATION PER SERVING: SERVING SIZE: 1 Appetizer • Calories 35 • Calories from Fat 20 • % Daily Value: Total Fat 2 g 3% • Saturated Fat 1 g 5% • Cholesterol 0 mg 0% • Sodium 85 mg 4% • Total Carbohydrate 3 g 1% • Dietary Fiber 0 g 0% • Sugars 1 g • Protein 1 g • Vitamin A 0% • Vitamin C 0% • Calcium 2% • Iron 0% • **Dietary Exchanges:** ½ Fat

EASY PESTO PINWHEELS; SHRIMP AND PINEAPPLE KABOBS, PAGE 162; SPICY HONEY CHICKEN DRUMMETTES, PAGE 157

Mediterranean Crescent Pinwheels

(Pictured on page 233.)

Use a serrated knife with a gentle sawing motion to slice the dough without squashing it.

PREP TIME: 25 MINUTES
(READY IN 45 MINUTES)
MAKES 20 APPETIZERS

1 (8-oz.) can refrigerated crescent dinner rolls

½ lb. prosciutto or cooked ham, thinly sliced

4 oz. (1 cup) crumbled feta cheese

½ teaspoon pepper

1 tablespoon olive or vegetable oil

6 tablespoons chopped fresh basil

1. Heat oven to 375°F. Spray cookie sheets with nonstick cooking spray. Separate dough into 4 rectangles; place on lightly floured surface. Firmly press perforations to seal. Press or roll each to form 8x5-inch rectangle.

2. Arrange ¼ of prosciutto slices evenly over each rectangle. In small bowl, combine cheese, pepper and oil; mix well. Sprinkle mixture evenly over prosciutto on each rectangle. Sprinkle with basil.

3. Starting at short side of each rectangle, roll up; seal long edges. With serrated knife, cut each roll into 5 slices. Place, cut side up, on sprayed cookie sheets.

4. Bake at 375°F. for 15 to 20 minutes or until golden brown. Immediately remove from cookie sheets.

make-ahead tip

Prepare pinwheels as directed in recipe; place on cookie sheet. Do not bake. Cover with plastic wrap; refrigerate up to 2 hours. Uncover; bake as directed in recipe.

NUTRITION INFORMATION PER SERVING: SERVING SIZE: 1 Appetizer • Calories 80 • Calories from Fat 45 • % Daily Value: Total Fat 5 g 8% • Saturated Fat 2 g 10% • Cholesterol 10 mg 3% • Sodium 310 mg 13% • Total Carbohydrate 5 g 2% • Dietary Fiber 0 g 0% • Sugars 1 g • Protein 4 g • Vitamin A 0% • Vitamin C 0% • Calcium 4% • Iron 2% • **Dietary Exchanges:** ½ Starch, ½ High-Fat Meat **OR** ½ Carbohydrate, ½ High-Fat Meat

Olive Crescent Twists

These tender breadsticks are studded with chopped olives and topped with a sprinkling of Parmesan.

PREP TIME: 30 MINUTES
MAKES 16 APPETIZERS

¾ cup well-drained mixed olives

1 tablespoon olive oil

¼ teaspoon garlic powder

1 (8-oz.) can refrigerated crescent dinner rolls

1 egg, beaten

2 tablespoons grated Parmesan cheese

1. Heat oven to 375°F. Lightly grease cookie sheets or spray with nonstick cooking spray. In food processor bowl with metal blade or blender container, combine olives, oil and garlic powder; process with on/off pulses until finely chopped.

2. Separate dough into 4 rectangles. Press each to form 7x4-inch rectangle, pressing perforations to seal. Brush dough rectangles with beaten egg. Evenly spread olive mixture on 2 of the rectangles. Top with remaining 2 rectangles, egg-brushed side down; press down.

3. With thin sharp knife, cut each filled rectangle crosswise into 8 strips. Place strips 1 inch apart on greased cookie sheets, twisting each 2 or 3 times. Brush tops of dough with beaten egg. Sprinkle strips lightly with cheese.

4. Bake at 375°F. for 10 to 13 minutes or until golden brown. Serve warm or cool.

make-ahead tip

Prepare twists as directed in recipe; place on cookie sheet. Do not bake. Cover with plastic wrap; refrigerate up to 2 hours. Uncover; bake as directed in recipe.

NUTRITION INFORMATION PER SERVING: SERVING SIZE: 1 Appetizer • Calories 90 • Calories from Fat 50 • % Daily Value: Total Fat 6 g 9% • Saturated Fat 1 g 5% • Cholesterol 15 mg 5% • Sodium 260 mg 11% • Total Carbohydrate 6 g 2% • Dietary Fiber 0 g 0% • Sugars 1 g • Protein 2 g • Vitamin A 0% • Vitamin C 0% • Calcium 0% • Iron 2% • **Dietary Exchanges:** ½ Starch, 1 Fat **OR** ½ Carbohydrate, 1 Fat

Flaky Crescent Twists

Look for the sun-dried tomato spread in the produce section of the supermarket.

PREP TIME: 15 MINUTES
(READY IN 35 MINUTES)
MAKES 16 APPETIZERS

¼ cup sun-dried tomato spread (from 9-oz. jar)

¼ cup grated Parmesan cheese

1 (8-oz.) can refrigerated crescent dinner rolls

1 egg, beaten

1. Heat oven to 375°F. Lightly spray cookie sheets with nonstick cooking spray. In small bowl, combine tomato spread and cheese; mix well.

2. Separate dough into 4 rectangles. Press each to form 7x4-inch rectangle, pressing perforations to seal. Evenly spread pesto mixture onto 2 of the rectangles. Top with remaining 2 rectangles; press down.

3. With thin sharp knife, cut each filled rectangle crosswise into 8 strips. Place strips 1 inch apart on greased cookie sheets, twisting each 2 or 3 times. Brush tops of dough with egg. Discard any remaining egg mixture.

4. Bake at 375°F. for 11 to 17 minutes or until golden brown. Serve warm or cool.

NUTRITION INFORMATION PER SERVING: SERVING SIZE: 1 Appetizer • Calories 80 • Calories from Fat 45 • % Daily Value: Total Fat 5 g 8% • Saturated Fat 1 g 5% • Cholesterol 15 mg 5% • Sodium 135 mg 6% • Total Carbohydrate 6 g 2% • Dietary Fiber 0 g 0% • Sugars 1 g • Protein 2 g • Vitamin A 0% • Vitamin C 0% • Calcium 2% • Iron 0% • **Dietary Exchanges:** ½ Starch, 1 Fat **OR** ½ Carbohydrate, 1 Fat

Pesto Crescent Twists with Feta Spread

The creamy cheese spread, flavored with a hint of pesto, is also a good spread for crackers or a dip for fresh cut-up vegetables.

PREP TIME: 20 MINUTES
(READY IN 40 MINUTES)
MAKES 16 APPETIZERS

TWISTS

2 (8-oz.) cans refrigerated crescent dinner rolls

½ cup purchased pesto

2 tablespoons finely chopped walnuts

SPREAD

¼ cup sour cream

4 oz. (1 cup) crumbled feta cheese

1 (3-oz.) pkg. cream cheese, softened

2 teaspoons olive oil

1 teaspoon purchased pesto

1. Heat oven to 375°F. Grease cookie sheets. Unroll 1 can of dough onto cutting board or sheet of waxed paper. Firmly press perforations to seal. Press or roll to form 13x7-inch rectangle. In small bowl, combine ½ cup pesto and walnuts; mix well. Spread mixture over dough.

2. Unroll remaining can of dough. Firmly press perforations to seal. Press or roll to form 13x7-inch rectangle. Carefully place dough rectangle over pesto and walnut filling. Cut filled dough in half crosswise to make two 7x6½-inch pieces. Cut each half into 8 strips. Twist each strip tightly; place on greased cookie sheets.

3. Bake at 375°F. for 14 to 19 minutes or until golden brown.

4. Meanwhile, in medium bowl, combine sour cream, feta cheese and cream cheese; mix until well blended. Place in small serving bowl. In another small bowl, combine oil and 1 teaspoon pesto. Drizzle over cheese mixture. With tip of knife, stir to marble. Serve warm twists with spread. Store any remaining spread in refrigerator.

NUTRITION INFORMATION PER SERVING: SERVING SIZE: 1 Appetizer • Calories 200 • Calories from Fat 140 • % Daily Value: Total Fat 15 g 23% • Saturated Fat 5 g 25% • Cholesterol 15 mg 5% • Sodium 370 mg 15% • Total Carbohydrate 12 g 4% • Dietary Fiber 0 g 0% • Sugars 3 g • Protein 4 g • Vitamin A 4% • Vitamin C 0% • Calcium 8% • Iron 4% • **Dietary Exchanges:** 1 Starch, 2½ Fat **OR** 1 Carbohydrate, 2½ Fat

Sausage Snack Wraps

These mini "pig-in-blanket" snacks may remind you of a cocktail party from a generation ago, and they are still snapped up just as quickly by kids and grown-ups alike.

PREP TIME: 15 MINUTES
(READY IN 30 MINUTES)
MAKES 48 APPETIZERS

2 (8-oz.) cans refrigerated crescent dinner rolls

48 fully cooked cocktail smoked sausage links or hot dogs

1. Heat oven to 375°F. Separate each can of dough into 8 triangles. Cut each triangle lengthwise into thirds. Place sausage on shortest side of each triangle. Roll up, starting at shortest side; roll to opposite point. Place on ungreased cookie sheets.

2. Bake at 375°F. for 12 to 15 minutes or until golden brown, switching position of cookie sheets halfway through baking. If desired, serve warm snack wraps with ketchup and mustard.

make-ahead tip

Prepare snacks as directed in recipe; place on cookie sheet. Do not bake. Cover with plastic wrap; refrigerate up to 2 hours. Uncover; bake as directed in recipe.

NUTRITION INFORMATION PER SERVING: SERVING SIZE: 1 Appetizer • Calories 60 • Calories from Fat 35 • % Daily Value: Total Fat 4 g 6% • Saturated Fat 1 g 5% • Cholesterol 5 mg 2% • Sodium 160 mg 7% • Total Carbohydrate 4 g 1% • Dietary Fiber 0 g 0% • Sugars 1 g • Protein 2 g • Vitamin A 0% • Vitamin C 0% • Calcium 0% • Iron 0% • **Dietary Exchanges:** ½ High-Fat Meat

Parmesan Spinach Roll-Ups

Sprinkle the work surface with cornmeal instead of flour, if you wish, to give a bit more texture to the outer surface of these cheese- and spinach-filled roll-ups.

PREP TIME: 20 MINUTES
(READY IN 45 MINUTES)
MAKES 20 APPETIZERS

1 egg

2 (10.6-oz.) pkg. refrigerated Parmesan breadsticks

1 (1-lb.) pkg. frozen cut leaf spinach, thawed, squeezed to drain

2 oz. (½ cup) shredded mozzarella cheese

1 teaspoon lemon juice

1 tablespoon all-purpose flour

1. Heat oven to 350°F. Lightly grease cookie sheets or use ungreased baking stone. In medium bowl, combine egg and contents of both containers of Parmesan spread from breadsticks; beat well with wire whisk. Add spinach, cheese and lemon juice; mix well.

2. Sprinkle work surface with flour. Unroll dough onto floured surface. Separate into 20 breadsticks. Press or roll each breadstick to form 7x1½-inch strip.

3. Spread each strip with about 1 tablespoon spinach mixture. Roll up, starting at one end; pinch end of dough to seal. Place rolls, cut side up, 3 inches apart on greased cookie sheets.

4. Bake at 350°F. for 20 to 25 minutes or until golden brown.

tip

To quickly thaw spinach, place in colander or strainer; rinse with warm water until thawed. Squeeze dry with paper towels.

NUTRITION INFORMATION PER SERVING: SERVING SIZE: 1 Appetizer • Calories 110 • Calories from Fat 45 • % Daily Value: Total Fat 5 g 8% • Saturated Fat 1 g 5% • Cholesterol 15 mg 5% • Sodium 300 mg 13% • Total Carbohydrate 12 g 4% • Dietary Fiber 1 g 4% • Sugars 1 g • Protein 5 g • Vitamin A 20% • Vitamin C 4% • Calcium 8% • Iron 6% • **Dietary Exchanges:** 1 Starch, 1 Fat **OR** 1 Carbohydrate, 1 Fat

Crescent Bacon 'n Olive Cheesies

A great bacon shortcut to keep in mind: Cook the bacon slices in the microwave oven, sandwiched between microwave-safe paper towels set on a plate. Two slices will cook up nice and crisp in about two minutes on HIGH power, and you'll have no frying pan to clean.

PREP TIME: 25 MINUTES
(READY IN 40 MINUTES)
MAKES 16 APPETIZERS

2 slices bacon

1 oz. (¼ cup) shredded Cheddar cheese

¼ cup finely chopped olives

2 tablespoons butter or margarine, softened

½ teaspoon dry mustard

¼ teaspoon paprika

1 (8-oz.) can refrigerated crescent dinner rolls

2 tablespoons sesame seed

2 tablespoons finely chopped fresh parsley

1. Heat oven to 375°F. Cook bacon until crisp. Drain on paper towel; crumble. In small bowl, combine crumbled bacon, cheese, olives, butter, dry mustard and paprika; mix well. Set aside.

2. Remove dough from can in 2 rolled sections; do not unroll. Coat each section with sesame seed. With serrated knife, cut each section into 8 slices. Place on ungreased cookie sheet.

3. With thumb, make indentation in center of each slice. Top each with about 1 teaspoon cheese mixture.

4. Bake at 375°F. for 10 to 12 minutes or until golden brown. Sprinkle with parsley. Serve warm. Store in refrigerator.

make-ahead tip

Prepare appetizers as directed in recipe; place on cookie sheet. Do not bake. Cover with plastic wrap; refrigerate up to 2 hours. Uncover; bake as directed in recipe. Sprinkle with parsley.

NUTRITION INFORMATION PER SERVING: SERVING SIZE: 1 Appetizer • Calories 90 • Calories from Fat 50 • % Daily Value: Total Fat 6 g 9% • Saturated Fat 2 g 10% • Cholesterol 5 mg 2% • Sodium 170 mg 7% • Total Carbohydrate 6 g 2% • Dietary Fiber 0 g 0% • Sugars 1 g • Protein 2 g • Vitamin A 2% • Vitamin C 0% • Calcium 2% • Iron 2% • **Dietary Exchanges:** ½ Starch, 1 Fat **OR** ½ Carbohydrate, 1 Fat

Olive-Cheese Bites

Everyone is familiar with sesame seed—but have you ever seen a sesame plant? Most of us haven't. It's an annual, cultivated for its seeds alone, which grow inside pods. The seeds are widely used in almost all parts of the world, raw or toasted, pressed into oil or ground into a paste called tahini.

PREP TIME: 35 MINUTES
MAKES 48 SERVINGS

1 (11-oz.) can refrigerated breadsticks

48 large pimiento-stuffed green olives, well drained

1 egg, beaten

3 tablespoons sesame seed, if desired

1 cup pasteurized process cheese sauce

3 tablespoons tomato juice

1/8 teaspoon ground red pepper (cayenne)

1. Heat oven to 375°F. Spray cookie sheets with nonstick cooking spray. Remove dough from can; separate into 12 strips. Cut each strip into 4 pieces; flatten each piece.

2. Place 1 olive in center of each piece of dough. Wrap dough around olive to completely cover, stretching dough to fit if necessary and pressing edges firmly to seal. Repeat with remaining dough pieces. Dip tops in beaten egg, then in sesame seed. Place, seam side down, on sprayed cookie sheets.

3. Bake at 375°F. for 11 to 14 minutes or until golden brown.

4. Meanwhile, in small saucepan, combine pasteurized process cheese sauce, tomato juice and ground red pepper. Cook over low heat for 3 to 4 minutes or until cheese sauce melts and mixture is well blended, stirring constantly. Serve warm olive-cheese bites with warm cheese sauce for dipping.

NUTRITION INFORMATION PER SERVING: SERVING SIZE: 1/48 of Recipe • Calories 40 • Calories from Fat 20 • % Daily Value: Total Fat 2 g 3% • Saturated Fat 1 g 5% • Cholesterol 10 mg 3% • Sodium 250 mg 10% • Total Carbohydrate 4 g 1% • Dietary Fiber 0 g 0% • Sugars 1 g • Protein 1 g • Vitamin A 0% • Vitamin C 0% • Calcium 2% • Iron 0% • **Dietary Exchanges:** 1/2 Starch **OR** 1/2 Carbohydrate

Chicken Curry Crescent Snacks

In India, traditional cooks grind and blend their curry spices daily, varying the proportions to suit the day's menu. The different brands of curry powder on supermarket shelves can vary widely, too, and can range from fairly mild to very hot.

PREP TIME: 10 MINUTES
(READY IN 30 MINUTES)
MAKES 8 APPETIZERS

1 (4.25-oz.) can white meat chicken spread

1/4 cup raisins

1/4 cup coarsely chopped salted cashews

1/2 teaspoon curry powder

1 (8-oz.) can refrigerated crescent dinner rolls

Mango chutney, if desired

1. Heat oven to 375°F. In small bowl, combine chicken spread, raisins, cashews and curry powder; mix well.

2. Separate dough into 8 triangles. Spoon about 1 tablespoon chicken mixture on shortest side of each triangle. Roll up, starting at shortest side of triangle and rolling to opposite point. Place rolls, point side down, on ungreased cookie sheet; curve into crescent shape.

3. Bake at 375°F. for 8 to 12 minutes or until golden brown. Cool 5 minutes. Serve topped with chutney.

make-ahead tip

Prepare snacks as directed in recipe; place on cookie sheet. Do not bake. Cover with plastic wrap; refrigerate up to 2 hours. Uncover; bake as directed in recipe.

NUTRITION INFORMATION PER SERVING: SERVING SIZE: 1 Appetizer • Calories 200 • Calories from Fat 90 • % Daily Value: Total Fat 10 g 15% • Saturated Fat 2 g 10% • Cholesterol 10 mg 3% • Sodium 410 mg 17% • Total Carbohydrate 22 g 7% • Dietary Fiber 1 g 4% • Sugars 9 g • Protein 5 g • Vitamin A 0% • Vitamin C 0% • Calcium 0% • Iron 6% • **Dietary Exchanges:** 1 1/2 Starch, 2 Fat **OR** 1 1/2 Carbohydrate, 2 Fat

Flaky Reuben Bites

The origins of the original Reuben aren't clear, but the corned beef-Swiss-sauerkraut combo remains firmly fixed in our culinary repertoire, whatever its roots. This version transforms the sandwich ingredients into flaky-crusted warm appetizer slices. If you wish, roll the dough in caraway seeds before baking to evoke the earthy flavor of deli rye bread.

PREP TIME: 25 MINUTES
MAKES 24 SERVINGS

ROLLS

1 (8-oz.) can refrigerated crescent dinner rolls

¼ lb. thinly sliced corned beef

2 oz. (½ cup) finely shredded Swiss cheese

⅓ cup well-drained sauerkraut

DIPPING SAUCE

½ cup purchased Thousand Island salad dressing

1 tablespoon milk

1. Heat oven to 375°F. Unroll dough into 2 long rectangles. Press each to form 12-inch-long rectangle; press perforations to seal.

2. Layer half of corned beef on each dough rectangle, cutting to fit if necessary. Top each with cheese and sauerkraut. Starting at long side, roll up each tightly; seal long edges. Place, seam side down, on ungreased cookie sheet; tuck edges under.

3. Bake at 375°F. for 12 to 14 minutes or until golden brown.

4. Meanwhile, in small bowl, combine dipping sauce ingredients; mix well.

5. To serve, cut warm rolls into 1-inch slices; place on serving platter. Serve warm slices with dipping sauce.

make-ahead tip

Prepare appetizers as directed in recipe; place on cookie sheet. Do not bake. Cover with plastic wrap; refrigerate up to 2 hours. Uncover; bake as directed in recipe.

NUTRITION INFORMATION PER SERVING: SERVING SIZE: ¹⁄₂₄ of Recipe • Calories 70 • Calories from Fat 45 • % Daily Value: Total Fat 5 g 8% • Saturated Fat 1 g 5% • Cholesterol 10 mg 3% • Sodium 170 mg 7% • Total Carbohydrate 5 g 2% • Dietary Fiber 0 g 0% • Sugars 1 g • Protein 2 g • Vitamin A 0% • Vitamin C 0% • Calcium 2% • Iron 0% • **Dietary Exchanges:** ½ Starch, 1 Fat **OR** ½ Carbohydrate, 1 Fat

Herb Bites with Brie

Herbes de Provence, a dried blend widely used in the South of France, typically includes marjoram, thyme, rosemary and basil; summer savory and other flavors—even lavender—sometimes figure in the mix, too.

PREP TIME: 35 MINUTES
MAKES 8 SERVINGS

1 (8-oz.) round Brie cheese

1 (11-oz.) can refrigerated breadsticks

2 tablespoons margarine or butter, melted

1 teaspoon sesame seed

½ teaspoon herbes de Provence

¼ teaspoon garlic powder

5 (1-inch) pieces roasted red bell peppers (from 7.5-oz. jar)

1 teaspoon chopped yellow bell pepper

3 large basil leaves

1. Heat oven to 375°F. Cut 15-inch piece of foil. Fold in half lengthwise; cut on fold to make 2 strips. Overlap 2 ends; fold together to make 29-inch strip. Fold lengthwise twice to make long strip 1½ inches wide. Overlap and fold remaining ends to form 8-inch diameter circle for collar. Spray inside of collar with nonstick cooking spray. Place on ungreased cookie sheet. Place cheese in center of collar.

2. Remove dough from can; separate into 12 strips. Cut each strip into 4 pieces; place in medium bowl. Drizzle dough with melted margarine. Sprinkle with sesame seed, herbes de Provence and garlic powder; toss to coat. Spoon breadstick pieces to fill space between cheese and foil collar on cookie sheet.

3. Bake at 375°F. for 15 minutes. Remove foil collar; bake an additional 5 to 10 minutes or until breadstick pieces are golden brown and cheese is soft.

4. Cut roasted pepper pieces into shapes to resemble poinsettia petals. Place in center of cheese. Sprinkle yellow bell pepper pieces in center of poinsettia. Place basil leaves around roasted pepper pieces to resemble leaves. Slide onto serving plate. Serve warm breadsticks with melted cheese.

NUTRITION INFORMATION PER SERVING: SERVING SIZE: ⅛ of Recipe • Calories 230 • Calories from Fat 120 • % Daily Value: Total Fat 13 g 20% • Saturated Fat 6 g 30% • Cholesterol 30 mg 10% • Sodium 500 mg 21% • Total Carbohydrate 19 g 6% • Dietary Fiber 1 g 4% • Sugars 3 g • Protein 9 g • Vitamin A 10% • Vitamin C 10% • Calcium 6% • Iron 6% • **Dietary Exchanges:** 1 Starch, 1 High-Fat Meat, 1 Fat **OR** 1 Carbohydrate, 1 High-Fat Meat, 1 Fat

Goat Cheese and Sun-Dried Tomato Bread Bites

A sprinkling of kosher (salt) gives the breadsticks an appealing pretzel-like finish. Kosher salt has larger grains than ordinary table salt and contains no additives.

PREP TIME: 30 MINUTES
(READY IN 50 MINUTES)
MAKES 24 APPETIZERS

1 (11-oz.) can refrigerated breadsticks

4 oz. (1 cup) crumbled chèvre (goat) cheese with basil and garlic or plain chèvre (goat) cheese

½ cup oil-packed sun-dried tomatoes, drained, coarsely chopped

1 egg

1 tablespoon water

Kosher or coarse salt, if desired

1. Heat oven to 375°F. Spray cookie sheet with nonstick cooking spray. Unroll dough; separate into breadsticks. Cut each in half crosswise to make 24 small breadsticks. Press each breadstick until 1½ inches wide.

2. With thumb, make indentation in center of each breadstick. Place 1 rounded teaspoon cheese in each indentation; top each with 1 teaspoon tomatoes. Roll up each jelly-roll fashion; place seam side down on sprayed cookie sheet.

3. In small bowl, combine egg and water; beat well. Lightly brush over tops of filled breadsticks. Sprinkle each with salt.

4. Bake at 375°F. for 12 to 17 minutes or until tops are light golden brown.

NUTRITION INFORMATION PER SERVING: SERVING SIZE: 1 Appetizer • Calories 60 • Calories from Fat 20 • % Daily Value: Total Fat 2 g 3% • Saturated Fat 1 g 5% • Cholesterol 10 mg 3% • Sodium 250 mg 10% • Total Carbohydrate 7 g 2% • Dietary Fiber 0 g 0% • Sugars 1 g • Protein 2 g • Vitamin A 0% • Vitamin C 2% • Calcium 0% • Iron 2% • Dietary Exchanges: ½ Starch, ½ Fat OR ½ Carbohydrate, ½ Fat

Mexican Cornbread Pizza Bites

Cornmeal, a Mexican staple, flavors the crust of this south-of-the-border interpretation of pizza.

PREP TIME: 15 MINUTES
(READY IN 30 MINUTES)
MAKES 32 APPETIZERS

1 (11.5-oz.) can refrigerated cornbread twists

1 teaspoon chili powder

⅓ cup taco sauce

1 teaspoon cumin

1 (2¼-oz.) can sliced ripe olives, drained

¼ cup chopped red or green bell pepper

2 tablespoons finely chopped onion

1 jalapeño chile, seeded, finely chopped

4 oz. (1 cup) shredded Monterey Jack cheese

2 tablespoons chopped fresh cilantro, if desired

1. Heat oven to 400°F. Unroll cornbread twists into ungreased 15x10x1-inch baking pan; press together to form 15x6-inch rectangle. Prick dough with fork; sprinkle with chili powder. Bake at 400°F. for 5 minutes.

2. Meanwhile, in small bowl, combine taco sauce and cumin; mix well.

3. Remove partially baked crust from oven. Spread taco sauce mixture over crust. Sprinkle with olives, bell pepper, onion, chile and cheese.

4. Return to oven; bake an additional 8 to 12 minutes or until edges are golden brown and cheese is melted. Sprinkle with cilantro. Cut in half lengthwise; cut into strips.

NUTRITION INFORMATION PER SERVING: SERVING SIZE: 1 Appetizer • Calories 60 • Calories from Fat 25 • % Daily Value: Total Fat 3 g 5% • Saturated Fat 1 g 5% • Cholesterol 3 mg 1% • Sodium 130 mg 5% • Total Carbohydrate 5 g 2% • Dietary Fiber 0 g 0% • Sugars 1 g • Protein 2 g • Vitamin A 2% • Vitamin C 4% • Calcium 4% • Iron 2% • Dietary Exchanges: ½ Starch, ½ Fat OR ½ Carbohydrate, ½ Fat

Mini Cheddar Popovers

Choose mild or sharp Cheddar according to your preference; either way, the eggy dough magically puffs in the center, leaving the characteristic hollow.

PREP TIME: 30 MINUTES
MAKES 24 POPOVERS

3 teaspoons oil

¾ cup milk

1 egg

1 egg white

¾ cup all-purpose flour

1⅓ oz. (⅓ cup) shredded Cheddar cheese

1. Heat oven to 425°F. Spray 24 miniature muffin cups with nonstick cooking spray. Place muffin pans on cookie sheet. Add ⅛ teaspoon oil to bottom of each cup.

2. In small bowl, combine milk, egg and egg white; beat well with wire whisk. Add flour; beat until smooth. Stir in cheese.

3. Place pans on cookie sheet in oven for several minutes to heat. Remove cookie sheet from oven; quickly divide batter evenly into hot muffin cups, filling each cup about ⅔ full.

4. Bake at 425°F. for 18 to 20 minutes or until popovers are puffed and deep golden brown. Immediately remove from muffin cups.

HIGH ALTITUDE (ABOVE 3500 FEET): Do not place muffin pan on cookie sheet; do not add oil to muffin cups. Do not preheat pan. If using dark pan, reduce oven temperature to 400°F.

NUTRITION INFORMATION PER SERVING: SERVING SIZE: 1 Popover • Calories 25 • Calories from Fat 10 • % Daily Value: Total Fat 1 g 2% • Saturated Fat 1 g 5% • Cholesterol 10 mg 3% • Sodium 20 mg 1% • Total Carbohydrate 3 g 1% • Dietary Fiber 0 g 0% • Sugars 0 g • Protein 1 g • Vitamin A 0% • Vitamin C 0% • Calcium 2% • Iron 0% • **Dietary Exchanges:** ½ Starch **OR** ½ Carbohydrate

Stilton Cheese Puffs

Stilton, English blue cheese, works well in this recipe because of its smooth texture when melted. Substitute Danish blue if you can't find Stilton.

PREP TIME: 40 MINUTES
MAKES 24 APPETIZERS

½ cup water

¼ cup butter, cut into small pieces

½ cup all-purpose flour

¼ teaspoon salt

⅛ teaspoon coarse-ground black pepper

2 eggs

2½ oz. (½ cup) crumbled Stilton cheese

1. Heat oven to 400°F. Line cookie sheet with parchment paper. In medium saucepan, combine water and butter; heat over medium heat until mixture comes to a boil and butter is melted.

2. Stir in flour, salt and pepper. Cook over medium heat for about 1 minute, stirring vigorously until mixture leaves sides of saucepan in smooth compact ball. Remove from heat.

3. Add eggs 1 at a time, beating with spoon for 1 minute after each addition until mixture is smooth and glossy. Stir in cheese; mix well. Drop mixture by rounded teaspoonfuls or pipe from decorating bag onto paper-lined cookie sheet to form 1-inch puffs.

4. Bake at 400°F. for 14 to 18 minutes or until puffed and golden brown.

make-ahead tip

Prepare puffs as directed in recipe. Cool completely. Place in covered container. To reheat, place puffs on cookie sheet. Heat at 400°F. for 3 to 6 minutes or until thoroughly heated.

HIGH ALTITUDE (ABOVE 3500 FEET): No change.

NUTRITION INFORMATION PER SERVING: SERVING SIZE: 1 Appetizer •
Calories 40 • Calories from Fat 25 • % Daily Value: Total Fat 3 g 5% •
Saturated Fat 2 g 10% • Cholesterol 25 mg 8% • Sodium 85 mg 4% •
Total Carbohydrate 2 g 1% • Dietary Fiber 0 g 0% • Sugars 0 g •
Protein 1 g • Vitamin A 2% • Vitamin C 0% • Calcium 0% • Iron 0% •
Dietary Exchanges: ½ Fat

Mushroom Pita Triangles

Pita bread, a Middle Eastern staple, bakes in a
very hot oven. The dough puffs during cooking,
leaving a hollow center that's ideal for pocket
sandwiches. Pitas are often cut into triangles
for dipping; here, the triangles get topped with
a Dijon-spiked mixture of Swiss cheese and
sliced mushrooms.

PREP TIME: 20 MINUTES
MAKES 12 APPETIZERS

1 tablespoon Dijon mustard

2 (6-inch) pocket (pita) breads

3 (¾-oz.) slices Swiss cheese

1 cup sliced fresh mushrooms

½ teaspoon dried Italian seasoning

1. Spread mustard on pocket breads. Cut each
pocket bread into 6 triangles; place on
ungreased cookie sheet.

2. Cut each cheese slice diagonally into 4 triangles; place 1 cheese triangle on each bread
triangle. Arrange mushroom slices over
cheese. Sprinkle with Italian seasoning.

3. Broil 4 to 6 inches from heat for 2 to
4 minutes or until cheese is melted.

NUTRITION INFORMATION PER SERVING: SERVING SIZE: 1 Appetizer •
Calories 50 • Calories from Fat 20 • % Daily Value: Total Fat 2 g 3% •
Saturated Fat 1 g 5% • Cholesterol 5 mg 2% • Sodium 100 mg 4% •
Total Carbohydrate 6 g 2% • Dietary Fiber 0 g 0% • Sugars 0 g •
Protein 3 g • Vitamin A 0% • Vitamin C 0% • Calcium 6% • Iron 2% •
Dietary Exchanges: ½ Starch, ½ Fat **OR** ½ Carbohydrate, ½ Fat

Pesto and Goat Cheese Appetizers

To get the most authentic roasted red-pepper
flavor, choose peppers packed in olive oil
rather than vinegar. The oil-packed peppers
are sometimes available at the deli counter or
self-serve grocery salad bars.

PREP TIME: 30 MINUTES
MAKES 24 APPETIZERS

1 (8-oz.) can refrigerated crescent dinner rolls

½ cup purchased pesto

2 oz. (½ cup) crumbled chèvre (goat) cheese

¼ cup coarsely chopped drained roasted red bell
     peppers (from 7.25-oz. jar) or sliced ripe olives

1. Heat oven to 375°F. Lightly spray cookie
sheet with nonstick cooking spray. Unroll
dough into 2 long rectangles. Cut each rectangle into 12 squares. Place squares on
sprayed cookie sheet.

2. Spread each square with pesto. Sprinkle
with crumbled cheese. Top with roasted
peppers.

3. Bake at 375°F. for 10 to 12 minutes or
until edges are golden brown.

NUTRITION INFORMATION PER SERVING: SERVING SIZE: 1 Appetizer •
Calories 70 • Calories from Fat 45 • % Daily Value: Total Fat 5 g 8% •
Saturated Fat 1 g 5% • Cholesterol 3 mg 1% • Sodium 120 mg 5% •
Total Carbohydrate 4 g 1% • Dietary Fiber 0 g 0% • Sugars 1 g •
Protein 2 g • Vitamin A 2% • Vitamin C 2% • Calcium 2% • Iron 0% •
Dietary Exchanges: ½ Starch, 1 Fat **OR** ½ Carbohydrate, 1 Fat

Mozzarella and Pesto Crescent Tarts

To seed the tomatoes, cut them in half and scoop out the seedy pulp with a tiny spoon. A baby's feeding spoon is ideal. If you prefer a juicier topping, skip the seeding step altogether.

PREP TIME: 20 MINUTES
(READY IN 35 MINUTES)
MAKES 16 SERVINGS

1 (8-oz.) can refrigerated crescent dinner rolls

2 tablespoons purchased pesto

2 medium tomatoes, seeded, sliced

1 small red onion, thinly sliced

1 to 2 teaspoons chopped fresh rosemary
   or 1/2 teaspoon dried rosemary leaves

2 oz. (1/2 cup) diced fresh mozzarella cheese or
   shredded mozzarella cheese

1 oz. (1/4 cup) shredded fresh Parmesan cheese

1. Heat oven to 425°F. Unroll dough into 2 long rectangles. Place 3 inches apart on ungreased cookie sheet. Firmly press perforations to seal. Press to form two 10x3-inch strips, forming rim around edge of dough.

2. Spread each strip with 1 tablespoon pesto. Top each with tomatoes, onion and rosemary. Sprinkle each with mozzarella and Parmesan cheese.

3. Bake at 425°F. for 10 to 14 minutes or until edges are golden brown and cheese is melted. Cut each into crosswise slices. Serve warm or cool.

Four medium Italian plum tomatoes can be substituted for the regular tomatoes.

NUTRITION INFORMATION PER SERVING: SERVING SIZE: 1/16 of Recipe • Calories 90 • Calories from Fat 45 • % Daily Value: Total Fat 5 g 8% • Saturated Fat 1 g 5% • Cholesterol 3 mg 1% • Sodium 170 mg 7% • Total Carbohydrate 7 g 2% • Dietary Fiber 0 g 0% • Sugars 2 g • Protein 3 g • Vitamin A 2% • Vitamin C 4% • Calcium 6% • Iron 2% • **Dietary Exchanges:** 1/2 Starch, 1 Fat **OR** 1/2 Carbohydrate, 1 Fat

Seeded Crescent Wedges

A crunchy trio of sunflower, sesame and caraway seeds coats mustard/bourbon-brushed crescent roll wedges. For a slightly different result, substitute dill seed or fennel for the caraway.

PREP TIME: 10 MINUTES
(READY IN 30 MINUTES)
MAKES 32 APPETIZERS

2 tablespoons shelled sunflower seeds

1 tablespoon caraway seed

1 tablespoon sesame seed

1 (8-oz.) can refrigerated crescent dinner rolls

2 tablespoons Dijon mustard

1 tablespoon bourbon whiskey or apple juice

1 tablespoon honey

1. Heat oven to 375°F. Spray large cookie sheet with nonstick cooking spray. In small bowl, combine sunflower seeds, caraway seed and sesame seed; mix well. Set aside.

2. Separate dough into 4 rectangles. Place on sprayed cookie sheet. Firmly press perforations to seal. Cut each rectangle into 8 wedges.

3. In small bowl, combine mustard, bourbon whiskey and honey; mix well. Brush over wedges. Separate wedges slightly. Sprinkle each wedge with seed mixture.

4. Bake at 375°F. for 9 to 14 minutes or until golden brown. Remove from cookie sheet. Cool 5 minutes. Serve warm or cool.

NUTRITION INFORMATION PER SERVING: SERVING SIZE: 1 Appetizer • Calories 40 • Calories from Fat 20 • % Daily Value: Total Fat 2 g 3% • Saturated Fat 0 g 0% • Cholesterol 0 mg 0% • Sodium 80 mg 3% • Total Carbohydrate 4 g 1% • Dietary Fiber 0 g 0% • Sugars 1 g • Protein 1 g • Vitamin A 0% • Vitamin C 0% • Calcium 0% • Iron 0% • **Dietary Exchanges:** 1/2 Starch **OR** 1/2 Carbohydrate

Baked Artichoke Squares

Hot artichoke dip, a longtime crowd pleaser, joins with spinach to become a luscious topping for a dinner roll base.

PREP TIME: 15 MINUTES
(READY IN 35 MINUTES)
MAKES 60 APPETIZERS

2 (8-oz.) cans refrigerated crescent dinner rolls

1 (14-oz.) can artichoke hearts, drained, chopped

1 (9-oz.) pkg. frozen spinach in a pouch, thawed, squeezed to drain

3/4 cup grated Parmesan cheese

2/3 cup mayonnaise

2/3 cup sour cream

1/8 teaspoon garlic powder

1. Heat oven to 375°F. Unroll dough into 4 long rectangles. Place crosswise in ungreased 15x10x1-inch baking pan; press over bottom and 1 inch up sides to form crust. Press perforations to seal.

2. Bake at 375°F. for 10 to 12 minutes or until light golden brown. Meanwhile, in medium bowl, combine all remaining ingredients; mix well.

3. Remove partially baked crust from oven. Spread artichoke mixture evenly over crust.

4. Return to oven; bake an additional 8 to 10 minutes or until topping is thoroughly heated. Cut into 1½-inch squares.

NUTRITION INFORMATION PER SERVING: SERVING SIZE: 1 Appetizer • Calories 60 • Calories from Fat 35 • % Daily Value: Total Fat 4 g 6% • Saturated Fat 1 g 5% • Cholesterol 4 mg 1% • Sodium 110 mg 5% • Total Carbohydrate 4 g 1% • Dietary Fiber 0 g 0% • Sugars 1 g • Protein 1 g • Vitamin A 4% • Vitamin C 0% • Calcium 2% • Iron 0% • **Dietary Exchanges:** 1 Vegetable, 1 Fat

Quick 'n Easy Herb Flatbread

To make this quick recipe even faster, spread the topping onto a prebaked pizza bread shell.

PREP TIME: 10 MINUTES
(READY IN 25 MINUTES)
MAKES 9 APPETIZERS

1 (10-oz.) can refrigerated pizza crust

1 tablespoon olive or vegetable oil

1/2 to 1 teaspoon dried basil leaves

1/2 to 1 teaspoon dried rosemary leaves, crushed

1/2 teaspoon minced garlic

1/8 teaspoon salt

1 small tomato

1 oz. (1/4 cup) shredded fresh Parmesan cheese

1. Heat oven to 425°F. Spray cookie sheet with nonstick cooking spray. Unroll dough; place on sprayed cookie sheet. Starting at center, press out dough with hands to form 12x8-inch rectangle.

2. In small bowl, combine oil, basil, rosemary and garlic; mix well. Brush over dough; sprinkle with salt.

3. Chop tomato; place in shallow bowl. With back of spoon, crush tomato. Spread tomato over dough.

4. Bake at 425°F. for 5 to 9 minutes or until edges are light golden brown.

5. Sprinkle cheese over tomato. Bake an additional 2 to 3 minutes or until cheese is melted and edges are golden brown. Cut into squares.

NUTRITION INFORMATION PER SERVING: SERVING SIZE: 1 Appetizer • Calories 100 • Calories from Fat 25 • % Daily Value: Total Fat 3 g 5% • Saturated Fat 1 g 5% • Cholesterol 2 mg 1% • Sodium 290 mg 12% • Total Carbohydrate 15 g 5% • Dietary Fiber 1 g 4% • Sugars 2 g • Protein 4 g • Vitamin A 0% • Vitamin C 0% • Calcium 4% • Iron 6% • **Dietary Exchanges:** 1 Starch, ½ Fat **OR** 1 Carbohydrate, ½ Fat

Country French Herb Flatbread

To maintain freshness, store *herbes de Provence* and other dried herbs in a dark, cool, dry place. The cabinet over the stove is a notoriously bad spot, as rising steam and heat will rob flavor.

PREP TIME: 15 MINUTES
(READY IN 35 MINUTES)
MAKES 20 APPETIZERS

1 (10-oz.) can refrigerated pizza crust

4½ teaspoons olive oil

2 teaspoons dried herbes de Provence

5 to 6 oil-packed sun-dried tomatoes, drained, chopped

⅓ cup chèvre (goat) cheese, softened

2 eggs

Dash pepper

Fresh thyme or rosemary sprigs, if desired

Red and/or yellow cherry tomatoes, if desired

1. Heat oven to 400°F. Spray 13x9-inch pan with nonstick cooking spray. Unroll dough; place in sprayed pan. Starting at center, press out dough with hands to edge of pan. With fingers, make indentations over surface of dough. Brush with 3 teaspoons of the oil. Sprinkle with 1 teaspoon of the herbes de Provence. Top with sun-dried tomatoes.

2. In medium bowl, combine cheese, eggs, remaining 1½ teaspoons oil and remaining 1 teaspoon herbes de Provence; mix well with wire whisk. Pour evenly over tomatoes; spread carefully.

3. Bake at 400°F. for 15 to 20 minutes or until edges are golden brown. Remove from oven; sprinkle with pepper. If necessary, loosen sides of bread from pan. Cut into squares. Arrange on serving platter. Garnish with thyme sprigs and cherry tomatoes.

tip

To substitute for herbes de Provence, combine ½ teaspoon each dried thyme, marjoram, rosemary and basil leaves.

NUTRITION INFORMATION PER SERVING: SERVING SIZE: 1 Appetizer • Calories 60 • Calories from Fat 20 • % Daily Value: Total Fat 2 g 3% • Saturated Fat 1 g 5% • Cholesterol 0 mg 0% • Sodium 95 mg 4% • Total Carbohydrate 7 g 2% • Dietary Fiber 0 g 0% • Sugars 1 g • Protein 2 g • Vitamin A 0% • Vitamin C 4% • Calcium 0% • Iron 4% • **Dietary Exchanges:** ½ Starch, ½ Fat **OR** ½ Carbohydrate, ½ Fat

Zesty Cheese Bread

Chopped cherry peppers—your choice of hot or sweet—can substitute for the chiles.

PREP TIME: 10 MINUTES
(READY IN 45 MINUTES)
MAKES 10 APPETIZERS

1 (10-oz.) can refrigerated pizza crust

1 (4.5-oz.) can chopped green chiles, well drained

2 oz. (½ cup) shredded sharp Cheddar cheese

2 oz. (½ cup) shredded hot pepper Monterey Jack cheese

¼ teaspoon garlic powder

1. Heat oven to 375°F. Spray cookie sheet with nonstick cooking spray.

2. Do not unroll dough. Place dough on sprayed cookie sheet. Starting at center, press out dough with hands to form 14x5-inch rectangle. Sprinkle chiles and cheeses over dough to within ½ inch of long sides. Bring long sides up over cheese; pinch center seam to seal. Pinch ends to seal. Sprinkle with garlic powder.

3. Bake on highest oven rack at 375°F. for 15 to 20 minutes or until golden brown. Cool 15 minutes. Cut into slices.

NUTRITION INFORMATION PER SERVING: SERVING SIZE: 1 Appetizer • Calories 120 • Calories from Fat 45 • % Daily Value: Total Fat 5 g 8% • Saturated Fat 3 g 15% • Cholesterol 10 mg 3% • Sodium 280 mg 12% • Total Carbohydrate 14 g 5% • Dietary Fiber 1 g 4% • Sugars 1 g • Protein 5 g • Vitamin A 2% • Vitamin C 4% • Calcium 10% • Iron 6% • **Dietary Exchanges:** 1 Starch, 1 Fat **OR** 1 Carbohydrate, 1 Fat

snacks & beverages

HERBED ITALIAN COCKTAIL MIX, PAGE 253;
BUBBLY APPLE-ORANGE REFRESHER, PAGE 279   **LF** (low-fat) = recipes that have 5 grams of fat or less per serving.

Popcorn Munch Mix

This is so easy and fun to make that kids can do most of the job. Slight deviations in measurements won't affect the success of the finished mix.

PREP TIME: 15 MINUTES
(READY IN 2 HOURS 15 MINUTES)
MAKES 6 CUPS

4 cups popped popcorn

1 cup bite-sized crispy wheat squares cereal

1 cup fish-shaped crackers

1 cup sesame cracker sticks or miniature pretzels

½ cup peanuts

¼ cup margarine or butter

¼ teaspoon seasoned salt

¼ teaspoon garlic powder

1½ teaspoons Worcestershire sauce

1. Heat oven to 250°F. In large bowl, combine popcorn, cereal, crackers, cracker sticks and peanuts. Set aside.

2. Place margarine in 13x9-inch pan. Place in oven until melted. Remove pan from oven. Stir in seasoned salt, garlic powder and Worcestershire sauce. Drizzle margarine mixture evenly over popcorn mixture in bowl; toss to coat. Place popcorn mixture in same 13x9-inch pan.

3. Bake at 250°F. for 1 hour, stirring every 15 minutes. Cool 1 hour or until completely cooled. Store in tightly covered container.

NUTRITION INFORMATION PER SERVING: SERVING SIZE: ½ Cup • Calories 170 • Calories from Fat 100 • % Daily Value: Total Fat 11 g 17% • Saturated Fat 2 g 10% • Cholesterol 0 mg 0% • Sodium 310 mg 13% • Total Carbohydrate 13 g 4% • Dietary Fiber 2 g 8% • Sugars 1 g • Protein 4 g • Vitamin A 4% • Vitamin C 0% • Calcium 2% • Iron 8% • **Dietary Exchanges:** 1 Starch, 2 Fat **OR** 1 Carbohydrate, 2 Fat

Spicy Popcorn and Peanuts

Besides being an irresistible party snack, the popcorn-peanut mixture also makes a thoughtful gift for a teacher or coworker. Package it in a wide-mouthed glass jar, and tie a square of gingham around the lid with a length of raffia.

PREP TIME: 40 MINUTES
(READY IN 1 HOUR 10 MINUTES)
MAKES 9 CUPS

8 cups popped popcorn

1 cup dry-roasted peanuts

3 tablespoons oil

1 teaspoon chili powder

¼ teaspoon garlic salt

⅛ teaspoon ground red pepper (cayenne)

1. Heat oven to 250°F. In 13x9-inch pan, combine popcorn and peanuts. In small bowl, combine all remaining ingredients; blend well. Drizzle evenly over popcorn mixture; toss to coat.

2. Bake at 250°F. for 30 minutes, stirring once or twice. Cool 30 minutes or until completely cooled. Store in tightly covered container.

NUTRITION INFORMATION PER SERVING: SERVING SIZE: ½ Cup • Calories 100 • Calories from Fat 70 • % Daily Value: Total Fat 8 g 12% • Saturated Fat 1 g 5% • Cholesterol 0 mg 0% • Sodium 135 mg 6% • Total Carbohydrate 5 g 2% • Dietary Fiber 1 g 4% • Sugars 0 g • Protein 2 g • Vitamin A 0% • Vitamin C 0% • Calcium 0% • Iron 0% • **Dietary Exchanges:** ½ Starch, 1½ Fat **OR** ½ Carbohydrate, 1½ Fat

Italian Snack Mix

Garlic, herbs and cheese are a classic trio of flavors in the Italian spirit.

PREP TIME: 30 MINUTES
(READY IN 1 HOUR)
MAKES 10 CUPS

4 cups popped popcorn

2 cups white Cheddar snack crackers

2 cups thin pretzel sticks, broken in half

2 cups miniature garlic-flavored bagel chips

1/4 cup margarine or butter, melted

2 tablespoons grated Parmesan-Romano cheese blend
   or grated Parmesan cheese

1/2 teaspoon dried Italian seasoning

1/4 teaspoon garlic powder

1. Heat oven to 300°F. In large bowl, combine popcorn, crackers, pretzel sticks and bagel chips.

2. In small bowl, combine all remaining ingredients; blend well. Drizzle evenly over popcorn mixture; toss to coat. Spread evenly in ungreased 15x10x1-inch baking pan.

3. Bake at 300°F. for 8 to 12 minutes or until thoroughly heated, stirring occasionally. Cool 30 minutes or until completely cooled. Store in tightly covered container.

NUTRITION INFORMATION PER SERVING: SERVING SIZE: 1/2 Cup • Calories 110 • Calories from Fat 50 • % Daily Value: Total Fat 6 g 9% • Saturated Fat 1 g 5% • Cholesterol 0 mg 0% • Sodium 260 mg 11% • Total Carbohydrate 13 g 4% • Dietary Fiber 1 g 4% • Sugars 1 g • Protein 2 g • Vitamin A 0% • Vitamin C 0% • Calcium 2% • Iron 4% • **Dietary Exchanges:** 1 Starch, 1 Fat **OR** 1 Carbohydrate, 1 Fat

Cheese Herb Snack Mix

Start with two irresistible finger foods—popcorn and pretzels—and add herbs and cheese for an even more tempting snack.

PREP TIME: 30 MINUTES
MAKES 6 CUPS

2 tablespoons grated Parmesan cheese

1/2 teaspoon dried basil leaves

1/2 teaspoon dried thyme leaves

3 cups low-salt fat-free miniature pretzel twists

3 cups air-popped popcorn

Nonstick cooking spray

1. Heat oven to 375°F. In small bowl, combine Parmesan cheese, basil and thyme; mix well.

2. In large bowl, combine pretzels and popcorn; spread in ungreased 15x10x1-inch baking pan. Spray pretzel mixture with nonstick cooking spray for 10 seconds to thoroughly coat. Sprinkle cheese mixture evenly over pretzel mixture; do not stir.

3. Bake at 375°F. for 6 minutes or until hot. Cool 15 minutes or until completely cooled.

NUTRITION INFORMATION PER SERVING: SERVING SIZE: 1/2 Cup • Calories 90 • Calories from Fat 10 • % Daily Value: Total Fat 1 g 2% • Saturated Fat 0 g 0% • Cholesterol 0 mg 0% • Sodium 240 mg 10% • Total Carbohydrate 16 g 5% • Dietary Fiber 1 g 4% • Sugars 1 g • Protein 3 g • Vitamin A 0% • Vitamin C 0% • Calcium 0% • Iron 6% • **Dietary Exchanges:** 1 Starch **OR** 1 Carbohydrate

Southwestern Snack Mix

This snack mix satisfies the craving for big flavors. Paprika, chili powder and cayenne lend a reddish tinge and spicy flavor.

PREP TIME: 10 MINUTES
MAKES 10 CUPS

4 cups popped popcorn

3 cups miniature pretzel twists

2 cups miniature garlic-flavored bagel chips

1 cup corn chips

3 tablespoons margarine or butter, melted

1 teaspoon paprika

3/4 teaspoon chili powder

1/2 teaspoon cumin

1/4 teaspoon onion powder

1/4 teaspoon garlic powder

Dash ground red pepper (cayenne)

1. In large bowl, combine popcorn, pretzels, bagel chips and corn chips.

2. In small bowl, combine all remaining ingredients; blend well. Drizzle evenly over popcorn mixture; toss gently to coat. Store in tightly covered container.

NUTRITION INFORMATION PER SERVING: SERVING SIZE: 1/2 Cup • Calories 110 • Calories from Fat 45 • % Daily Value: Total Fat 5 g 8% • Saturated Fat 1 g 5% • Cholesterol 0 mg 0% • Sodium 280 mg 12% • Total Carbohydrate 14 g 5% • Dietary Fiber 1 g 4% • Sugars 1 g • Protein 2 g • Vitamin A 4% • Vitamin C 0% • Calcium 0% • Iron 4% • **Dietary Exchanges:** 1/2 Starch, 1/2 Fruit, 1 Fat **OR** 1 Carbohydrate, 1 Fat

Herbed Italian Cocktail Mix

(Pictured on page 248.)

This satisfying mix is very quick to toss together. The only cooking is to melt the margarine in the microwave.

PREP TIME: 10 MINUTES
MAKES 10 CUPS

1 (7-oz.) pkg. gourmet round onion- and garlic-flavored croutons

1 (5.6-oz.) pkg. corn nuts

3 cups bite-sized crispy multi-bran squares cereal

2 cups miniature garlic-flavored bagel chips

1/4 cup margarine or butter, melted

1/4 cup chopped fresh basil or 1 teaspoon dried basil leaves

1/2 teaspoon onion powder

2 tablespoons grated Parmesan cheese

1. In large bowl, combine croutons, corn nuts, cereal and bagel chips.

2. In small bowl, combine margarine, basil and onion powder; blend well. Drizzle evenly over crouton mixture. Sprinkle with Parmesan cheese; toss gently. Store in tightly covered container.

NUTRITION INFORMATION PER SERVING: SERVING SIZE: 1/2 Cup • Calories 140 • Calories from Fat 50 • % Daily Value: Total Fat 6 g 9% • Saturated Fat 1 g 5% • Cholesterol 0 mg 0% • Sodium 270 mg 11% • Total Carbohydrate 19 g 6% • Dietary Fiber 2 g 8% • Sugars 1 g • Protein 3 g • Vitamin A 2% • Vitamin C 8% • Calcium 2% • Iron 15% • **Dietary Exchanges:** 1 1/2 Starch, 1 Fat **OR** 1 1/2 Carbohydrate, 1 Fat

Spicy Cheesy Popcorn

Spicy Cheesy Popcorn rivals any other snack mix for flavor, but it has just 30 calories per serving.

PREP TIME: 5 MINUTES
MAKES 10 CUPS

10 cups cheese-flavored popcorn

½ teaspoon garlic powder

1½ teaspoons chili powder

¼ teaspoon ground red pepper (cayenne)

Butter-flavored nonstick cooking spray

1. Spread popcorn in ungreased 15x10x1-inch baking pan.

2. In small bowl, combine garlic powder, chili powder and ground red pepper; mix well. Spray popcorn for 7 to 8 seconds with nonstick cooking spray. Immediately sprinkle with chili powder mixture; toss to coat. Store in tightly covered container.

NUTRITION INFORMATION PER SERVING: SERVING SIZE: ½ Cup • Calories 30 • Calories from Fat 20 • % Daily Value: Total Fat 2 g 3% • Saturated Fat 0 g 0% • Cholesterol 0 mg 0% • Sodium 50 mg 2% • Total Carbohydrate 3 g 1% • Dietary Fiber 1 g 4% • Sugars 0 g • Protein 1 g • Vitamin A 0% • Vitamin C 0% • Calcium 0% • Iron 0% • **Dietary Exchanges:** ½ Fat

Party Snack Mix

For a party on a limited budget, use peanuts in this mix. To splurge, use cashews, almonds, hazelnuts or even pistachios.

PREP TIME: 10 MINUTES
(READY IN 1 HOUR 10 MINUTES)
MAKES 12 CUPS

4 cups bite-sized crispy corn squares cereal

2 cups bite-sized crispy wheat squares cereal

2 cups pretzel sticks

2 cups Spanish peanuts or mixed nuts

½ cup butter, melted

1 tablespoon Worcestershire sauce

1 teaspoon salt

¼ teaspoon garlic powder

⅛ teaspoon hot pepper sauce

1. Heat oven to 325°F. In large bowl, combine cereals, pretzel sticks and peanuts.

2. In small bowl, combine all remaining ingredients; blend well. Drizzle evenly over cereal mixture; toss to coat. Spread in ungreased 15x10x1-inch baking pan.

3. Bake at 325°F. for 25 to 30 minutes or until lightly toasted, stirring occasionally. Cool 30 minutes or until completely cooled. Store in tightly covered container.

NUTRITION INFORMATION PER SERVING: SERVING SIZE: ½ Cup • Calories 180 • Calories from Fat 90 • % Daily Value: Total Fat 10 g 15% • Saturated Fat 2 g 10% • Cholesterol 0 mg 0% • Sodium 410 mg 17% • Total Carbohydrate 17 g 6% • Dietary Fiber 2 g 8% • Sugars 1 g • Protein 5 g • Vitamin A 4% • Vitamin C 8% • Calcium 0% • Iron 20% • **Dietary Exchanges:** 1 Starch, 2 Fat **OR** 1 Carbohydrate, 2 Fat

Trail Mix

Use the recipe as a general guideline for this lightly seasoned blend. You can substitute rice or wheat cereal squares, peanuts, popcorn or other small crackers for any of the crunchy ingredients listed.

PREP TIME: 20 MINUTES
(READY IN 35 MINUTES)
MAKES 3 CUPS

¾ cup oat cereal rings

¾ cup corn cereal squares

¾ cup oyster crackers

¾ cup cheese-flavored fish-shaped crackers

¾ cup broken pretzel sticks

4 teaspoons soy sauce

1½ teaspoons Dijon mustard

¾ teaspoon garlic powder

¾ teaspoon onion powder

1. Heat oven to 350°F. Spray 15x10x1-inch baking pan with nonstick cooking spray. In large bowl, combine cereal rings, cereal squares, oyster crackers, fish-shaped crackers and pretzel sticks.

2. In small bowl, combine all remaining ingredients; blend well. Drizzle over cereal-cracker mixture; toss to coat. Spread mixture evenly in sprayed pan.

3. Bake at 350°F. for 5 minutes. Stir mixture; bake an additional 3 to 5 minutes. Cool 15 minutes or until completely cooled. Store in tightly covered container.

NUTRITION INFORMATION PER SERVING: SERVING SIZE: ½ Cup • Calories 150 • Calories from Fat 35 • % Daily Value: Total Fat 4 g 6% • Saturated Fat 1 g 5% • Cholesterol 0 mg 0% • Sodium 680 mg 28% • Total Carbohydrate 24 g 8% • Dietary Fiber 1 g 4% • Sugars 2 g • Protein 4 g • Vitamin A 4% • Vitamin C 4% • Calcium 4% • Iron 10% • **Dietary Exchanges:** 1½ Starch, 1 Fat **OR** 1½ Carbohydrate, 1 Fat

Crunchy Snack Mix

The all-purpose Greek seasoning in this recipe is a blend of oregano, onion powder, and parsley. Look for it in the spice section of the supermarket.

PREP TIME: 40 MINUTES
MAKES 5 CUPS

2 cups bite-sized pieces of unsalted baked tortilla chips (about 2 oz.)

1 cup (about 25) miniature fat-free pretzels

1 cup (about 15) fat-free white Melba snacks, broken into bite-sized pieces

1 cup (about 6) bagel chips, broken into bite-sized pieces

Olive oil nonstick cooking spray

1½ teaspoons all-purpose Greek seasoning

1. Heat oven to 250°F. In large bowl or plastic bag, combine tortilla chips, pretzels, Melba snacks and bagel chips.

2. Spray mixture with nonstick cooking spray for 3 to 4 seconds; mix or shake well. Repeat 2 more times.

3. Add 1 teaspoon of the Greek seasoning; mix or shake well. Spread mixture in ungreased 15x10x1-inch baking pan. Spray with cooking spray for 3 to 4 seconds. Sprinkle with remaining ½ teaspoon Greek seasoning.

4. Bake at 250°F. for 7 minutes. Stir mixture; bake an additional 8 minutes. Cool 15 minutes or until completely cooled.

NUTRITION INFORMATION PER SERVING: SERVING SIZE: ½ Cup • Calories 110 • Calories from Fat 25 • % Daily Value: Total Fat 3 g 5% • Saturated Fat 0 g 0% • Cholesterol 0 mg 0% • Sodium 290 mg 12% • Total Carbohydrate 17 g 6% • Dietary Fiber 1 g 4% • Sugars 1 g • Protein 3 g • Vitamin A 0% • Vitamin C 0% • Calcium 0% • Iron 2% • **Dietary Exchanges:** 1 Starch, ½ Fat **OR** 1 Carbohydrate, ½ Fat

Crunchy Canyon Snack Mix

To keep snack mixes crisp, store them in airtight containers or heavy resealable food storage plastic bags, especially in humid weather.

PREP TIME: 25 MINUTES
(READY IN 55 MINUTES)
MAKES 8 CUPS

3 cups miniature pretzel twists

2½ cups bite-sized wedge-shaped Cheddar cheese snack crackers

2 cups miniature garlic-flavored bagel chips or mini garlic-flavored rye toast

1 (3¼-oz.) pkg. Italian-flavored breadsticks, broken into thirds

⅓ cup margarine or butter, melted

1 tablespoon Worcestershire sauce

1 teaspoon lemon juice

½ teaspoon garlic powder

½ teaspoon seasoned salt

⅛ teaspoon ground red pepper (cayenne)

1. Heat oven to 350°F. In large bowl, combine pretzel twists, crackers, bagel chips and breadsticks.

2. In small bowl, combine all remaining ingredients; blend well. Drizzle evenly over pretzel mixture; toss to coat. Spread mixture evenly in ungreased 15x10x1-inch baking pan.

3. Bake at 350°F. for 10 to 15 minutes or until crisp, stirring occasionally. Cool 30 minutes or until completely cooled. Store in tightly covered container.

NUTRITION INFORMATION PER SERVING: SERVING SIZE: ½ Cup • Calories 200 • Calories from Fat 80 • % Daily Value: Total Fat 9 g 14% • Saturated Fat 2 g 10% • Cholesterol 0 mg 0% • Sodium 490 mg 20% • Total Carbohydrate 25 g 8% • Dietary Fiber 1 g 4% • Sugars 1 g • Protein 4 g • Vitamin A 4% • Vitamin C 0% • Calcium 0% • Iron 8% • **Dietary Exchanges:** 1½ Starch, 1½ Fat **OR** 1½ Carbohydrate, 1½ Fat

Fire-It-Up Snack Mix

This salty-fiery-sweet mix is addictive.

PREP TIME: 40 MINUTES
(READY IN 1 HOUR 10 MINUTES)
MAKES 10 CUPS

2 cups corn chips

2 cups small pretzel twists

2 cups oyster crackers

2 cups honey-roasted peanuts

2 cups pumpkin seeds

⅓ cup margarine or butter, melted

3 tablespoons firmly packed brown sugar

3 teaspoons chili powder

1½ teaspoons ground red pepper (cayenne)

1 teaspoon hot pepper sauce

1. Heat oven to 300°F. In large bowl, combine corn chips, pretzel twists, oyster crackers, peanuts and pumpkin seeds.

2. In small bowl, combine all remaining ingredients; blend well. Drizzle margarine mixture evenly over corn chip mixture; toss to coat. Place in 2 ungreased 15x10x1-inch baking pans.

3. Bake at 300°F. for 25 to 30 minutes or until peanuts are golden brown, stirring every 10 minutes. Cool 30 minutes or until completely cooled. (Mixture crisps as it cools.) Store in tightly covered container.

NUTRITION INFORMATION PER SERVING: SERVING SIZE: ½ Cup • Calories 300 • Calories from Fat 170 • % Daily Value: Total Fat 19 g 29% • Saturated Fat 3 g 15% • Cholesterol 0 mg 0% • Sodium 340 mg 14% • Total Carbohydrate 24 g 8% • Dietary Fiber 3 g 12% • Sugars 7 g • Protein 9 g • Vitamin A 6% • Vitamin C 0% • Calcium 2% • Iron 20% • **Dietary Exchanges:** 1½ Starch, ½ High-Fat Meat, 3 Fat **OR** 1½ Carbohydrate, ½ High-Fat Meat, 3 Fat

Seaside Snack Mix

(Pictured on page 256.)

This mix is perfect for a beach party. Spooned into cellophane party bags and tied with ribbons, it also makes a good party favor.

PREP TIME: 5 MINUTES
MAKES 10½ CUPS

1 (7-oz.) pkg. deep sea-shaped Cheddar-flavored snack crackers

1 (6-oz.) pkg. tiny fish-shaped Parmesan cheese crackers

2 cups oyster crackers

1½ cups thin pretzel sticks, broken in half

In large bowl, combine all ingredients; toss gently. Store in tightly covered container.

NUTRITION INFORMATION PER SERVING: SERVING SIZE: ½ Cup • Calories 130 • Calories from Fat 45 • % Daily Value: Total Fat 5 g 8% • Saturated Fat 2 g 10% • Cholesterol 0 mg 0% • Sodium 290 mg 12% • Total Carbohydrate 17 g 6% • Dietary Fiber 1 g 4% • Sugars 1 g • Protein 3 g • Vitamin A 0% • Vitamin C 0% • Calcium 2% • Iron 6% • **Dietary Exchanges:** 1 Starch, 1 Fat **OR** 1 Carbohydrate, 1 Fat

Orange-Spiced Sugared Almonds

Consider these delicately spiced nuts as an alternative to Jordan almonds for a bridal shower or wedding favor.

PREP TIME: 15 MINUTES
(READY IN 45 MINUTES)
MAKES 3 CUPS

1 cup sugar

½ teaspoon cinnamon

¼ teaspoon salt

¼ teaspoon allspice

⅛ teaspoon nutmeg

¼ cup orange juice

2 cups unblanched whole almonds

1. Line cookie sheet with foil; grease foil. In medium saucepan, combine all ingredients except almonds. Cook over medium heat until candy thermometer reaches soft-ball stage (234°F.).

2. Remove from heat. Add almonds; toss until well glazed. Spread in single layer on greased foil-lined cookie sheet. Cool 30 minutes or until completely cooled. Break apart, if necessary. Store in tightly covered container.

NUTRITION INFORMATION PER SERVING: SERVING SIZE: 2 Tablespoons • Calories 110 • Calories from Fat 50 • % Daily Value: Total Fat 6 g 9% • Saturated Fat 0 g 0% • Cholesterol 0 mg 0% • Sodium 25 mg 1% • Total Carbohydrate 11 g 4% • Dietary Fiber 1 g 4% • Sugars 9 g • Protein 3 g • Vitamin A 0% • Vitamin C 0% • Calcium 4% • Iron 4% • **Dietary Exchanges:** ½ Fruit, ½ High-Fat Meat, ½ Fat **OR** ½ Carbohydrate, ½ High-Fat Meat, ½ Fat

Sherried Walnuts and Cashews

Set out this elegant mix for an early evening cocktail party. Handle the corn syrup mixture carefully—cooked sugar can cause burns very easily.

PREP TIME: 20 MINUTES
(READY IN 1 HOUR 10 MINUTES)
MAKES 4 CUPS

2 tablespoons brown sugar

1/4 teaspoon cinnamon

1/4 cup dry sherry

2 tablespoons corn syrup

2 tablespoons butter

2 cups walnut halves

2 cups cashew halves

1. Heat oven to 250°F. Line 15x10x1-inch baking pan with foil. In large skillet, combine brown sugar, cinnamon, sherry, corn syrup and butter. Bring to a boil over medium heat, stirring constantly.

2. Stir in walnuts and cashews; cook and stir 4 to 7 minutes or until liquid is absorbed. Spread nuts in foil-lined pan.

3. Bake at 250°F. for 15 to 20 minutes or until glazed. Cool on foil for 30 minutes or until completely cooled. Store in tightly covered container.

NUTRITION INFORMATION PER SERVING: SERVING SIZE: 2 Tablespoons • Calories 110 • Calories from Fat 80 • % Daily Value: Total Fat 9 g 14% • Saturated Fat 2 g 10% • Cholesterol 0 mg 0% • Sodium 10 mg 0% • Total Carbohydrate 5 g 2% • Dietary Fiber 1 g 4% • Sugars 2 g • Protein 2 g • Vitamin A 0% • Vitamin C 0% • Calcium 0% • Iron 4% • **Dietary Exchanges:** 1/2 Fruit, 1/2 High-Fat Meat, 1 Fat **OR** 1/2 Carbohydrate, 1/2 High-Fat Meat, 1 Fat

Peppy Roasted Pumpkin Seeds

Seasoned and baked to a golden crisp, the seeds are arguably the tastiest part of the pumpkin.

PREP TIME: 40 MINUTES
MAKES 1 CUP

1 cup pumpkin seeds from fresh pumpkin

2 teaspoons oil

2 teaspoons taco seasoning mix (from 1.25-oz. pkg.)

1. Heat oven to 350°F. Rinse pumpkin seeds; remove any pulp and fiber. Pat seeds dry with paper towels. Spread seeds in ungreased 15x10x1-inch baking pan. Sprinkle with oil; stir to coat.

2. Bake at 350°F. for 15 to 20 minutes or until deep golden brown and crisp, stirring once.

3. Sprinkle warm seeds with taco seasoning mix. Cool 10 minutes or until completely cooled. Store in tightly covered container.

NUTRITION INFORMATION PER SERVING: SERVING SIZE: 2 Tablespoons • Calories 110 • Calories from Fat 80 • % Daily Value: Total Fat 9 g 14% • Saturated Fat 2 g 10% • Cholesterol 0 mg 0% • Sodium 50 mg 2% • Total Carbohydrate 4 g 1% • Dietary Fiber 1 g 4% • Sugars 0 g • Protein 4 g • Vitamin A 0% • Vitamin C 0% • Calcium 0% • Iron 15% • **Dietary Exchanges:** 1/2 Starch, 1/2 Medium-Fat Meat, 1 Fat **OR** 1/2 Carbohydrate, 1/2 Medium-Fat Meat, 1 Fat

Gin and Tonic Cocktail

Cut a slit in the lime slice and rub the citrus around the entire rim before anchoring it to the edge of the glass holding this cool summer classic.

PREP TIME: 5 MINUTES
MAKES 1 SERVING

2/3 cup small ice cubes

3 to 4 tablespoons gin

2/3 cup tonic water

1 lime slice

1 lemon slice, if desired

Place ice cubes in tall glass. Pour gin over ice cubes. Add tonic water; stir gently. Garnish with lime and lemon slices.

NUTRITION INFORMATION PER SERVING: SERVING SIZE: 1 Recipe • Calories 210 • Calories from Fat 0 • % Daily Value: Total Fat 0 g 0% • Saturated Fat 0 g 0% • Cholesterol 0 mg 0% • Sodium 10 mg 0% • Total Carbohydrate 15 g 5% • Dietary Fiber 0 g 0% • Sugars 14 g • Protein 0 g • Vitamin A 0% • Vitamin C 4% • Calcium 0% • Iron 0% • **Dietary Exchanges:** 1 Fruit, 3 Fat **OR** 1 Carbohydrate, 3 Fat

Martini Cocktails

Chilling the cocktail glasses and straining out ice from the martini mixture cools the drink without diluting it. Nevertheless, this is a drink meant to be sipped slowly, no matter how cold!

PREP TIME: 10 MINUTES
MAKES 4 (1/3-CUP) SERVINGS

1/2 cup small ice cubes or shaved ice

2/3 cup gin

2/3 cup dry vermouth

4 pimiento-stuffed green olives

4 cocktail onions

1. Chill four 3-oz. stemmed glasses in freezer.

2. To serve, place olive in each chilled glass. Place ice cubes in martini shaker or pitcher. Add gin and vermouth; shake or stir until blended. Pour into glasses, straining out ice. Garnish each with olive and onion.

NUTRITION INFORMATION PER SERVING: SERVING SIZE: 1/3 Cup • Calories 120 • Calories from Fat 0 • % Daily Value: Total Fat 0 g 0% • Saturated Fat 0 g 0% • Cholesterol 0 mg 0% • Sodium 120 mg 5% • Total Carbohydrate 0 g 0% • Dietary Fiber 0 g 0% • Sugars 0 g • Protein 0 g • Vitamin A 0% • Vitamin C 0% • Calcium 0% • Iron 0% • **Dietary Exchanges:** 3 Fat

Manhattan Cocktails

Vermouth—fortified, sweetened wine flavored with herbs—is a key ingredient in the martini, the Manhattan and other classic cocktails.

PREP TIME: 10 MINUTES
MAKES 4 (¼-CUP) SERVINGS

4 maraschino cherries with stems

½ cup small ice cubes or cracked ice

⅔ cup bourbon or whiskey

⅓ cup sweet vermouth

⅛ to ¼ teaspoon bitters (4 dashes)

1. Chill four 3-oz. stemmed glasses in freezer.

2. To serve, place cherry in each chilled glass. Place ice cubes in pitcher. Add bourbon, vermouth and bitters; stir until blended. Pour into glasses, straining out ice.

NUTRITION INFORMATION PER SERVING: SERVING SIZE: ¼ Cup • Calories 110 • Calories from Fat 0 • % Daily Value: Total Fat 0 g 0% • Saturated Fat 0 g 0% • Cholesterol 0 mg 0% • Sodium 15 mg 1% • Total Carbohydrate 1 g 1% • Dietary Fiber 0 g 0% • Sugars 1 g • Protein 0 g • Vitamin A 0% • Vitamin C 0% • Calcium 0% • Iron 0% • **Dietary Exchanges:** 2½ Fat

Sunrise Mimosas

These pink- and orange-tinged mimosas are perfect for a celebration brunch or evening aperitif. Make one batch with sparkling wine and one with club soda—mark them clearly—so that children and those who don't drink alcohol can enjoy the "bubbly," too.

PREP TIME: 10 MINUTES
MAKES 12 (¾-CUP) SERVINGS

1 (10-oz.) pkg. frozen strawberries in syrup, thawed, undrained

3 cups 100% tangerine juice (made from frozen concentrate)

2 (750-ml) bottles champagne or 7 cups club soda, chilled

6 strawberries with stems, halved, if desired

1. Place strainer over medium bowl; pour strawberries with syrup into strainer. Press berries with back of spoon through strainer to remove seeds; discard seeds.

2. In nonmetal bowl or pitcher, combine strawberry puree, tangerine juice and sparkling wine; stir gently. Serve over ice in stemmed goblets. Garnish each glass with strawberry half.

NUTRITION INFORMATION PER SERVING: SERVING SIZE: ¾ Cup • Calories 140 • Calories from Fat 0 • % Daily Value: Total Fat 0 g 0% • Saturated Fat 0 g 0% • Cholesterol 0 mg 0% • Sodium 0 mg 0% • Total Carbohydrate 16 g 5% • Dietary Fiber 1 g 4% • Sugars 12 g • Protein 0 g • Vitamin A 8% • Vitamin C 50% • Calcium 0% • Iron 0% • **Dietary Exchanges:** 1 Fruit, 1½ Fat **OR** 1 Carbohydrate, 1½ Fat

Cranberry-Raspberry Wine Coolers

White zinfandel, a "blush" wine, is actually pale pink. Refreshing chilled on a summer evening, it mixes well with berries and juice in this jewel-colored cooler.

PREP TIME: 20 MINUTES
(READY IN 3 HOURS 50 MINUTES)
MAKES 12 (½-CUP) SERVINGS

1 (10-oz.) pkg. frozen raspberries in syrup, thawed

2 cups raspberry-cranberry juice drink blend, chilled

3 cups white zinfandel wine, chilled

1½ cups lemon-lime flavored carbonated beverage, chilled

12 fresh orange or star fruit slices

1. In medium bowl, combine raspberries and ½ cup of the raspberry-cranberry drink; mix well. Spoon into 12 sections of ice cube tray. Freeze 3½ hours or until firm.

2. To serve, place 1 ice cube in each of 12 wine glasses. In large pitcher, combine remaining raspberry-cranberry drink, wine and carbonated beverage; stir gently. Pour into glasses. Garnish with orange slices.

NUTRITION INFORMATION PER SERVING: SERVING SIZE: ½ Cup • Calories 110 • Calories from Fat 0 • % Daily Value: Total Fat 0 g 0% • Saturated Fat 0 g 0% • Cholesterol 0 mg 0% • Sodium 5 mg 0% • Total Carbohydrate 18 g 6% • Dietary Fiber 1 g 4% • Sugars 16 g • Protein 0 g • Vitamin A 0% • Vitamin C 45% • Calcium 0% • Iron 2% • **Dietary Exchanges:** 1 Fruit, 1 Fat **OR** 1 Carbohydrate, 1 Fat

Banana Daiquiri Slush

A batch of icy, tart-sweet daiquiri slush brings the Caribbean islands to you.

PREP TIME: 15 MINUTES
(READY IN 5 HOURS 15 MINUTES)
MAKES 8 (1-CUP) SERVINGS

2 ripe bananas, peeled, cut up

1 (12-oz.) can frozen limeade concentrate, thawed

1½ cups light rum

4 cups lemon-lime flavored carbonated beverage, chilled

1. In blender container, combine bananas and limeade concentrate. Cover; blend until smooth.

2. In large nonmetal freezer container, combine banana mixture, rum and 2 cups of the carbonated beverage; mix well. Cover container; freeze at least 5 hours or until frozen.

3. Twenty to 30 minutes before serving time, remove mixture from freezer. To serve, add remaining 2 cups carbonated beverage to banana mixture; stir until slushy. Spoon into glasses. Garnish as desired.

NUTRITION INFORMATION PER SERVING: SERVING SIZE: 1 Cup • Calories 280 • Calories from Fat 0 • % Daily Value: Total Fat 0 g 0% • Saturated Fat 0 g 0% • Cholesterol 0 mg 0% • Sodium 15 mg 1% • Total Carbohydrate 46 g 15% • Dietary Fiber 1 g 4% • Sugars 41 g • Protein 0 g • Vitamin A 0% • Vitamin C 15% • Calcium 0% • Iron 0% • **Dietary Exchanges:** 3 Fruit, 2 Fat **OR** 3 Carbohydrate, 2 Fat

Piña Colada Slush

This nonalcoholic slush omits the rum usually included in the pineapple-coconut drink. If you wish, reserve a few cubes of pineapple to garnish each glass.

PREP TIME: 10 MINUTES
(READY IN 4 HOURS 10 MINUTES)
MAKES 14 (1-CUP) SERVINGS

4 cups cubed fresh pineapple (1 medium)

1 (15-oz.) can cream of coconut

2 cups orange juice

7 cups lemon-lime flavored carbonated beverage (from 2-liter bottle), chilled

1. In blender container or food processor bowl with metal blade, combine half each of the pineapple, cream of coconut and orange juice; blend until smooth. Pour into 1½-quart nonmetal freezer container. Repeat with remaining pineapple, cream of coconut and orange juice. Cover container; freeze 4 to 6 hours or until icy, stirring twice.

2. To serve, spoon ½ cup frozen mixture into each glass. Add ½ cup carbonated beverage to each glass; stir gently.

NUTRITION INFORMATION PER SERVING: SERVING SIZE: 1 Cup • Calories 160 • Calories from Fat 50 • % Daily Value: Total Fat 6 g 9% • Saturated Fat 5 g 25% • Cholesterol 0 mg 0% • Sodium 30 mg 1% • Total Carbohydrate 25 g 8% • Dietary Fiber 1 g 4% • Sugars 20 g • Protein 1 g • Vitamin A 0% • Vitamin C 35% • Calcium 0% • Iron 2% • **Dietary Exchanges:** 1½ Fruit, 1½ Fat **OR** 1½ Carbohydrate, 1½ Fat

Peachy Keen Slush

If you're serving a crowd and don't have enough glasses for everyone, check with a party rental outlet—you may find that renting glassware isn't much more expensive than purchasing disposables.

PREP TIME: 15 MINUTES
(READY IN 3 HOURS 15 MINUTES)
MAKES 22 (¾-CUP) SERVINGS

¼ cup sugar

2 cups water

1 (12-oz.) can frozen orange juice concentrate, thawed

1 (12-oz.) can frozen lemonade concentrate, thawed

3 cups water

2½ cups peach-flavored schnapps

⅓ cup lemon juice

1 (2-liter) bottle (8½ cups) ginger ale, chilled

1. In medium saucepan, combine sugar and 2 cups water; mix well. Bring to a boil. Boil 3 minutes. Set aside to cool slightly.

2. In large nonmetal freezer container, combine concentrates, 3 cups water, schnapps and lemon juice; blend well. Stir in sugar mixture. Cover container; freeze 3 to 4 hours or until frozen, stirring 2 or 3 times after 2 hours.

3. To serve, spoon ½ cup slush mixture into each glass. Add about ⅓ cup ginger ale to each glass; stir gently.

NUTRITION INFORMATION PER SERVING: SERVING SIZE: ¾ Cup • Calories 200 • Calories from Fat 0 • % Daily Value: Total Fat 0 g 0% • Saturated Fat 0 g 0% • Cholesterol 0 mg 0% • Sodium 10 mg 0% • Total Carbohydrate 38 g 13% • Dietary Fiber 0 g 0% • Sugars 34 g • Protein 1 g • Vitamin A 0% • Vitamin C 50% • Calcium 0% • Iron 2% • **Dietary Exchanges:** 2½ Fruit, 1 Fat **OR** 2½ Carbohydrate, 1 Fat

Blue Hawaii Freeze

Blue Hawaii Freeze is frosty, grown-up lemonade. Serve the drink in either clear glasses or brightly colored glassware, if you have it, and garnish the rim of each glass with a slice of orange, lemon or fresh strawberry.

PREP TIME: 5 MINUTES
MAKES 5 (1-CUP) SERVINGS

2 cups lemonade

½ cup blue orange-flavored liqueur (curaçao)

1 tablespoon sugar

1 teaspoon lime juice

2 cups coarsely crushed ice cubes

1. Chill five 10-oz. glasses in freezer.

2. In blender container, combine all ingredients; blend until smooth. Pour into chilled glasses.

NUTRITION INFORMATION PER SERVING: SERVING SIZE: 1 Cup • Calories 130 • Calories from Fat 0 • % Daily Value: Total Fat 0 g 0% • Saturated Fat 0 g 0% • Cholesterol 0 mg 0% • Sodium 0 mg 0% • Total Carbohydrate 22 g 7% • Dietary Fiber 0 g 0% • Sugars 19 g • Protein 0 g • Vitamin A 0% • Vitamin C 6% • Calcium 0% • Iron 0% • **Dietary Exchanges:** 1½ Fruit, 1 Fat **OR** 1½ Carbohydrate, 1 Fat

Lemon Margaritas

To extract as much juice as possible from a lime, roll it firmly on the counter with your hand before you slice and squeeze it.

PREP TIME: 20 MINUTES
MAKES 4 (1-CUP) SERVINGS

Coarse salt or sugar

¾ cup tequila

½ cup fresh lime juice (6 to 8 medium limes)

¼ cup orange-flavored liqueur

¾ cup frozen lemonade concentrate, thawed (half 12-oz. can)

3 cups small ice cubes

1. Dip tops of cocktail glasses in water; dip in salt to coat.

2. In blender container, combine all remaining ingredients; blend until slushy. Pour tequila mixture carefully into each glass. Garnish as desired.

NUTRITION INFORMATION PER SERVING: SERVING SIZE: 1 Cup • Calories 260 • Calories from Fat 0 • % Daily Value: Total Fat 0 g 0% • Saturated Fat 0 g 0% • Cholesterol 0 mg 0% • Sodium 1410 mg 59% • Total Carbohydrate 34 g 11% • Dietary Fiber 0 g 0% • Sugars 28 g • Protein 0 g • Vitamin A 0% • Vitamin C 20% • Calcium 0% • Iron 2% • **Dietary Exchanges:** 2 Fruit, 3 Fat **OR** 2 Carbohydrate, 3 Fat

Mock Margaritas

Here's the punch without the punch, suitable and satisfying for all ages. For children, dip the rim of the glass in sugar instead of salt.

PREP TIME: 10 MINUTES
MAKES 10 (½-CUP) SERVINGS

Lime slices, if desired

Coarse salt, if desired

¾ cup frozen lemonade concentrate, thawed (half 12-oz. can)

¾ cup frozen limeade concentrate, thawed (half 12-oz. can)

¼ cup powdered sugar

3 cups crushed ice

2 cups club soda, chilled

1. Rub tops of glasses with lime slices; dip in salt to coat.

2. In blender container, combine lemonade and limeade concentrates, powdered sugar and ice; blend until slushy. Add club soda; stir gently. Pour mixture carefully into each glass. Garnish with lime slices.

NUTRITION INFORMATION PER SERVING: SERVING SIZE: ½ Cup • Calories 100 • Calories from Fat 0 • % Daily Value: Total Fat 0 g 0% • Saturated Fat 0 g 0% • Cholesterol 0 mg 0% • Sodium 10 mg 0% • Total Carbohydrate 24 g 8% • Dietary Fiber 0 g 0% • Sugars 22 g • Protein 0 g • Vitamin A 0% • Vitamin C 10% • Calcium 0% • Iron 0% • **Dietary Exchanges:** 1½ Fruit **OR** 1½ Carbohydrate

Sangría

Choose a clear glass *jarra* (pitcher) to show off the burgundy wine and fruit slices. A little chopped apple could also be added, and a traditional Spanish sangría often has a bit of brandy, too.

PREP TIME: 10 MINUTES
(READY IN 2 HOURS 10 MINUTES)
MAKES 8 (¾-CUP) SERVINGS

¾ cup sugar

¾ cup fresh lemon juice

¾ cup orange juice

⅓ cup orange-flavored liqueur

5 cups burgundy wine

1 lemon, sliced

1 orange, sliced

1. In 4-quart nonmetal container, combine sugar, lemon juice, orange juice, liqueur and wine. Refrigerate at least 2 hours or until thoroughly chilled.

2. Just before serving, pour sangría into pitcher. Add lemon and orange slices. Serve over ice in glasses.

NUTRITION INFORMATION PER SERVING: SERVING SIZE: ¾ Cup • Calories 250 • Calories from Fat 0 • % Daily Value: Total Fat 0 g 0% • Saturated Fat 0 g 0% • Cholesterol 0 mg 0% • Sodium 10 mg 0% • Total Carbohydrate 33 g 11% • Dietary Fiber 2 g 8% • Sugars 28 g • Protein 1 g • Vitamin A 0% • Vitamin C 70% • Calcium 4% • Iron 6% • **Dietary Exchanges:** 2 Fruit, 3 Fat **OR** 2 Carbohydrate, 3 Fat

Grape Juice and Fruit Sangría

This nonalcoholic punch resembles traditional sangría but you won't have to check IDs before serving. For a whimsical touch, freeze the ice cubes in trays shaped like little hearts or stars.

PREP TIME: 10 MINUTES
MAKES 6 (1-CUP) SERVINGS

1 quart (4 cups) grape juice, chilled

1 small lemon, sliced

1 lime, cut into wedges

1 small orange, sliced

2 cups lemon-lime flavored carbonated beverage, chilled

2 cups ice cubes

1. In 3-quart nonmetal pitcher, combine grape juice and fruit, slightly squeezing lemon, lime and orange slices into juice.

2. To serve, add carbonated beverage and ice cubes; stir gently.

NUTRITION INFORMATION PER SERVING: SERVING SIZE: 1 Cup • Calories 150 • Calories from Fat 0 • % Daily Value: Total Fat 0 g 0% • Saturated Fat 0 g 0% • Cholesterol 0 mg 0% • Sodium 15 mg 1% • Total Carbohydrate 36 g 12% • Dietary Fiber 1 g 4% • Sugars 0 g • Protein 1 g • Vitamin A 0% • Vitamin C 20% • Calcium 0% • Iron 2% • **Dietary Exchanges:** 2½ Fruit **OR** 2½ Carbohydrate

White Wine Sangría

For those who don't care for red wine, sangría can also be made with white wine. Make sure the mulled mixture is completely cooled (it can be made ahead of time) before adding the wine.

PREP TIME: 30 MINUTES
MAKES 24 (½-CUP) SERVINGS

1 cup sugar

1 cup water

1 cinnamon stick

2 medium oranges, sliced

1 lemon, sliced

1 lime, sliced

3 (750-ml) bottles dry white wine, chilled

3 cups club soda, chilled

1. In medium saucepan, combine sugar, water and cinnamon stick; mix well. Simmer 5 minutes over low heat. Remove from heat. Add fruit. Cool 20 minutes or until completely cooled.

2. Remove cinnamon stick from fruit mixture. Pour into large punch bowl. Add wine and club soda; stir gently.

NUTRITION INFORMATION PER SERVING: SERVING SIZE: ½ Cup • Calories 100 • Calories from Fat 0 • % Daily Value: Total Fat 0 g 0% • Saturated Fat 0 g 0% • Cholesterol 0 mg 0% • Sodium 10 mg 0% • Total Carbohydrate 11 g 4% • Dietary Fiber 1 g 4% • Sugars 10 g • Protein 0 g • Vitamin A 0% • Vitamin C 20% • Calcium 2% • Iron 2% • **Dietary Exchanges:** ½ Fruit, 1½ Fat **OR** ½ Carbohydrate, 1½ Fat

Champagne Raspberry Floats

Festive and fancy, these fizzy floats make a good party punch on a hot summer day. Tie satin ribbons in a variety of colors on the glassware stems or punch cup handles, to help guests identify their own glasses.

PREP TIME: 5 MINUTES
MAKES 12 (½-CUP) SERVINGS

1 (10-oz.) pkg. frozen raspberries in syrup, thawed

1 (750-ml) bottle (3¼ cups) dry white champagne or 1 (25.4-oz.) bottle sparkling white grape juice, chilled

1 pint (2 cups) raspberry sherbet, softened

1. In blender container, puree raspberries until smooth. To remove seeds, press mixture through strainer into small bowl with back of spoon; discard seeds.

2. In large pitcher or punch bowl, combine raspberry puree, champagne and softened sherbet; stir until frothy and well blended. Serve immediately in frosted champagne glasses or punch cups.

NUTRITION INFORMATION PER SERVING: SERVING SIZE: ½ Cup • Calories 120 • Calories from Fat 10 • % Daily Value: Total Fat 1 g 2% • Saturated Fat 0 g 0% • Cholesterol 0 mg 0% • Sodium 15 mg 1% • Total Carbohydrate 17 g 6% • Dietary Fiber 1 g 4% • Sugars 13 g • Protein 1 g • Vitamin A 0% • Vitamin C 8% • Calcium 2% • Iron 0% • **Dietary Exchanges:** 1 Fruit, 1½ Fat **OR** 1 Carbohydrate, 1½ Fat

Mango-Passion Fruit Slush

The homely passion fruit, grown in the tropics, is larger than a golf ball, with wrinkly purple-black skin. Inside, however, the orange flesh has a bright, sweet, amazing flavor that adds life to many kinds of beverages.

PREP TIME: 10 MINUTES
(READY IN 6 HOURS 10 MINUTES)
MAKES 16 (1-CUP) SERVINGS

2 ripe mangoes, peeled, seed removed and flesh cut up

2 (11.5-oz.) cans frozen passion fruit flavored juice cocktail concentrate, thawed

1½ cups water

1½ cups light rum

8 cups lemon-lime flavored carbonated beverage (from 2-liter bottle), chilled

1. Place mango flesh in food processor bowl with metal blade. Add juice cocktail concentrate; process until smooth. Pour into 2-quart nonmetal freezer container. Stir in water and rum. Cover container; freeze 6 to 8 hours or until icy, stirring twice.

2. To serve, spoon ½ cup frozen mixture into each glass. Add ½ cup carbonated beverage to each glass; stir gently.

NUTRITION INFORMATION PER SERVING: SERVING SIZE: 1 Cup • Calories 220 • Calories from Fat 0 • % Daily Value: Total Fat 0 g 0% • Saturated Fat 0 g 0% • Cholesterol 0 mg 0% • Sodium 55 mg 2% • Total Carbohydrate 42 g 14% • Dietary Fiber 0 g 0% • Sugars 40 g • Protein 0 g • Vitamin A 20% • Vitamin C 10% • Calcium 0% • Iron 0% • **Dietary Exchanges:** 3 Fruit, 1 Fat **OR** 3 Carbohydrate, 1 Fat

Strawberry Champagne Punch

An unexpected ingredient—strawberry-flavored gelatin—gives this punch a bright red color and the strawberry flavor.

PREP TIME: 30 MINUTES
MAKES 24 (½-CUP) SERVINGS

1 cup water

1 (3-oz.) pkg. strawberry flavor gelatin

¾ cup frozen lemonade concentrate, thawed (half 12-oz. can)

2 cups cold water

1 (750-ml) bottle rosé wine, chilled

1 (750-ml) bottle champagne, chilled

1 pint (2 cups) fresh strawberries with stems, frozen

1. Bring water to a boil in small saucepan. Add gelatin; stir until gelatin is dissolved. Cool 15 minutes.

2. In punch bowl, combine lemonade concentrate, cold water and gelatin mixture; mix well.

3. Just before serving, stir in wine, champagne and frozen strawberries.

NUTRITION INFORMATION PER SERVING: SERVING SIZE: ½ Cup • Calories 80 • Calories from Fat 0 • % Daily Value: Total Fat 0 g 0% • Saturated Fat 0 g 0% • Cholesterol 0 mg 0% • Sodium 10 mg 0% • Total Carbohydrate 10 g 3% • Dietary Fiber 0 g 0% • Sugars 9 g • Protein 0 g • Vitamin A 0% • Vitamin C 15% • Calcium 0% • Iron 0% • **Dietary Exchanges:** 1 Fruit, ½ Fat **OR** 1 Carbohydrate, ½ Fat

Tropical Rum Punch

The fruit and rum flavors blend wonderfully while chilling, but the club soda should be added at the last minute to preserve the fizz.

PREP TIME: 10 MINUTES
(READY IN 2 HOURS 10 MINUTES)
MAKES 24 (½-CUP) SERVINGS

1 (46-oz.) can (5¾ cups) pineapple juice, chilled

¾ cup frozen limeade concentrate, thawed (half 12-oz. can)

1½ to 2 cups rum

1 (1-liter) bottle (4¼ cups) club soda, chilled

Dash bitters

1. In large nonmetal pitcher or punch bowl, combine pineapple juice, limeade concentrate and rum; mix well. Refrigerate at least 2 hours or until thoroughly chilled.

2. Just before serving, stir in club soda and bitters. Serve over ice in glasses. If desired, garnish each serving with wedge of fresh pineapple and maraschino cherry.

NUTRITION INFORMATION PER SERVING: SERVING SIZE: ½ Cup • Calories 90 • Calories from Fat 0 • % Daily Value: Total Fat 0 g 0% • Saturated Fat 0 g 0% • Cholesterol 0 mg 0% • Sodium 10 mg 0% • Total Carbohydrate 12 g 4% • Dietary Fiber 0 g 0% • Sugars 11 g • Protein 0 g • Vitamin A 0% • Vitamin C 10% • Calcium 0% • Iron 0% • **Dietary Exchanges:** 1 Fruit, ½ Fat **OR** 1 Carbohydrate, ½ Fat

Strawberry Margarita Slush

As a beverage or as dessert, this is a fruity, cool antidote to the heat of summer.

PREP TIME: 10 MINUTES
(READY IN 4 HOURS 10 MINUTES)
MAKES 10 (1-CUP) SERVINGS

1 (16-oz.) pkg. frozen whole strawberries

⅓ cup sugar

1 (12-oz.) can frozen limeade concentrate

1½ cups water

1½ cups tequila

4 cups lemon-lime flavored carbonated beverage, chilled

1. In food processor bowl with metal blade or blender container, combine strawberries, sugar and limeade concentrate; process until strawberries are chopped and mixture is blended. Slowly add ½ to 1 cup of the water, blending well.

2. Pour into nonmetal freezer container. Add remaining ½ to 1 cup water, tequila and 1½ cups of the carbonated beverage; mix well. Cover container; freeze 4 to 5 hours or until icy, stirring 2 or 3 times after 2 hours.

3. To serve, stir mixture; spoon into 10 glasses. Top each serving with ¼ cup carbonated beverage.

NUTRITION INFORMATION PER SERVING: SERVING SIZE: 1 Cup • Calories 250 • Calories from Fat 0 • % Daily Value: Total Fat 0 g 0% • Saturated Fat 0 g 0% • Cholesterol 0 mg 0% • Sodium 10 mg 0% • Total Carbohydrate 43 g 14% • Dietary Fiber 1 g 4% • Sugars 40 g • Protein 0 g • Vitamin A 0% • Vitamin C 30% • Calcium 0% • Iron 2% • **Dietary Exchanges:** 3 Fruit, 1½ Fat **OR** 3 Carbohydrate, 1½ Fat

Frosty Raspberry Iced Tea

This iced tea is a match for the muggiest summer day. It's laced with fresh ginger, a traditional "cure" for hot weather.

PREP TIME: 5 MINUTES
(READY IN 10 HOURS)
MAKES 20 (1-CUP) SERVINGS

4 cups water

1 (¼-inch) slice gingerroot

3 tea bags

1 (12-oz.) can frozen concentrated raspberry juice blend, thawed

10 cups lemon-lime flavored carbonated beverage (from two 2-liter bottles), chilled

1. In 1-quart glass jar, combine water, gingerroot and tea bags. Cover; set in sunny location for 2 to 3 hours or until tea is extracted.

2. Remove and discard tea bags and gingerroot. In 2-quart nonmetal freezer container, combine tea, concentrate and 2 cups of the carbonated beverage. Cover container; freeze at least 8 hours or until icy, stirring twice.

3. To serve, spoon about ½ cup frozen tea mixture into each glass. Add scant ½ cup chilled carbonated beverage to each glass; stir gently.

NUTRITION INFORMATION PER SERVING: SERVING SIZE: 1 Cup • Calories 90 • Calories from Fat 0 • % Daily Value: Total Fat 0 g 0% • Saturated Fat 0 g 0% • Cholesterol 0 mg 0% • Sodium 25 mg 1% • Total Carbohydrate 23 g 8% • Dietary Fiber 0 g 0% • Sugars 21 g • Protein 0 g • Vitamin A 0% • Vitamin C 30% • Calcium 0% • Iron 0% • **Dietary Exchanges:** 1½ Fruit **OR** 1½ Carbohydrate

Golden Aztec Cooler

For a thicker granita-style treat, omit the club soda and serve the slush with spoons.

PREP TIME: 5 MINUTES
MAKES 6 (¾-CUP) SERVINGS

¾ cup sugar

½ cup lime juice

½ cup orange juice

½ cup water

1 cup crushed ice

1½ cups club soda, chilled

1. In blender container, combine all ingredients except club soda; blend until slushy.

2. Pour mixture into nonmetal pitcher. Stir in club soda.

NUTRITION INFORMATION PER SERVING: SERVING SIZE: ¾ Cup • Calories 120 • Calories from Fat 0 • % Daily Value: Total Fat 0 g 0% • Saturated Fat 0 g 0% • Cholesterol 0 mg 0% • Sodium 15 mg 1% • Total Carbohydrate 29 g 10% • Dietary Fiber 0 g 0% • Sugars 27 g • Protein 0 g • Vitamin A 0% • Vitamin C 15% • Calcium 0% • Iron 0% • **Dietary Exchanges:** 2 Fruit **OR** 2 Carbohydrate

Party Punch

Fresh berries, lemon slices or orange slices can be frozen right into the ice. For an ice ring that won't dilute the punch, try freezing white grape juice in the mold.

PREP TIME: 10 MINUTES
MAKES 15 (½-CUP) SERVINGS

¾ cup frozen lemonade concentrate, thawed (half 12-oz. can)

¾ cup frozen orange juice concentrate, thawed (half 12-oz. can)

2 cups white Catawba grape juice, chilled

1 (1-liter) bottle (4¼ cups) lemon-lime flavored carbonated beverage, chilled

Ice ring or ice mold, if desired

1. Just before serving, in punch bowl, combine lemonade and orange juice concentrates; blend well.

2. Add grape juice and carbonated beverage; stir gently. Place ice ring in bowl.

NUTRITION INFORMATION PER SERVING: SERVING SIZE: ½ Cup • Calories 100 • Calories from Fat 0 • % Daily Value: Total Fat 0 g 0% • Saturated Fat 0 g 0% • Cholesterol 0 mg 0% • Sodium 10 mg 0% • Total Carbohydrate 25 g 8% • Dietary Fiber 0 g 0% • Sugars 23 g • Protein 1 g • Vitamin A 0% • Vitamin C 35% • Calcium 0% • Iron 0% • **Dietary Exchanges:** 1½ Fruit **OR** 1½ Carbohydrate

Apricot Cooler

The cherry ice cubes are prepared in a two-step process so that the cherries don't float up and stick out of the cubes. If you make the cherry ice cubes ahead of time, store them in a heavy resealable plastic bag to preserve the flavor. If your tap water is heavily chlorinated, consider using bottled water for making these special ice cubes.

PREP TIME: 5 MINUTES
(READY IN 2 HOURS 5 MINUTES)
MAKES 16 (½-CUP) SERVINGS

16 maraschino cherries

Water

1 (46-oz.) can apricot nectar, chilled

¾ cup frozen lemonade concentrate, thawed (half 12-oz. can)

2 cups lemon-lime flavored carbonated beverage, chilled

1. To make cherry ice cubes, place 1 maraschino cherry in each section of ice cube tray. Fill each section halfway with water; freeze 1 hour or until firm. Fill tray completely with water; freeze at least 1 hour or until serving time.

2. In large nonmetal pitcher or punch bowl, combine apricot nectar and lemonade concentrate; mix well.

3. Just before serving, add carbonated beverage. Serve over cherry ice cubes in cups or glasses.

NUTRITION INFORMATION PER SERVING: SERVING SIZE: ½ Cup • Calories 100 • Calories from Fat 0 • % Daily Value: Total Fat 0 g 0% • Saturated Fat 0 g 0% • Cholesterol 0 mg 0% • Sodium 5 mg 0% • Total Carbohydrate 24 g 8% • Dietary Fiber 1 g 4% • Sugars 22 g • Protein 0 g • Vitamin A 25% • Vitamin C 4% • Calcium 0% • Iron 2% • **Dietary Exchanges:** 1½ Fruit **OR** 1½ Carbohydrate

Grapefruit Citrus Cooler

This tart, refreshing cooler has just enough sweetness to keep your mouth from puckering.

PREP TIME: 5 MINUTES
MAKES 16 (½-CUP) SERVINGS

3½ cups ruby red grapefruit juice, chilled

¼ cup lemon juice

3 tablespoons lime juice

½ cup sugar

4 cups club soda, chilled

1. In large nonmetal punch bowl or pitcher, combine juices and sugar; mix well.

2. Just before serving, add club soda; stir gently. Serve over ice in glasses.

NUTRITION INFORMATION PER SERVING: SERVING SIZE: ½ Cup • Calories 50 • Calories from Fat 0 • % Daily Value: Total Fat 0 g 0% • Saturated Fat 0 g 0% • Cholesterol 0 mg 0% • Sodium 15 mg 1% • Total Carbohydrate 12 g 4% • Dietary Fiber 0 g 0% • Sugars 12 g • Protein 0 g • Vitamin A 0% • Vitamin C 30% • Calcium 0% • Iron 0% • **Dietary Exchanges:** 1 Fruit **OR** 1 Carbohydrate

Cranberry Fizz

A bowl of cranberry fizz is a friendly way to welcome guests to a holiday gathering.

PREP TIME: 5 MINUTES
MAKES 16 (½-CUP) SERVINGS

1 quart (4 cups) cranberry juice cocktail, chilled

1 cup grapefruit juice, chilled

1 cup orange juice, chilled

½ cup sugar

2 cups ginger ale, chilled

1. In large nonmetal pitcher or punch bowl, combine cranberry juice cocktail, grapefruit juice, orange juice and sugar; blend well.

2. Just before serving, add ginger ale; stir gently.

NUTRITION INFORMATION PER SERVING: SERVING SIZE: ½ Cup • Calories 80 • Calories from Fat 0 • % Daily Value: Total Fat 0 g 0% • Saturated Fat 0 g 0% • Cholesterol 0 mg 0% • Sodium 0 mg 0% • Total Carbohydrate 21 g 7% • Dietary Fiber 0 g 0% • Sugars 21 g • Protein 0 g • Vitamin A 0% • Vitamin C 50% • Calcium 0% • Iron 0% • **Dietary Exchanges:** 1½ Fruit **OR** 1½ Carbohydrate

Cranberry Wassail

A little wassail, or simmering wine punch, warms the spirit.

PREP TIME: 20 MINUTES
MAKES 12 (¾-CUP) SERVINGS

6 whole cloves

6 whole allspice

1 (48-oz.) bottle cranberry juice cocktail

½ cup firmly packed brown sugar

½ teaspoon nutmeg

1 (750-ml) bottle dry red wine

Cinnamon sticks, if desired

1. Tie whole spices in 2 layers of cheesecloth or place in tea ball.

2. In large saucepan or Dutch oven, combine cranberry juice cocktail, brown sugar and nutmeg; mix well. Add spices; cook over medium heat until sugar dissolves, stirring occasionally. Reduce heat; cover and simmer 10 minutes.

3. Add wine; cook until thoroughly heated. Remove spices. If desired, garnish with cinnamon sticks.

NUTRITION INFORMATION PER SERVING: SERVING SIZE: ¾ Cup • Calories 150 • Calories from Fat 0 • % Daily Value: Total Fat 0 g 0% • Saturated Fat 0 g 0% • Cholesterol 0 mg 0% • Sodium 10 mg 0% • Total Carbohydrate 28 g 9% • Dietary Fiber 0 g 0% • Sugars 27 g • Protein 0 g • Vitamin A 0% • Vitamin C 50% • Calcium 0% • Iron 4% • **Dietary Exchanges:** 2 Fruit, ½ Fat **OR** 2 Carbohydrate, ½ Fat

SPEEDWAY PUBLIC LIBRARY
SPEEDWAY, INDIANA

Lively Lemon Tingler

Cooking sugar and water together creates a simple syrup that keeps the beverage uniformly sweet, without the sugar sinking to the bottom of the glass.

PREP TIME: 10 MINUTES
(READY IN 1 HOUR)
MAKES 6 (1-CUP) SERVINGS

1½ cups sugar

1 cup water

1½ cups fresh lemon juice (about 8 lemons)

3 cups ginger ale, chilled

1. In small saucepan, combine sugar and water; cook over medium heat, stirring constantly until sugar is dissolved. Remove from heat; cool to room temperature.

2. Add lemon juice; stir to blend. Store base mixture in tightly covered nonmetal container or jar in refrigerator.

3. For each serving, in tall glass, combine ½ cup chilled base mixture and ½ cup ginger ale. If desired, add ice.

NUTRITION INFORMATION PER SERVING: SERVING SIZE: 1 Cup • Calories 260 • Calories from Fat 0 • % Daily Value: Total Fat 0 g 0% • Saturated Fat 0 g 0% • Cholesterol 0 mg 0% • Sodium 10 mg 0% • Total Carbohydrate 66 g 22% • Dietary Fiber 0 g 0% • Sugars 62 g • Protein 0 g • Vitamin A 0% • Vitamin C 45% • Calcium 0% • Iron 0% • **Dietary Exchanges:** 4½ Fruit **OR** 4½ Carbohydrate

Guava Lemonade Coolers

Bright red grenadine syrup is made with pomegranate seeds.

PREP TIME: 10 MINUTES
MAKES 6 (¾-CUP) SERVINGS

1 (12-oz.) can frozen lemonade concentrate, thawed

2 cups guava fruit juice drink

2 cups lemon-lime flavored carbonated beverage, chilled

2 tablespoons grenadine syrup

6 lime slices

6 lemon slices

1. In large nonmetal pitcher, combine lemonade concentrate, guava drink, carbonated beverage and grenadine syrup; mix well. Refrigerate until serving time.

2. To serve, place ice cubes in tall glasses. Pour guava mixture into glasses. Garnish with lime and lemon slices.

NUTRITION INFORMATION PER SERVING: SERVING SIZE: ¾ Cup • Calories 240 • Calories from Fat 0 • % Daily Value: Total Fat 0 g 0% • Saturated Fat 0 g 0% • Cholesterol 0 mg 0% • Sodium 30 mg 1% • Total Carbohydrate 61 g 20% • Dietary Fiber 1 g 4% • Sugars 52 g • Protein 0 g • Vitamin A 0% • Vitamin C 70% • Calcium 0% • Iron 4% • **Dietary Exchanges:** 4 Fruit **OR** 4 Carbohydrate

Bubbly Apple–Orange Refresher

(Pictured on page 248.)

Garnish this nonalcoholic drink with slices of star fruit, kiwi or melon shapes (cut from sliced cantaloupe or honeydew with small cookie cutters). Press the fruit slices onto the rim of the glass.

PREP TIME: 10 MINUTES
MAKES 25 (½-CUP) SERVINGS

1 quart (4 cups) apple juice, chilled

1 quart (4 cups) orange juice, chilled

¾ cup frozen lemonade concentrate, thawed (half 12-oz. can)

1 (1-liter) bottle (4¼ cups) lemon-lime flavored carbonated beverage, chilled

1. In 4-quart nonmetal pitcher or punch bowl, combine juices and lemonade concentrate; stir until well blended. Serve immediately or refrigerate until serving time.

2. Just before serving, slowly add carbonated beverage; stir gently to blend. Serve over ice in glasses. Garnish as desired.

NUTRITION INFORMATION PER SERVING: SERVING SIZE: ½ Cup • Calories 70 • Calories from Fat 0 • % Daily Value: Total Fat 0 g 0% • Saturated Fat 0 g 0% • Cholesterol 0 mg 0% • Sodium 10 mg 0% • Total Carbohydrate 17 g 6% • Dietary Fiber 0 g 0% • Sugars 0 g • Protein 0 g • Vitamin A 0% • Vitamin C 30% • Calcium 0% • Iron 0% • **Dietary Exchanges:** 1 Fruit **OR** 1 Carbohydrate

Orange-Ginger Iced Tea with Fruit Stirrers

You can make this beautifully garnished tea with standard orange pekoe tea bags, or with fruit-flavored herbal teas, especially for an evening gathering where people might prefer to avoid caffeine.

PREP TIME: 5 MINUTES
(READY IN 3 HOURS 5 MINUTES)
MAKES 8 (1-CUP) SERVINGS

TEA

6 tea bags

1 (1-inch) piece gingerroot, cut into thin slices

1 medium orange, quartered

8 cups water

FRUIT STIRRERS

8 strawberries

8 orange, lemon or lime wedges

8 cantaloupe or honeydew melon balls

8 slices star fruit, if desired

8 (6-inch) bamboo skewers

1. In 2-quart nonmetal pitcher, combine all tea ingredients. Cover; let stand in sun for 2 hours.

2. Strain tea; discard tea bags, gingerroot and orange from tea. Refrigerate at least 1 hour or until chilled.

3. To serve, alternately thread fruit onto skewers. Place ice cubes in glasses; pour tea over ice. Place 1 fruit stirrer in each glass. If desired, serve with sugar and/or sweetener.

NUTRITION INFORMATION PER SERVING: SERVING SIZE: 1 Cup with Fruit • Calories 15 • Calories from Fat 0 • % Daily Value: Total Fat 0 g 0% • Saturated Fat 0 g 0% • Cholesterol 0 mg 0% • Sodium 0 mg 0% • Total Carbohydrate 4 g 1% • Dietary Fiber 1 g 4% • Sugars 4 g • Protein 0 g • Vitamin A 10% • Vitamin C 40% • Calcium 0% • Iron 0% • **Dietary Exchanges:** ½ Fruit **OR** ½ Carbohydrate

Rich and Creamy Eggnog

This thick, creamy eggnog can also serve as dessert. For a slightly slimmer version, use nonfat or low-fat milk.

PREP TIME: 10 MINUTES
(READY IN 1 HOUR 10 MINUTES)
MAKES 10 (½-CUP) SERVINGS

- 4 cups milk
- 1 (3.4-oz.) pkg. instant vanilla pudding and pie filling mix
- 1 (8-oz.) carton (1 cup) refrigerated or frozen fat-free egg product, thawed
- 1 teaspoon vanilla
- 1 teaspoon rum extract or ¼ cup light rum
- ¼ teaspoon salt
- ¼ teaspoon nutmeg
- Whipped cream, if desired
- Nutmeg, if desired

1. In large bowl, combine 2 cups of the milk and pudding mix; beat 1 minute or until smooth.

2. Add remaining 2 cups milk, egg product, vanilla, rum extract, salt and ¼ teaspoon nutmeg; beat well. Cover; refrigerate at least 1 hour before serving.

3. To serve, pour eggnog into cups. Top each with whipped cream and a sprinkle of nutmeg.

NUTRITION INFORMATION PER SERVING: SERVING SIZE: ½ Cup • Calories 130 • Calories from Fat 45 • % Daily Value: Total Fat 5 g 8% • Saturated Fat 3 g 15% • Cholesterol 20 mg 7% • Sodium 280 mg 12% • Total Carbohydrate 16 g 5% • Dietary Fiber 0 g 0% • Sugars 14 g • Protein 6 g • Vitamin A 8% • Vitamin C 0% • Calcium 15% • Iron 2% • **Dietary Exchanges:** ½ Starch, ½ Low-Fat Milk, ½ Fat **OR** 1 Carbohydrate, ½ Fat

Rosy Mulled Punches

Part of the pleasure of these mulled punches is the aroma of sweet spices from the simmering pot, a pleasure that's repeated in the fragrant steam rising from each cup.

PREP TIME: 25 MINUTES
(READY IN 3 HOURS 25 MINUTES)
MAKES 14 (½-CUP) SERVINGS EACH

SYRUP

- 2 cups water
- 1 cup sugar
- 1 teaspoon whole cloves
- 1 teaspoon whole allspice
- 2 cinnamon sticks
- 1 lemon, sliced
- 1 orange, sliced

NONALCOHOLIC PUNCH

- 1½ quarts (6 cups) raspberry-cranberry drink

ALCOHOLIC PUNCH

- 2 (750-ml) bottles (6 cups) dry red wine

1. In small saucepan, combine all syrup ingredients; mix well. Cook over medium heat until mixture comes to a boil, stirring constantly. Reduce heat; simmer 10 minutes.

2. Strain syrup. Cool slightly. Refrigerate syrup at least 3 hours or until serving time.

3. At serving time, place half of prepared syrup (about 1¼ cups) in each of 2 large saucepans. To one add raspberry-cranberry drink. To the other add wine. Simmer each over low heat until thoroughly heated. Serve hot with cinnamon sticks and citrus twists, if desired.

NUTRITION INFORMATION PER SERVING: SERVING SIZE: ½ Cup NONALCOHOLIC PUNCH • Calories 100 • Calories from Fat 0 • % Daily Value: Total Fat 0 g 0% • Saturated Fat 0 g 0% • Cholesterol 0 mg 0% • Sodium 0 mg 0% • Total Carbohydrate 24 g 8% • Dietary Fiber 1 g 4% • Sugars 23 g • Protein 0 g • Vitamin A 0% • Vitamin C 50% • Calcium 0% • Iron 0% • **Dietary Exchanges:** 1½ Fruit **OR** 1½ Carbohydrate

NUTRITION INFORMATION PER SERVING: SERVING SIZE: ½ Cup ALCOHOLIC PUNCH • Calories 50 • Calories from Fat 0 • % Daily Value: Total Fat 0 g 0% • Saturated Fat 0 g 0% • Cholesterol 0 mg 0% • Sodium 0 mg 0% • Total Carbohydrate 9 g 3% • Dietary Fiber 0 g 0% • Sugars 8 g • Protein 0 g • Vitamin A 0% • Vitamin C 8% • Calcium 0% • Iron 0% • **Dietary Exchanges:** ½ Fruit **OR** ½ Carbohydrate

index

Page numbers in *italics* refer to photographs.

282

Titles by Pillsbury

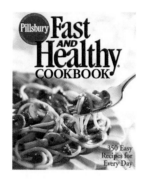

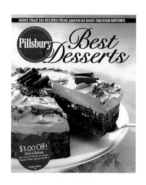

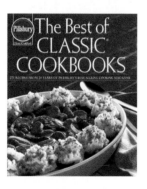

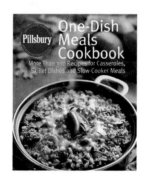

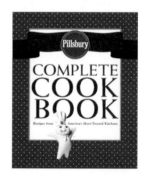